PHILOSOPHY, PSYCHOLOGY AND SOCIAL PRACTICE

JOHN DEWEY

Philosophy, Psychology and Social Practice

Essays Selected, Edited and with a Foreword by

Joseph Ratner

FOUNDED 1838

GPPS

G. P. PUTNAM'S SONS
NEW YORK

Copyright © 1963 by G. P. Putnam's Sons

Library of Congress Catalog
Card Number: 63-16188

PRINTED IN THE UNITED STATES OF AMERICA

EDITORIAL NOTE

ALL except two of the essays in this volume have never before been published in book form. The two exceptions—"The Reflex Arc Concept in Psychology" and "Interpretation of the Savage Mind"—appeared in the collection of essays entitled *Philosophy and Civilization* (Minton, Balch and Company, 1931).

The essays are arranged chronologically by year, save for "Psychology and Social Practice," which is in the ultimate, instead of penultimate, place. If the chronological arrangement were rigidly by month as well as by year of original publication, essays 4 and 12 would have to exchange places with essays 5 and 13 respectively; this would be undesirable.

Visible editorial changes are enclosed in square brackets; the invisible—deletions of internal and superannuated page references and other such mechanical matters—are not indicated.

For permission to reprint twelve essays, thanks are due: The American Psychological Association, the Editor of *Mind,* and The Editorial Board of *The Philosophical Review.* The remaining six essays originally appeared in journals which have, for varying lengths of time, been enjoying their eternal reward.

J. R.

CONTENTS

FOREWORD

JOHN DEWEY began his philosophic career as a devoted, one might almost say devout, adherent and defender of a variety of Hegelian Absolute Idealism. The first nine essays in this volume are the products of that devotion. The second nine reveal the emergence of the original, creative thinker working on the foundations of his own philosophy, a philosophy that was destined to become the most comprehensive and influential in the history of American culture.

A philosopher of John Dewey's power and originality of mind does not become a disciple of Hegelian Absolutism merely because the professor of philosophy at Johns Hopkins happens to be an Hegelian; nor because of any other external or adventitious circumstance. The twenty-three-year-old Dewey succumbed to the spell of George Sylvester Morris's teaching because there was something in Hegelianism which answered a fundamental need. What that need was, John Dewey had occasion to explain nearly half a century later. In his autobiographical sketch "From Absolutism to Experimentalism," he explained that Hegel's thought "supplied a demand for unification that was doubtless an intense emotional craving, and yet was a hunger that only an intellectualized subject-matter could satisfy. It is more than difficult, it is impossible, to recover that early mood. But the sense of divisions and separations that were, I suppose, borne in upon me as a consequence of a heritage of New England culture, divisions by way of isolation of self from the world, of soul from body, of nature from God, brought a painful oppression

—or, rather, they were an inward laceration. My earlier philosophic study had been an intellectual gymnastic. Hegel's
synthesis of subject and object, matter and spirit, the divine
and the human, was, however, no mere intellectual formula;
it operated as an immense release, a liberation. Hegel's treatment of human culture, of institutions and the arts, involved
the same dissolution of hard-and-fast dividing walls, and had
a special attraction for me." *

Hegel's philosophy was the first, indeed probably the only
philosophy that even for a short time seemed completely to
satisfy Dewey's intense emotional hunger. But some five years
before Hegel entered the life of his mind, Dewey had had a
vivid intimation of what a philosophy that would satisfy "his
head and his heart" ought to be or do. In his junior year at
the University of Vermont he had a short, non-laboratory
course in physiology, "a book of Huxley's being the text." He
"derived from that study"—to continue with Dewey's recol-
lections—"a sense of interdependence and interrelated unity
that gave form to intellectual stirrings that had been previously inchoate, and created a kind of type or model of a view
of things to which material in any field ought to conform.
Subconsciously, at least, I was led to desire a world and a life
that would have the same properties as had the human organism in the picture of it derived from study of Huxley's treatment." Whether or not Hegel's philosophy ever seemed to
the young Dewey as admirably integrated as the human organism, it obviously seemed integrated enough, "organic"
enough, to win his undivided allegiance.

The power, rather than the originality, of Dewey's mind
is in evidence during his Hegelian period. In the very first
essay, published while Dewey was a graduate student at Johns
Hopkins, the young philosopher already shows a marked
ability to cut through the details to the solid bone of philosophic contention. His polemic also shows notable power.
Interestingly enough, although his argument is in behalf of

* Thanks are due George Allen and Unwin, Ltd. for permission to quote
from the sketch referred to which appeared in *Contemporary American
Philosophy: Personal Statements*, Vol. II (1930).

Hegelianism, his polemical method owes nothing to Hegel and everything to Aristotle—to the old rules of logic which Hegel's logic sought to displace. Each step in the argument consists in reducing the particular issue there at stake to two mutually exclusive propositions. One must be true and the other false and no middle ground is possible. Throughout the series of either-or confrontations the truth, of course, invariably comes up on the Hegelian side. In the second essay, also published while Dewey was working for his doctorate, the old rules of logic carry the burden of the polemic, but Hegel's logic for the first time boldly appears in the exposition, sometimes with an evangelical flicker in its eye: ". . . a Reason which differentiates itself that it may integrate itself into fuller riches, a Reason that denies itself that it may become itself." As Dewey's mind became more deeply saturated with Hegelianism, his argumentation became more heavily laden with Hegelian peculiarities of thought and expression. But at no time was the saturation so complete that the old rules of logic, the common-sense habits of mind, disappeared without leaving a trace. New England culture lacerated the young Dewey's heart, but it also steadied his head. The tender-mindedness of Hegelian Idealism never could quite overcome or destroy the tough-mindedness of his Vermont heritage.

The advantage of wholehearted discipleship to Hegelianism—if advantage it may be called—is that what would otherwise be difficult is easy to understand and insoluble problems are really no problems at all. This characteristic of the true Hegelian disciple is, I think, most strikingly manifest in the long essay "Soul and Body." There is much in it which bore valuable fruit in Dewey's post-Hegelian development, but as an argument defending and expounding the Idealist doctrine it is redolent with the simplicity of unquestioning discipleship. The common belief that the relation of the soul to the body is uncomprehended, even incomprehensible, is due, so runs the nub of Dewey's argument, to an almost childish confusion of "pictures" and "principles." If we just get rid of this confusion, if we just realize that "principles," not "pictures," have explanatory power, then practically *ipso facto* the problem of the soul-body relation is gotten rid of too. What that relation is then reveals itself as clearly as does the noonday sun in an azure sky. "The soul is immanent in the body only because, and in so far as, it has realized itself in the body. The body is its organ because the soul has *made* the body its organ. . . . The body as an organ of the soul is the result of the informing, creating activity of the soul itself . . . the soul is immanent in the body, not by virtue of the body as mere body, but because, being transcendent, it has expressed and manifested its nature in the body. . . . It is a living and acting force which has formed, and is constantly forming the body, as its own mechanism. . . . It has tabernacled in the flesh and transformed that flesh into its own manifestation. The body is the bodying forth of the soul." These quotations give the "positive" truth expounded in the essay; the major "negative" truth is the comforting admonition: "Let it be no surprsie that physiological psychology has revealed no new truth concerning the relations of soul and body"—and in view of the absolute finality of the "positive" truth, necessarily never can reveal new truth.

Aristotle has been made a party to so many different philosophic revelations, it is hardly surprising that Dewey should make him a party to this one, too. And when we remember the cultural time, Dewey's evangelical upbringing and Morris's unclouded conviction that Hegelianism "scientifically" vindicated the basic tenets of Christianity—when we remember just this (not to mention much more) with requisite vividness, it is not surprising that Dewey should also hail Christ, Saint Paul and the Apostle's Creed as witnesses for the Truth he delivers. The ease with which Dewey accomplishes the task of converting these three normally hostile into indubitably favorable witnesses is impressive; it is, indeed, little short of masterful.

To be a true and faithful disciple of Hegel—or of anybody else—was not the role Dewey was born to fulfill. His bent to originality was too decided, his creative urge too strong, to let him rest content with reproducing and disseminating another man's doctrine. In the essay "Psychology as Philosophic Method," the direction in which his creative Hegelian ambition was then moving is revealed. He had "no doubt" that Hegel had "successfully and thoroughly" accomplished the job of exposing and correcting the root error in Kant's philosophy. Nevertheless, something important remained to be done on Kant's work "and only when this has been done, will, for the first time, the presuppositions latent in the work of Hegel, which give it its convincing force and validity, be brought out." For Dewey to see himself doing this bringing out is, to be sure, no vaulting ambition, but when all the fundamentals of the Philosophic Truth are already discovered and known, there is neither occasion nor room for vaulting.

In his first essay, the twenty-three-year-old Dewey caustically points out, in criticizing the doctrine of Sensationalism: "There is also a self-contradiction in the theory so glaring that it might well have made anyone pause who was not so mastered by the presuppositions of his system as to be blind to the rules of ordinary logic." Just when Dewey himself began to recover from the blindness induced in him by his devotion to the presuppositions of Hegelianism, latent and otherwise, is a difficult, in fact impossible, thing to determine precisely. Nor is it possible to determine precisely to what he owed the return of normal vision. For many new experiences of varying power and influence had, each in its own way, been boring through his complement of Hegelian presuppositions. His cure was the cumulative result of the impact upon his mind of persons and practical exigencies of life rather than of books—with one notable exception, William James's *Principles of Psychology* which appeared in 1890.

Dewey's espousal of Hegelianism, which lasted in full force for about seven years, undoubtedly left "a permanent deposit" in his mind. The significance of this "deposit," though not to be underestimated, can easily be exaggerated. What attracted Dewey to Hegel in the first place is far more important in his subsequent, post-Hegelian development than anything he derived or retained from Hegel.

Emancipation from Hegelianism did not liberate Dewey

from the imperious pressures of his deep inner craving for a unified world. Hegelianism had satisfied that craving for a time. Although the Hegelian unification had, alas, turned out to be deceptive, the ideal, the objective, of unification was not thereby discredited. Because Hegel had not really succeeded did not mean that success was really impossible and the quest for unification should be abandoned. Short of changing his fundamental character, of extinguishing the basic need of his nature, Dewey could not abandon this quest. And as a matter of fact, throughout his long life of ceaseless philosophic activity, he never did.

Before Dewey's mind was captured and enclosed by Hegel, it had been opened and enlivened by Huxley. When he began to see through Hegel he, in effect, went back to Huxley, not directly, to be sure, but indirectly, via William James. The singular effectiveness of the *Principles* in helping Dewey get his new philosophic bearings was due, above all, to its sustained and vivid demonstration of the biological function of thought.

Although James integrated the most abstract, even abstruse, intellectual operations with biological function, he never carried his psychological reconstruction to the point of eliminating the traditional "subjective" element from his *Psychology*. In fact, he both explicitly and implicitly accepts the standard dualistic position as one of the psychologist's necessary presuppositions; to go beyond dualism is to forsake the proper province of the psychologist and to wander into the domain of the metaphysician. Dewey could not possibly agree to James's delimitation of the field of psychology because it would saddle psychology with an incurable dualism. Hence it is that Dewey first steps out—in "The Ego as Cause" —as James's critic rather than as his admirer and follower. The objective of overcoming dualism in psychology is the underlying motive, the dynamic, of all Dewey's essays in the field. "The Reflex Arc Concept in Psychology" is his greatest, most influential, single contribution to this end.

Hegel did not create the world. He did not even discover the world or any part of it. He was not an explorer or creative scientist. He was a philosopher pure and simple and, like every other of his kind, he sought to interpret the world, to make it intelligible. His distinctive contribution to the common philosophic effort is to be found not in any material content but in the system of categories, the explanatory principles, the conceptual pattern he developed for rendering this unintelligible whole perspicuous to the mind. Hegel's schematism, his pattern of thought, has a life of its own, independent of his particular use of it. Karl Marx, for example, in his post-Hegelian stretch of life, retained the Hegelian schematism but applied it in just the opposite sense. Hegel stood the world on its head. Marx turned Hegelianism upside down, believing that he thereby put the world on its feet again. John Dewey, for a period of several years, tried to do something similar. He tried to reinterpret Hegel's categories in conformity with his own ideas. Had such reinterpretation been successful, the benefit would have been intellectually enormous. Dewey would then have had, at the outset of his post-Hegelian career, a system of concepts for organizing and systematizing his own developing thought. The reinterpretation, however, proved to be impossible. By 1897-1898, Dewey finally and definitively realized this. He stopped trying to pour his new wine into Hegel's old bottles. From that time on, Dewey was completely on his own—as completely on his own as any philosopher can be who is acutely sensitive to the intellectual and practical world about him and restlessly seeks to absorb and transform it so that it may become intelligible to himself, and his vision, mayhap, be seen by others and be found illuminating too.

JOSEPH RATNER

PHILOSOPHY, PSYCHOLOGY AND SOCIAL PRACTICE

1

KNOWLEDGE AND THE RELATIVITY
OF FEELING

THE doctrine of the Relativity of Knowledge is one of the most characteristic theories of modern thought. To many, indeed, it seems the sum of all modern wisdom. That we cannot know Being, but must confine ourselves to sequences among phenomena—this appears to many the greatest achievement of thought: a discovery whose full meaning it was reserved for the nineteenth century to penetrate, and one which, if mastered, will put an end to all the idle speculation which is supposed to have disgraced the philosophical thought of the past, and turn intellectual activity into the fruitful fields of real knowledge.

The doctrine has been reached in at least four different ways, and held by as many schools. There is the Positivist, who claims to have reached the doctrine as the result of history, and not from any system of Metaphysics, and who is among the loudest in proclaiming it the panacea for all ills which intellect is heir to. There is the school who profess to have reached it from a philosophical examination of thought itself, and to have found it involved in "imbecilities" at every attempt to overstep phenomena—the school whose chief representative is Hamilton, but more lately given to calling up the greater shade of Kant to conjure by. Then there is the Associationalist, who, after Hume had made wreck of Sensationalism by showing that its methods and presuppositions left no basis for any objective knowledge—no, nor for objec-

From *The Journal of Speculative Philosophy*, January, 1883; 56-70.

tive existence either—had before him the sorry task of keeping the method and yet avoiding the result. His instrument was the "association of ideas," and by it he attempted to reach results compatible with everyday thought and the established facts of physical science. But to whatever extent he succeeded (and we are not concerned with that question at present), he found himself confined within the limits of his subjective capacity for association, and he, too, took Relativity for his shibboleth.

But with the development of the theory of evolution arose a school that wielded a mightier weapon. Here was an established scientific theory which assumed objective existence, and also, in one of its highest generalizations, included man, and showed that he, and presumably his intellect and knowledge, had in the progress of the cycles been developed from these original existences and forces. Here, then, is a theory which, in a certain form, may deny all creating and constructive thought, and consequently be thoroughly sensationalistic. Furthermore, by extending indefinitely the sphere and time of operations, it bridged the gaps and strengthened the weak points of former sensationalism; and, above all, it postulated objective existence. Here, then, is a theory which may satisfy the demands of physical science and of "common sense" as to existence independent of subjective feeling; pay a compliment to the former by adopting its methods and results, and at the same time forever silence all who claim that we have absolute knowledge. For, notice how this theory is also compelled to assume the form of Relativity. According to it, in the form we are considering, all knowledge is, through a nervous organism, constructed through evolution from the lowest form of life, or from matter. Accordingly, it must be conditioned by the state and quality of the organism, and cannot represent or copy objective existence. It is therefore relative to the subject. But since, according to the realistic assumptions of the theory, there is objective existence, this must remain forever unknown and unknowable. To know it would be possible only through the contradiction of a feeling not relative to the subject. This, then, is the position of that form of the doctrine of the Relativity of Knowledge which is probably most widely influential at present. All knowledge is derived from feeling; feeling is conditioned upon the existence of external objects, and expresses the way in which the sentient subject is affected by them, and not what they are in themselves. All knowledge is through feeling, and all feeling is relative. Such are its dogmas.

What we intend in this paper is to examine into the theory of the Relativity of Knowledge in so far as it bases itself upon the fact of the relativity of feeling to a subject. Were we to examine it exhaustively in its relations to the theory of evolution, with which in its fourth form it is connected, it would be necessary to ask how the scientific theory of evolution, by hypothesis an exact and correct statement of a universal law, is compatible with any such supposed origin of knowledge. But we pass over this for the present, and will inquire simply into the mutual relations of the two parts of any sensationalistic theory of the relativity of knowledge.

That we may have the work thoroughly before us, it must be noticed, first, that Relative here signifies subjective as opposed to objective, phenomenal as opposed to ontological. It denotes an imperfection of thought, not its essence. Secondly, this theory in its present form is not a psychological theory. It does not simply state certain facts regarding the method in which we get to know the world, but claims to be a Philosophy, and so gives epistemological conclusions regarding the knowableness of Being, and, therefore, ontological conclusions regarding the nature of Being, viz., that it is unrelated to Thought.

Plausible as the theory seems at first sight, by reason of its supposed basis in well-established scientific facts, it is impossible, upon further reflection, to suppress certain questionings. These formulate themselves as follows: How is it possible to assume at the same time the truth of the sensationalist hypothesis and that of the Relativity of Feeling? Are these two doctrines ultimately reconcilable? Does not the possibility of knowing the relativity of our feelings imply an element in knowledge besides these feelings? Could a merely feeling consciousness ever arrive at the knowledge that there were objects as referred to which its feelings were purely relative? In a word: Can a consciousness made up exclusively of feelings which are *ex hypothesi* relative ever transcend this relativity, and make assertions regarding an absolute object as referred to which alone they could be termed relative?

What I wish to present are some suggestions in answer of this question; and incidentally, if possible, to throw some light upon the ultimate ontological bearings of any theory of the relativity of feeling.

It is to be noticed, first, that this theory assumes that there is an absolute object or objects. There can be no relative except as referred to an Absolute. It is only by assuming that there is something Non-relative that we can know our feelings to be relative. Relative and absolute are correlate terms, and one without the other is meaningless, or rather impossible. Were it not postulated that there is a Non-relative existence as referred to which our present actual feelings *are* relative, it is evident that the feelings themselves would be the ultimate and absolute, thus contradicting the hypothesis. There is no need to occupy space in stating these truisms, for, besides their self-evident character, they are admitted, or rather claimed, by the chief modern representative of the doctrine we are examining. Says Mr. Spencer: "The proposition, that whatever we feel has an existence which is relative to ourselves only, cannot be proved, nay, cannot even be intelligibly expressed, without asserting directly, or by implication, an external existence which is not relative to ourselves." . . . The hypothesis "that the active antecedents of each primary feeling exist independently of consciousness is the only thinkable one. It is the one implicitly asserted in the very proposition that feelings are relative to our own nature, and it is taken for granted in every step of every argument by which the proposition is proved." And, again: "More certain than the relativity of relations, as we conceive them, is the existence of non-relative forms to which they refer; since proof of the first involves perpetual assumption of the last."

It being admitted, then, that knowledge of the relativity of

[22]

feeling implies knowledge of a non-relative existence, the question arises as to the compatibility of this position with the theory it accompanies, *viz.*, that all knowledge is derived from feeling. Is it logically possible to hold that all knowledge comes from feeling, and yet that there is knowledge of the existence of an Absolute? Rather, does not one position exclude the other? We will put the case in its simplest form. Either there is knowledge of something Non-relative or there is not. If the latter be the case, then, as we have already seen, the relativity of feeling could never be known, nay, the question as to its relativity could never have occurred to consciousness. The former alternative is the one adopted. We must admit that there is knowledge of the existence of an absolute object. But how is this knowledge obtained? Since all knowledge comes from feeling, this must also. In other words, since sensation-knowledge we must have sensation that there is an absolute existence. But on this theory (that every feeling is relative) an absolute sensation is a contradiction in terms. We may give up the sensationalist hypothesis, and, admitting that we have knowledge not derived from feeling (*viz.*, that an Absolute exists), hold that feeling is relative. Or we may give up the Relativity theory and hold, so far at least as this point is concerned, that Sensationalism is true. But to attempt to hold them together is suicidal. If all our knowledge comes from feeling, since we can never have a feeling of the absolute object, we never can have knowledge of it; and we cannot have a feeling of it, since, by the theory, the absolute is precisely that which is *not* conditioned by feeling. Or, on the other hand, if we know that all feeling is relative, we do know that there is an absolute object, and hence have knowledge not derived from sensation. When these alternatives are once fairly faced, it will be seen that one or the other must be definitely adopted. Both cannot be accepted. To attempt it is to show that neither position is understood.

Such is the fact. The reason for it is not far to seek. By the sensationalist hypothesis, we know only our feelings; according to the relativity theory, we must know the relation of our feelings to an object; this the feelings cannot give, except by transcending their relativity—except, in short, by ceasing to be feelings. Hume showed once for all that if the sensationalist presuppositions be adopted, the "perceptions" themselves were ultimate and final, and that any supposed reference of them to an object is a fiction to be accounted for as best may be.

An examination of the method by which Mr. Spencer attempts to unite with his sensationalism the position that the existence of an Absolute is known will confirm us in the conclusions just drawn, for we shall see that the best which he can offer is a virtual surrender. His argument was substantially given in the passages cited from him, and is similar to that given in the First Principles for the existence of an absolute object in general. Briefly, it is as follows: "The existence of a Non-relative is unavoidably asserted in every chain of reasoning by which relativity is proved." This is apparently offered as a serious argument in proof of the existence of an absolute object; at least it is all that is offered. Its worth may be made evident by a parallel example. To prove A, we must assume B; by its assumption A is proved. But B is involved in the proof of A; therefore B is also proved. It is evident, or ought to be, that we have here no proof of the existence of either A or B, of the Relative or Non-relative, but simply that there can be no A without B, no Relative without an Absolute—an undoubted fact, but one which leaves the existence of either in as much doubt as before. In truth, it is not a solution of the difficulty, but a statement of it. It says that unless there be an absolute object, our feelings cannot be known as relative; while the question is precisely *how* is this absolute object known. Mr. Spencer's legitimate conclusions from his argument are either that there is no absolute object, and hence the feelings are not relative, or we do know they are relative, and hence know that there is an absolute object, and have knowledge which is *not* relative. To attempt, as he does, to prove the existence of one from the assumed existence of the other is to reason in a circle. It cannot be that we know there is a Non-relative because we know that our feelings are relative, for the latter point is just the one in question, and cannot be proved, as Mr. Spencer himself shows, without assumption of the former. The knowledge of the existence of the Relative cannot be made to depend upon the assumption of a Non-relative, and knowledge of the existence of the Non-relative upon that of the Relative, at one and the same time. But it is only by this most illogical procedure that Mr. Spencer gets the Absolute, which, as he recognizes, is necessary to the proof of the relativity hypothesis.

We conclude, then, that we are justified in reasserting our original statement. To know that our sensations are relative, we must know that there is an Absolute. To know that there is an Absolute is, on the sensationalist hypothesis, to assert the *contradictio in adjecto* of an absolute feeling, or else to reason in the wholly illegitimate manner just examined. Hence, the two positions of Sensationalism and Relativity of sensations are wholly irreconcilable.

So far we have confined ourselves to the simplest assumption of these theories as conjoined—the assumption that there *is* an absolute object or objects. We have not concerned ourselves with the question, *What* is this absolute object? This, however, can no longer be kept in the background. Even admitting what we have seen it impossible to admit on the hypothesis that we have knowledge of the existence of a Non-relative, we have yet to decide whether the relativity of feeling can be proved without knowing *what* this Non-relative is. The sensationalist must hold, of course, that it can be. To hold that sensations can tell us what an absolute existence is, is a contradiction even greater (if there be degrees in contradiction) than the one we have just seen the theory involved in. And so we find that the absolute object is for Mr. Spencer beyond consciousness, independent of consciousness, unknowable. In fact, Absolute and non-relativeness to consciousness are synonymous terms with him and the Sensationalists generally. Our question, therefore, is: Can we prove the relativity of feelings on the hypothesis that they are relative to an unknown something by reference of them to something out of and independent of consciousness?

In reply, we ask the following questions: 1. Is it possible to know *that* something is, if we have absolutely no knowledge *what* that something is? Can we know that an Absolute is, if we don't know what Absolute means? 2. Is it possible to know the existence of anything which is *ex hypothesi* out of relation to consciousness, and, further, know that this is the Absolute? 3. Is it possible to refer the whole content of consciousness to something which is beyond consciousness? Since the relative is so only as referred to an Absolute, can such a ratio between that which is in consciousness and that which is out of it be discovered as to demonstrate the relative character of the former? All these questions must, I conceive, be answered in the negative. As to the first, the predication of existence of an Unknowable seems to be a psychological impossibility. If there be any meaning in the assertion that X is, I confess I cannot see it. When it is said that something *is,* it is meant that *something* is. The predication must be of something; it cannot be of a pure Non-entity, like the Unknowable. The subject must *mean* something before it can be said either to be or not to be, or have any other intelligible proposition regarding it made. And so, as matter of fact, it is only as Mr. Spencer identifies his Unknowable with an Absolute, and thus takes advantage of the popular connotations of the word, that he is able to say that the Unknowable is; it is only as he smuggles some degree of qualification, however slight, into the subject that he can make it the subject of a proposition.

The question as to the possibility of knowledge of anything beyond consciousness, while presenting, since unknowable, the same difficulties to an affirmative answer as the question just considered, must, in addition, be answered negatively, on grounds of self-consistency. To say that something beyond consciousness is known to exist, is merely to say that the same thing is and is not in consciousness. Its special characteristic is to be *out* of consciousness; but, so far as it is known to exist, it is in and for consciousness. To suppose otherwise is to suppose that consciousness can in some way get outside of or "beyond" itself, and be conscious of that which is not in consciousness—a proposition as absurd as that a man can stand on his own shoulders, or outstrip his shadow.

If we go further and give to the Absolute any positive signification, if it becomes anything more than the blank negation
of all determinate relations, the bare *is*, which nevertheless is
a qualification by thought, we are only adding further relations to consciousness; we are only qualifying it further by
thought relations. Can the theory we are examining avoid
such determinations? This brings us to our third question:
Can a mere *x*, an absolutely unrelated object, afford us any
ground for asserting the relativity of specific objects in consciousness as they actually exist? If the absolute object is entirely out of relation to consciousness, it certainly cannot be
related to feelings, the supposed content of consciousness.
Even were it granted that we could know the existence of an
unknowable object and know that it was absolute, we should
not be justified in saying that our actual feelings were relative; to effect this, the Absolute must be brought into specific
relations with specific feelings. As long as its sole characteristic
is unrelatedness to consciousness, it and the content of consciousness have nothing to do with each other; and to make
one the ground of asserting anything regarding the real nature
of the other is absurd. Indeed, not only *must* specific relations
between the object and feelings be asserted, but we find as
matter of fact at least one such implicitly posited, *viz.*, that of
cause and effect. The absolute object is the cause, the feeling
is the effect. Now, remember that by this same theory all
knowledge comes from feeling, and then ask how is it possible
for the feeling consciousness to know this relation. At most,
sensationalism can mean by causation regular succession of
feelings; but the characteristics of the supposed cause in this
case are precisely that it is *not* a feeling, and (since it is unknowable) that the succession has never been once observed,
but it is only by making this self-destructive assumption that
the theory can get the slightest footing.

We conclude on this point, therefore, that, to prove the
Relativity of Feeling, it must be assumed that there is an
absolute object; that this object must be in consciousness, and
specifically related to the content of consciousness, and that
these relations cannot be in the way of feeling. We must know

that there is such an object; we must know *what* it is, and the what must consist in its relation to thought. Perhaps a method of stating this conclusion which would appear less formal, though not less expressive of the difficulty, would be to say that whatever is explained must be explained by reference to the known and not the unknown. Even were it admitted, *e.g.,* that the cause of our feelings and that force have some transcendental existence entirely unrelated to ourselves and entirely unknown, it would not be by such unknowns that the relative character of our present feelings could be shown. To show or to explain is to bring the thing into relation with something known. Explanation of the unknown by the known, not of the known by the unknown, is the order of science.

An examination of the specific feelings which are said to be relative to the subject will both bring this point into clearer light, and reveal in what, positively, their relativity does consist. In a concrete case: Why is the feeling of color as given in immediate consciousness said to be relative? Is the knowledge that it is such obtained by reference to a known or an unknown object? The question thus put answers itself. The sensation of color is said to be relative to ourselves because it is known to be dependent upon vibrations of ether and the retinal structure of the eye. It is merely the relation between these two as given in consciousness. Unless I know that there is such a retinal structure and such waves, or something corresponding to them, it is absurd to speak of the feeling of color as relative. It is only because I may know what light is as objective that I may know that what it seems to be in feeling is relative and subjective. And so with sound and taste. The subjectivity of taste, *e.g.,* means that in the object unrelated to a nervous organism there is such and such a physical or chemical structure, and that the sensation of taste is the relation between that structure and a corresponding organic structure. Clearly, then, our knowledge of subjectivity or relativity depends upon knowledge of something objective. But it must be especially noticed that this something objective is not given in feeling, and, therefore, is not relative to sense. These objects—the waves of ether, the structure of the retina, etc.—are not themselves feelings, and never have been: were they feelings, there would be no reason to assert the relative character of the feelings following upon them. Consequently, if it should be said that these so-called objects, the vibrations, etc., although not themselves feelings, yet have meaning attached to them only in so far as they represent *possibilities* of feeling—and mean only that under certain conditions they would become feelings, and that even now they possess signification only as symbolized by actual sensations—the answer is ready. But, before giving it, we will state the objection more fully. It may be said that the objects we have supposed, the vibrations, etc., are, as known, themselves conditioned by the affection of the nervous organism through some other object, and so on indefinitely, so that, after all, our knowledge of them is entirely relative.

But any such objection, to be of value, must hold that this process goes on *ad infinitum,* as otherwise there would be something known not through feeling, and, therefore, not relative. But if it does go on *ad infinitum,* it is clear that we fall into our original difficulty: nothing will ever be known except the immediate feelings, and to refer them to anything existing out of or beyond themselves will be impossible. The mere fact that one feeling is the antecedent of another could never give any reason for asserting that that feeling was relative in comparison with an unknown object. To suppose that it could, is to suppose that a feeling may transcend its own relativity. Therefore, on this theory of the infinite regress, it can never be known that there is an absolute object, and, therefore, immediately present feelings can never be referred to such an object; *i.e.,* can never be known to be relative. They become themselves absolute and absolutely known.

We conclude, therefore, that to prove the relativity of feeling is impossible without assuming that there are objects which are known not through feeling. In short, Sensationalism and the Relativity hypothesis again prove themselves utterly incompatible. The theory of the Relativity of Feeling, therefore, is so far from proving the subjectivity of our knowledge that it is impossible, except upon a theory which assumes that we do have objective knowledge.

The removal of a possible misapprehension and an objection are needed to complete the discussion of this point. It will perhaps be said that, since the relativity of feeling was known long before there was knowledge of what the objects really were, and that since now it is possible or probable, in some cases, that we do not really know the objective order, our account cannot be correct. But it must be noticed that this account does not depend for its correctness upon the question whether objects are really what we think they are, but simply upon the question whether the theory of the Relativity of Feeling does not assume and require that it is *possible* to so know them. And this question is implicitly answered in the affirmative in this very objection; for, if our present knowledge is incorrect, this can be shown only by reference to an established objective order to which, by greater knowledge, it shall be shown that our present theories do not correspond.

Or, again, it may be said our account is incorrect, because the real reason for calling a feeling relative is not because we have any knowledge of the object as referred to which it is relative, but simply because under the same objective conditions different persons have different sensations, or even the same person at different times. But nothing is gained by this change in expression, since it assumes that there are permanent objective conditions, which must be known. For the two differing feelings are either known to refer to the same object or they are not. If not, all ground for calling them relative disappears. But, if they are, of course this object must be known. By any method of stating the theory, it will be found impossible to avoid reference to a known order objectively existing. In this connection it may not be without interest to quote Mr. Spencer's summary of the theory as admitting implicitly, though unconsciously, just this point. He says: "The quality and the quantity of the sensation produced by a given amount of a given external force vary not only with the structure of the organism, specific and individual, as well as the structure of the part affected, but also with the age, the constitutional state of the part as modified by temperature, circulation, and previous use, and even with the relative motion of subject and object." What we desire to call attention to are the two admissions or claims which he makes, all unconscious of their bearing upon his theory. (1) That there is objectively *"a given amount of a given force";* and (2) that some nine objectively existing causes of the modification of this force as given in feeling can be shown. In short, it is assumed that there is an objective force, the kind and amount of which is known, and that the causes which produce the variations of this in immediate feeling can be shown, and, consequently, eliminated.

So far, our conclusions as to the relation of the theory of Relativity of Feeling to the theory of knowledge have been negative, and consisted in pointing out that it was not consistent with Sensationalism. But we are now prepared to draw a positive conclusion and say that the real meaning of the theory of Relativity of Feeling is that a feeling is a specific determinate relation or reaction given in consciousness between two bodies, one a sensitive, the other a non-sensitive object. It is possible to hold it, therefore, only in conjunction with a theory which allows knowledge of these objects; furthermore, since we have knowledge of these objective conditions, the knowledge of their relation as given in feeling, though relative indeed to the subject, is not for that reason a detraction from our knowledge of objects, but rather an addition. One certainly cannot see *a priori* any reason why the knowledge of the reactions of, say, gold in the presence of an acid should be an interesting addition to our knowledge of these substances, while the knowledge of its relation to a sensitive organism as given in feeling should be a deprivation of real knowledge. Except upon the theory that the real nature of things is their nature out of relation to everything, knowledge of the mode of relation between an object and an organism is just as much genuine knowledge as knowledge of its physical and chemical properties, which in turn are only its relations.

Leaving the subject of feelings, we come to that of relations between feelings which it has also been attempted to demonstrate to be purely relative to the subject, giving no knowledge of objective relations. There is no reason to draw upon the patience of readers to examine this view. It is subject to all the difficulties which we have made out against the like theory regarding feelings, besides laboring under the additional difficulty of having to show that these relations are themselves naught but feelings. Since we have already shown that the relativity of feelings to the subject cannot be proved without assuming objective relations, the case stands, *a fortiori,* against any such attempt as the present. There is also a self-contradiction in the theory so glaring that it might well have made anyone pause who was not so mastered by the presuppositions of his system as to be blind to the rules of ordinary logic. Sensationalism must and does hold that all relations are reducible to feelings; are themselves, indeed, but kinds of feeling. But the theory of relativity supposes a relation between the subjective feeling and the unknown object which is the absolute. But, according to Sensationalism, this relation must be a feeling. Hence nothing exists but feelings, and relativity is a myth! If there be no real relations, there can be no relativity; and, conversely, to say that feelings are *really* relative is to say that a relation really and objectively is, and is known. But to say this is to abandon the position that relation is a kind of feeling, and thereby to abandon Sensationalism. The fact that the two positions are so often held in conjunction is only evidence of how slightly the real meaning of either is grasped.

We summarize our results as follows: The doctrine of the Relativity of Feeling is incompatible with Sensationalism, and is so for two reasons. First, Sensationalism can never give knowledge of the *sine qua non* of the Relativity theory: the existence of an absolute object. For the very reason that sensation *is* relative to the subject, it can never transcend that relativity and make assertions regarding something absolute. Secondly, even if the existence of the absolute object were assured, feeling *qua* feeling can never demonstrate its own relativity. The Absolute here as an unknown Universal can never be known to be the Absolute which constitutes the relativity of the present content of consciousness. The feelings must be definitely referred to that absolute object. For feeling itself to make any such reference assumes that it can transcend its relativity, and know not only an absolute object, but what it is and what relations subsist between the two.

But if this knowledge of the existence of an absolute object and of its determinate relations is not given by feeling, we are justified in saying that it is given by a consciousness which by its relations determines the object. For, as we have shown that these objects must be related to consciousness, and cannot be related in the way of feeling, what they can be except as determined and constituted by relations of this consciousness it is not easy to see. Since a feeling can be known as relative only when referred to an object, this object cannot be a feeling, nor constituted by a feeling. The object must, then, be relative to a thinking consciousness.

There are two points which every theory of the Relativity of Feeling must include and explain: (*a*) In what does the relative character of the feelings consist? (*b*) What is the nature of the correlate absolute? The sensationalist hypothesis breaks down, as we have seen, at both these points. But our present theory, that relativity consists in a specific ratio between a sensitive and a non-sensitive object, which are constituted by relations to self-consciousness, proves itself, I think, amply adequate. Since relativity, according to it, consists not in relation to a nervous organism, but to consciousness, the possibility of knowledge is provided for. And, on the other hand, since this self-consciousness is the ground and source of relations, it cannot be subject to them. It is itself the true Absolute, then. This does not mean that it is the Unrelated, but that it is not conditioned by those conditions which determine its objects. Thus, we are saved the absurdity of believing in a relative which has no correlate absolute.

We have thus considered the theory of the Relativity of Knowledge in that form where it unites itself with and bases itself upon feeling. The reader may see for himself how large a portion of it would also apply to any theory of the Relativity of Knowledge. In closing, we must repeat the caution with which we began: that we are not dealing with the theory of relativity of feeling as a psychological theory. The correctness of the theory is undoubted. The philosophical interpretation of it is the point in question. Its conditions and implications need development, and we have attempted to show that when they are developed the theory is compatible neither with Sensationalism, nor with Subjectivism, nor with Agnosticism; that it is compatible only with a theory which admits the constitutive power of Thought, as itself ultimate Being, determining objects.

2

KANT AND PHILOSOPHIC METHOD

ON its subjective side, so far as individuals are concerned, philosophy comes into existence when men are confronted with problems and contradictions which common sense and the special sciences are able neither to solve nor resolve. There is felt the need of going deeper into things, of not being content with haphazard views or opinions derived from this or that science, but of having some principle which, true on its account, may also serve to judge the truth of all besides. It is no matter of accident that modern philosophy begins, in Descartes, with a method which doubts all, that it may find that wherewith to judge all; nor is it meaningless that Kant, the founder of modernist philosophy, commences his first great work with a similar demand, and "calls upon Reason to undertake the most difficult of tasks, self-knowledge, and establish a tribunal to decide all questions according to its own eternal and unchangeable laws." This self-knowledge of Reason, then, is the Method and criterion which Kant offers.

Before we may see what is involved in this, it is necessary to see what in gist the previous methods had been, and why they had failed. The method of "intellectualism" begun by Descartes and presented to Kant through Wolff was (in one word): Analysis of conceptions, with the law of identity or noncontradiction for criterion. To discover truth is to analyze the problem down to those simple elements which cannot be thought away, and reach a judgment whose predicate may be

From *The Journal of Speculative Philosophy*, April, 1884; 162-174.

clearly and distinctly seen to be identical with its subject. Analytic thought, proceeding by the law of identity, gives the method for philosophic procedure. Now, Kant in his pre-critical period [1] had become convinced that analysis does not explain such a conception as that which we have of causation: "How one thing should arise out of another, when it is not connected with it, according to the law of identity, this is a thing which I should much like to have explained." Nor again, while it may be, and undoubtedly is, the method for pure thought, does it give any means for passing from thought to existence. This, he would say, is no predicate of anything; it is part of no conception, and can be got by no analysis. Reality is added to our notions from without, not evolved from them. But, if logical thought is not adequate to such notions as cause, nor able to reach existence, it can be no method for discovering Absolute truth.

So Kant finds himself thrown into the arms of the Empiricists. It is experience which shows us the origin of an effect in a cause, and experience which adds reality or existence to our thoughts. What, then, is the method of "Empiricism"? Beginning with Bacon, at first it merely asserted that the mind must be freed from all subjective elements, and become a mirror, to reflect the world of reality. But this, as criterion, is purely negative, and required the positive complement of Locke. This method in a word is, *Analysis of perceptions with agreement as criterion.* In contrast with the intellectual school, which began with conceptions supposed to be found ready-made in the human mind, it begins with the perceptions impressed upon that blank tablet, the Mind, by external objects, and finds "knowledge to consist in the perception of the connection or agreement or disagreement of these ideas." But two questions arise: If truth or knowledge consists in perceptions, how, any more than from conceptions, shall we get to an external world? This question was answered by Berkeley in showing that, if knowledge were what this theory made it to be, the external world was just

[1] See especially his essay on attempt to introduce the idea of negative quantity into philosophy.

that whose *esse* is *percipi*. The second question is: What is agreement of perception? Agreement certainly means, as Locke said, "connexion," that is, mutual reference, or Synthesis. But how can this synthesis occur? The mind is a blank, a wax tablet, a *tabula rasa*, whose sole nature is receptivity, and certainly it can furnish no synthesis. Locke had avoided the difficulty by assuming that ideas come to us or are "given" more or less conjoined—that one has naturally some bond of union with another. But this, of course, cannot be. Simple impressions or perceptions are, as Hume stated, such as admit of no distinction or separation, and these are the ultimate sensations. These have no connection with each other, except perhaps the accidental one of following or occurring together in time, and so it is that "every distinct perception is a separate existence." Necessary connection among them, therefore, there can be none. Sensations are purely contingent, accidental, and external in their relations to each other, with no bonds of union. Any agreement is the result of chance or blind custom. Knowledge as the necessary connection of perceptions does not exist.

Kant consequently discovers, by a more thorough study of empiricism, that it too betrays him. It, no more than his former guides, can furnish him with a way of getting to an external world nor to knowledge at all. Nay, even self, some ghost of which was left him by the other method, has disappeared too.

What has been the difficulty? Descartes did not come to a standstill at once, for he had tacitly presupposed the synthetic power of thought in itself—had even laid the ground for a theory of it in his reference to the Ego, or self-consciousness. But his successors, neglecting this, and developing only the analytic aspect of thought, had produced a vacuum, where no step to existence or actual relations, being synthetic, could be taken. "Conceptions are empty." Nor had Locke been estopped immediately, for he presupposed some synthesis in the objective world; but it turns out that he had no right to it, and world, self, and all actual relations, being synthetic, have gone. "Perceptions are blind." The problem, then, is

[37]

clearly before Kant, as is the key to its solution. Synthesis is the *sine qua non*. Knowledge is synthesis, and the explanation of knowledge or truth must be found in the explanation of synthesis. Hence the question of Method is now the question: How are synthetic judgments *a priori* possible? *A priori* means simply belonging to Reason in its own nature, so the question is, How and to what extent is Reason the source of synthesis?

The case stands thus: Pure thought is purely analytic; experience *per se* gives only a blind rhapsody of particulars, without meaning or connection—actual experience, or knowledge involves, *is* synthesis. How shall it be got? One path remains open. We may suppose that while thought *in itself* is analytic, it is synthetic when applied to a material given it, and that from this material, by its functions, it forms the objects which it knows. And such, in its lowest terms, is the contribution Kant makes. The material, the manifold, the particulars, are furnished by Sense in perception; the conceptions, the synthetic functions from Reason itself, and the union of these two elements are required, as well for the formation of the object known, as for its knowing.

To characterize Kant's contribution to Method, it remains to briefly examine these two sides of his theory: First, for the part played by the synthetic functions or the categories. These, in first intention, are so many conceptions of the understanding, and, as such, subject to analysis according to the law of identity, and thus furnish the subject matter of Logic. But they also have relation to objects, and, as such, are synthetic and furnish the subject matter of Transcendental Logic, whose work is to demonstrate and explain their objective validity. This is done by showing that "the categories make experience and its objects for the first time possible." That is to say, Kant, after showing that the principles of identity and contradiction, though the highest criteria of logical thought, can give no aid in determining the truths of actual experience, inquires what is the criterion of truth for the latter, or what comes to the same thing, of the synthetic use of the categories as Transcendental Logic—and the answer he finds to be "possible experience" itself. In other words, the categories have objective validity or synthetic use because without them no experience would be possible. If Hume, for example, asks how we can have assurance that the notion of causality has any worth when applied to objects, he is answered by showing that without this notion experience as an intelligible connected system would not exist. By the categories the objects of experience are constituted, and hence their objective validity.

It follows, accordingly, that the system of experience may be determined, as to its form, by a completely made out system of categories. In them, as synthetic functions, constituting experience, we find the criterion of truth. But they themselves have a higher condition. As synthetic functions, they must all be functions of a higher unity which is subject to none of them. And this Kant calls the synthetic *unity* of Apperception or, in brief, self-consciousness. This is the highest condition of experience, and in the developed notion of self-consciousness we find the criterion of truth. The theory of self-consciousness is Method.

But this abstract statement must be further developed. It comes to saying, on the one hand, that the criterion of the categories is possible experience, and on the other, that the criterion of possible experience is the categories and their supreme condition. This is evidently a circle, yet a circle which, Kant would say, exists in the case itself, which expresses the very nature of knowledge. It but states that in knowledge there is naught but knowledge which knows or is known—the only judge of knowledge, of experience, is experience itself. And experience is a system, a real whole made up of real parts. It as a whole is necessarily implied in every fact of experience, while it is constituted in and through these facts. In other terms, the relation of categories to experience is the relation of members of an organism to a whole. The criterion of knowledge is neither anything outside of knowledge, nor a particular conception within the sphere of knowledge which is not subject to the system as a whole; it is just this system which is constituted, so far as its form is concerned, by the categories.

Philosophic Method, or the discovering of the criterion of truth, will consist, then, in no setting up of a transcendent object as the empiricists did, or of an abstract principle after the manner of the intellectual school. Since the categories, in and through self-consciousness, constitute experience, Method will consist in making out a complete table of these categories in all their mutual relations, giving each its proper placing, with the full confidence that when so placed each will have its proper place in experience, *i.e.*, its capacity for expressing reality determined.

But we have now strayed far from Kant. While having said nothing which is not deducible from his Transcendental Logic, we have abstracted from the fact that this holds only of the *form* of our knowledge; that there is also an *aesthetic*, and that thought is synthetic, not in itself, but only upon a material supplied to it from without. Turning to this, we find the aspect of affairs changed. Though the categories make experience, they make it out of a foreign material to which they bear a purely external relation. They constitute objects, but these objects are not such in universal reference, but only to beings of like capacities of receptivity as ourselves. They respect not existence in itself, but ourselves as *affected* by that existence. The system of categories furnishes the criterion for all the knowledge we have, but this turns out to be no real knowledge. It is, Hegel says, as if one ascribed correct insight to a person, and then added that he could see only into the untruth, not the truth. Nor does the deficiency of our method end here. We had previously assumed that the categories as a system, or in their organic relation to self-consciousness, could be known. But it now turns out that nothing can be known except that to which this feeling of external matter through sensibility is given. To know this subject, or self-consciousness, is to make an object of it, and every object is sensible, that is, has a feeling which tells us how we are affected. But such a knowledge is evidently no knowledge of self-consciousness in its own nature. Thus, so far as knowledge is concerned, it must remain a bare form of self-identity, of "I = I," into definite organic relations with which the categories can never be brought. Hence, it appears that our picture of a method was doubly false—false in that after all it could not reach truth; false in that after all no such method was in itself possible. Our organic system of categories cannot constitute absolute truth—and no such organic system is itself knowable. Criterion and method we are still without. The golden prize, which seemed just within our hands as long as we confined ourselves to the Transcendental Logic, turns out to be a tinsel superfluity.

Yet, none the less, there was the suggestion of a method there, which is exactly what we wish. The only question is: Is its reference to the Aesthetic necessary? Is the latter a necessary part of Kant's theory, or, so far as it concerns the reception of external matter, an excrescence? The question is just here: Previous methods failed because they made no allowance for synthesis—Kant's because the synthesis can occur only upon matter foreign to it. Thought in the previous theories was *purely* analytic; in Kant's it is *purely* synthetic, in that it is synthesis of foreign material. Were thought at once synthetic *and* analytic, differentiating and integrating in its own nature, both affirmative and negative, relating to self at the same time that it related to other—indeed, through this relation to other—the difficulty would not have arisen.

Is the state of the case as Kant supposes? Must we say that Reason is synthetic only upon condition that material be given it to act upon, or, may it be, that while we must say that for the individual the material, nay, the form as indissolubly connected with the material, is given, yet, to Reason itself, nothing is given in the sense of being foreign to it?

A slight examination will show us that, at least as far as Kant is concerned, the former supposition is but an arbitrary limitation or assumption which Kant imposed upon himself, or received without question from previous philosophy. On one side, he had learned that pure thought is analytic; on the other, that the individual is affected with sensations impressed upon it by external objects. At the same time that he corrects both of these doctrines with his own deduction of the categories, he formally retains both errors.

So we have him asking at the very outset, as a matter of course: "In what other way is it to be conceived that the knowing power can be excited to activity, except by objects which affect our senses?" That is to say, he assumes at the outset that there is something external to Reason by which it must be excited. He perceives, what all admit, that an individual organized in a certain specific way with certain senses, and external things acting upon these senses, are conditions to our knowledge, and then proceeds to identify respectively this individual with the subject, and these things with the object, in the process of knowledge. But here it is that we ask with what right does he make this identification. If it is made, then surely the case stands with Reason as he says it does— it acts only upon a material foreign to it. Yet this individual and these things are but known objects already constituted by the categories, and existing only for the synthetic unity of apperception or self-consciousness. This, then, is the real subject, and the so-called subject and object are but the forms in which it expresses its own activity. In short, the relation of subject and object is not a "transcendent" one, but an "immanent," and is but the first form in which Reason manifests that it is both synthetic and analytic; that it separates itself from itself, that it may thereby reach higher unity with itself. It is the highest type of the law which Reason follows everywhere. The material which was supposed to confront Reason as foreign to it is but the manifestation of Reason itself. Such, at least, are the results which we reach in the Transcendental Deduction, and such are the results we consider ourselves justified to keep in opposition to Kant's pure assumptions.

We see the same thing in Kant's theory of phenomenon. Just as, concerning the process of knowledge, he assumes that subject and object are in external relation to each other, and hence Reason in contact with a foreign material, so here he assumes that the character of phenomenality consists in relation to an unknowable noumenon. The phenomenon is referred to something outside of experience, instead of being defined by its relation within experience—in which case it would be seen to be a phenomenon in its own nature, in that the categories which constitute it as such are not adequate to truth.

We have but to turn to Kant's derivation of the categories, to be again assured that Kant's theory of Reason as synthetic only in reference to foreign material is one purely assumed. As is notorious, these he took from the Logic of the School, which he held to give a complete table of all the forms of pure thought. When we turn to this table we find the highest point reached in it to be reciprocity. Now, reciprocity is precisely that external relation of two things to each other that we have already found existing, in Kant's theory, between subject and object in Knowledge—the relations of things that are independent of each other but mutually act upon each other. So, too, it is but another way of stating that Thought, analytic in itself, is synthetic when applied to an external material, or that this material, blind and haphazard in itself, is formed by something acting upon it. When Kant tells us, therefore, that the categories are not limited in their own nature, but become so when applied, as they must be, to determine space and time, we have in our hands the means of correcting him. They are limited, and express just the limitation of Kant himself. And Kant confesses their insufficiency as soon as he takes up the questions of moral and aesthetic experience and of life itself. Here we find the categories of freedom determined by ends, free production, organism to be everywhere present, while all through his *Critiques* is woven in the notion of an intuitive understanding which is the ultimate criterion of all truth, and this understanding is just what we have already met as the organic system of experience or self-consciousness.

Whether we consider the relations of subject and object, or the nature of the categories, we find ourselves forced into the presence of the notion of organic relation. The relation between subject and object is not an external one; it is one in a higher unity which is itself constituted by this relation. The only conception adequate to experience as a whole is organism. What is involved in the notion of organism? Why, precisely the Idea which we had formerly reached of a Reason which is both analytic and synthetic, a Reason which differentiates itself that it may integrate itself into fuller riches, a Reason that denies itself that it may become itself. Such a Reason, and neither an analytic Thought, nor an analytic Experience, nor a Reason which is analytic in itself, and synthetic for something else, is the ultimate criterion of truth, and the theory of this Reason is the Philosophic Method.

The two defects which we found before in Kant's theory now vanish. The method is no longer one which can reach untruth only, nor is it a method which cannot be made out. The track which we were upon in following the course of the Transcendental Deduction was the right one. The criterion of experience is the system of categories in their organic unity in self-consciousness, and the method consists in determining this system and the part each plays in constituting it. The method takes the totality of experience to pieces, and brings before us its conditions in their entirety. The relations of its content, through which alone this content has character and meaning, whereby it becomes an intelligible, connected whole, must be made to appear.

It was the suggestion of this method, it was the suggestion of so many means for its execution, it was the actual carrying of it out in so many points that makes Kant's *Philosophy* the *critical* philosophy, and his work the *crisis,* the separating, dividing, turning point of modern philosophy, and this hurried sketch would not be complete if we did not briefly point out what steps have been taken toward the fulfilling of the Ideal. This is found chiefly in Hegel and his *Logic*. We can only discuss in the light of what has already been said why Hegel begins with Logic; why the negative plays so important a part in his philosophy, and what is the meaning of Dialectic. (1) Logic. One of Hegel's repeated charges against Kant is, that he examines the categories with reference to their *objective* character, and not to determine their own meaning and worth. At first it might seem as if this were the best way to determine their worth, but it ought now to be evident that such a procedure is both to presuppose that they are subjective in themselves, and that we have a ready-made conception of object by which to judge them—in short, it amounts to saying that these conceptions are purely analytic, and have meaning only in relation to an external material. Hence the method must examine the categories without any reference to subjective or objective existences; or, to speak properly, since we now see that there are no purely subjective or objective existences, without any relation to things and thoughts as two distinct spheres. The antithesis between them is not to be blinked out of sight, but it must be treated as one which exists within Reason, and not one with one term in and the other out. The categories which, for the individual, determine the nature of the object, and those which state how the object is brought into the subjective form of cognition, must be deduced from Reason alone. A theory performing this task is what Hegel calls Logic, and is needed not only to overcome Kant's defects, but is immediately suggested by his positive accomplishments. In our account of the Transcendental Deduction we saw that self-consciousness was the supreme condition of all the categories, and hence can be subject in itself to none of them. When it is made subject we have no longer the absolute self-consciousness, but the empirical ego, the object of the inner sense. In short, the categories constitute the individuals as an object of experience, just as much as they do the material known. Hence they are no more subjective than objective. We may call them indifferently neither or both. The truth is, they belong to a sphere where the antithesis between subject and object is still potential, or *an sich*. It is evident, therefore, that logic, in the Hegelian use, is just that criterion of truth which we thought at first to find in Kant's transcendental Logic—it is an account of the conceptions or categories of Reason which constitute experience, internal and external, subjective and objective, and an account of them as a system, an organic unity in which each has its own place fixed. It is the completed Method of Philosophy.

(2) The Negative in Hegel. It ought now to be evident that

any Philosophy which can pretend to be a Method of Truth must show Reason as both Analytic *and* Synthetic. If History can demonstrate anything, it has demonstrated this, both by its successes and its failures. Reason must be that which separates itself, which differentiates, goes forth into differences, that it may then grasp these differences into a unity of its own. It cannot unite unless there be difference; there can be no synthesis where there is not analysis. On the other hand, the differences must remain forever foreign to Reason unless it brings them together; there can be no analysis where there is not synthesis, or a unity to be dirempted. If there be no synthesis in Reason, we end in the impotence of the former school of intellectualism, or in the helpless skepticism of Hume; if Reason be synthetic only upon a foreign material, we end in the contradictions of Kant. If there is to be *knowledge,* Reason must include both elements within herself. It is Hegel's thorough recognition of this fact that causes him to lay such emphasis on the negative. Pure affirmation or identity reaches its summit in Spinoza, where all is lost in the infinite substance of infinite attributes, as waves in the sea. Yet even Spinoza was obliged to introduce the negative, the determinations, the modes, though he never could succeed in getting them by any means from his pure affirmation. In Hume we find pure difference or negation, the manifold particularization of sensations, but even he is obliged to introduce synthetic principles in the laws of association, though he never succeeds in legitimately deriving them from sensations, for a "consistent sensationalism is speechless." Kant had tried a compromise of the principle, synthesis from within, difference from without. That, too, failed to give us knowledge or a criterion of Truth. Hegel comprehends the problem, and offers us Reason affirmative *and* negative, and affirmative only in and through its own negations, as the solution.

(3) Dialectic. We have now the notion of Dialectic before us in its essential features. We have seen that the desired object is a theory of the Conceptions of Reason in an organic system, and that Reason is itself both integrating and differentiating. Dialectic is the construction by Reason, through its

successive differentiations and resumptions of these differences into higher unities, of just this system. If we take any single category of Reason—that is to say, some conception which we find involved in the system of experience—this is one specific form into which Reason has unified or "synthesized" itself. Reason itself is immanent in this category; but, since Reason is also differentiating or analytic, Reason must reveal itself as such in this category, which accordingly passes, or is reflected, or develops into its opposite, while the two conceptions are then resumed into the higher unity of a more concrete conception.

Since the system of knowledge is implicit in each of its members, each category must judge itself, or rather, Reason, in its successive forms, passes judgment on its own inadequacy until the adequate is reached—and this can be nothing but Reason no longer implicit, but devolped into its completed system. Reason must everywhere, and in all its forms, propose itself as what it is, *viz.,* absolute or adequate to the entire truth of experience; but, since at first its *form* is still inadequate, it must show what is absolutely implicit in it, *viz.,* the entire sysem. That at first it does, by doing what it is the nature of the Reason which it manifests to do, by differencing itself, or passing into its opposite, its other; but, since Reason is also synthetic, grasping together, these differences must resolve themselves into a higher unity. Thus, Reason continues until it has developed itself into the conception which is in form equal to what itself is in content, or, until it has manifested all that it is implicitly. A twofold process has occurred. On the one hand, each special form of Reason or Category has been placed; that is, its degree of ability to state absolute truth fixed by its place in the whole organic system. On the other, the system itself has been developed; that is to say, as Reason goes on manifesting its own nature through successive differences and unities, each lower category is not destroyed, but retained—but retained at its proper value. Each, since it is Reason, has its relative *truth;* but each, since Reason is not yet adequately manifested, has only a *relative* truth. The Idea is the completed category, and this has for its meaning or content Reason made explicit or manifested; that is, all the stages or types of Reason employed in reaching it. "The categories are not errors, which one goes through on the way to the truth, but phases of truth. Their completed system in its organic wholeness is *the* Truth." And such a system is at once philosophic Method and Criterion; method, because it shows us not only the way to reach truth, but truth itself in construction; criterion, because it gives us the form of experience to which all the facts of experience as organic members must conform.

It will be seen, I hope, that we have not left our subject, "Kant's Relation to Philosophic Method"; for a crisis is nothing in itself. It is a crisis only as it is the turning point; and a turning point is the old passing into the new, and can be understood only as the old and the new are understood. The criterion of Kant is just this turning point; it is the transition of the old abstract thought, the old meaningless conception of experience, into the new concrete thought, the ever growing, ever rich experience.

3

THE NEW PSYCHOLOGY

BACON'S dictum regarding the proneness of the mind, in explanation, toward unity and simplicity, at no matter what sacrifice of material, has found no more striking exemplification than that offered in the fortunes of psychology. The least developed of the sciences, for a hundred years it has borne in its presentations the air of the one most completely finished. The infinite detail and complexity of the simplest psychical life, its interweavings with the physical organism, with the life of others in the social organism—created no special difficulty; and in a book like James Mill's *Analysis* we find every mental phenomenon not only explained, but explained by reference to one principle. That rich and colored experience, never the same in two nations, in two individuals, in two moments of the same life—whose thoughts, desires, fears, and hopes have furnished the material for the ever-developing literature of the ages, for a Homer and a Chaucer, a Sophocles and a Shakespeare, for the unwritten tragedies and comedies of daily life—was neatly and carefully dissected, its parts labeled and stowed away in their proper pigeonholes, the inventory taken, and the whole stamped with the stamp of *un fait accompli*. Schematism was supreme, and the air of finality was over all.

We know better now. We know that that life of man whose unfolding furnishes psychology its material is the most difficult and complicated subject which man can investigate. We have some consciousness of its ramifications and of its con-

From *The Andover Review*, September, 1884; 278-289.

nections. We see that man is somewhat more than a neatly dovetailed psychical machine who may be taken as an isolated individual, laid on the dissecting table of analysis and duly anatomized. We know that his life is bound up with the life of society, of the nation in the *ethos* and *nomos;* we know that he is closely connected with all the past by the lines of education, tradition, and heredity; we know that man is indeed the microcosm who has gathered into himself the riches of the world, both of space and of time, the world physical and the world psychical. We know also of the complexities of the individual life. We know that our mental life is not a syllogistic *sorites,* but an enthymeme most of whose members are suppressed; that large tracts never come into consciousness; that those which do get into consciousness, are vague and transitory, with a meaning hard to catch and read; are infinitely complex, involving traces of the entire life history of the individual, or are vicarious, having significance only in that for which they stand; that psychical life is a continuance, having no breaks into "distinct ideas which are separate existences"; that analysis is but a process of abstraction, leaving us with a parcel of parts from which the *"geistige Band"* is absent; that our distinctions, however necessary, are unreal and largely arbitrary; that mind is no compartment box nor bureau of departmental powers; in short, that we know almost nothing about the actual activities and processes of the soul. We know that the old psychology gave descriptions of that which has for the most part no existence, and which at the best it but described and did not explain.

I do not say this to depreciate the work of the earlier psychologists. There is no need to cast stones at those who, having a work to do, did that work well and departed. With Sir William Hamilton and J. Stuart Mill the school passed away. It is true that many psychologists still use their language and follow their respective fashions. Their influence, no doubt, is yet everywhere felt. But changed conditions are upon us, and thought, no more than revolution, goes backward. Psychology can live no better in the past than physiology or physics; but there is no more need for us to revile Hume and Reid for not giving birth to a full and complete science, than there is for complaining that Newton did not anticipate the physical knowledge of today, or Harvey the physiological.

The work of the earlier psychologists bore a definite and necessary relation both to the scientific conditions and the times in which it was done. If they had recognized the complexity of the subject and attempted to deal with it, the science would never have been begun. The very condition of its existence was the neglect of the largest part of the material, the seizing of a few schematic ideas and principles, and their use for universal explanation. Very mechanical and very abstract to us, no doubt, seems their division of the mind into faculties, the classification of mental phenomena into the regular, graded, clear-cut series of sensation, image, concept, etc.; but let one take a look into the actual processes of his own mind, the actual course of the mental life there revealed, and he will realize how utterly impossible were the description, much more the explanation, of what goes on there, unless the larger part of it were utterly neglected, and a few broad schematic rubrics seized by which to reduce this swimming chaos to some semblance of order.

Again, the history of all science demonstrates that much of its progress consists in bringing to light problems. Lack of consciousness of problems, even more than lack of ability to solve them, is the characteristic of the non-scientific mind. Problems cannot be solved till they are seen and stated, and the work of the earlier psychologists consisted largely in this sort of work. Further, they were filled with the *Zeitgeist* of their age, the age of the eighteenth century and the *Aufklärung,* which found nothing difficult, which hated mystery and complexity, which believed with all its heart in principles, the simpler and more abstract the better, and which had the passion of completion. By this spirit, the psychologists as well as the other thinkers of the day were mastered, and under its influence they thought and wrote.

Thus their work was conditioned by the nature of science itself, and by the age in which they lived. This work they did, and left to us a heritage of problems, of terminology, and of principles which we are to solve, reject, or employ as best we may. And the best we can do is to thank them, and then go about our *own* work; the worst is to make them the dividing lines of schools, or settle in hostile camps according to *their* banners. We are not called upon to defend them, for their work is in the past; we are not called upon to attack them, for *our* work is in the future.

It will be of more use briefly to notice some of the movements and tendencies which have brought about the change of attitude, and created what may be called the "New Psychology."

Not the slightest of these movements has been, of course, the reaction of the present century, from the abstract, if clear, principles of the eighteenth, toward concrete detail, even though it be confused. The general failure of the eighteenth century in all but destructive accomplishment forced the recognition of the fact that the universe is not so simple and easy a matter to deal with, after all; that there are many things in earth, to say nothing of heaven, which were not dreamed of in the philosophy of clearness and abstraction, whether that philosophy had been applied along the lines of the state, society, religion, or science. The world was sated with system and longed for fact. The age became realistic. That the movement has been accompanied with at least temporary loss in many directions, with the perishing of ideals, forgetfulness of higher purpose, decay of enthusiasm, absorption in the petty, a hard contentedness in the present, or a cynical pessimism as to both present and future, there can be no doubt. But neither may it be doubted that the movement was a necessity to bring the Antaeus of humanity back to the mother soil of experience, whence it derives its strength and very life, and to prevent it from losing itself in a substanceless vapor where its ideals and purposes become as thin and watery as the clouds toward which it aspires.

Out of this movement and as one of its best aspects came that organized, systematic, tireless study into the secrets of nature, which, counting nothing common or unclean, thought no drudgery beneath it, or rather thought nothing drudgery—that movement which with its results has been the great revelation given to the nineteenth century to make. In this movement psychology took its place, and in the growth of physiology which accompanied it I find the first if not the greatest occasion of the development of the New Psychology.

It is a matter in everyone's knowledge that, with the increase of knowledge regarding the structure and functions of the nervous system, there has arisen a department of science known as physiological psychology, which has already thrown great light upon psychical matters. But unless I entirely misapprehend the popular opinion regarding the matter, there is very great confusion and error in this opinion, regarding the relations of this science to psychology. This opinion, if I rightly gather it, is that physiological psychology is a science which does, or at least claims to, explain all psychical life by reference to the nature of the nervous system. To illustrate: very many professed popularizers of the results of scientific inquiry, as well as laymen, seem to think that the entire psychology of vision is explained when we have a complete knowledge of the anatomy of the retina, of its nervous connection with the brain, and of the center in the latter which serves for visual functions; or that we know all about memory if we can discover that certain brain cells store up nervous impressions, and certain fibers serve to connect these cells—the latter producing the association of ideals, while the former occasion their reproduction. In short, the commonest view of physiological psychology seems to be that it is a science which shows that some or all of the events of our mental life are physically conditioned upon certain nerve structures, and thereby *explains* these events. Nothing could be further from the truth. So far as I know, all the leading investigators clearly realize that explanations of psychical events, in order to *explain,* must themselves be psychical and not physiological. However important such knowledge as that of which we have just been speaking may be for physiology, it has *of itself* no value for psychology. It tells simply what and how physiological elements serve as a basis for psychical acts; what the latter *are,* or how they are to be explained, it tells us not at all. Physiology can no more, of itself, give us the what, why, and how of psychical life, than the physical geography of a country can enable us to construct or explain the history of the nation that has dwelt within that country. However important, however indispensable the land with all its qualities is as a basis for that history, that history itself can be ascertained and explained only through historical records and historic conditions. And so psychical events can be observed only through psychical means, and interpreted and explained by psychical conditions and facts.

What can be meant, then, by saying that the rise of this physiological psychology has produced a revolution in psychology? This: that it has given a new instrument, introduced a new *method*—that of experiment, which has supplemented and corrected the old method of introspection. Psychical facts still remain psychical, and are to be explained through psychical conditions; but our means of ascertaining what these facts are and how they are conditioned have been indefinitely widened. Two of the chief elements of the method of experiment are variation of conditions at the will and under the control of the experimenter, and the use of quantitative measurement. Neither of these elements can be applied through any introspective process. Both may be through physiological psychology. This starts from the well-grounded facts that the psychical events known as sensations arise through bodily stimuli, and that the psychical events known as volitions result in bodily movements; and it finds in these facts the possibility of the application of the method of experimentation. The bodily stimuli and movements may be directly controlled and measured, and thereby, indirectly, the psychical states which they excite or express.

` There is no need at this day to dwell upon the advantages derived in any science from the application of experiment. We know well that it aids observation by indefinitely increasing the power of analysis and by permitting exact measurement, and that it equally aids explanation by enabling us so to vary the constituent elements of the case investigated as to select the indispensable. Nor is there need to call attention to the especial importance of experiment in a science where introspection is the only direct means of observation. We are sufficiently aware of the defects of introspection. We know that it is limited, defective, and often illusory as a means of observation, and can in no way directly explain. To explain is to mediate; to connect the given fact with an unseen principle; to refer the phenomenon to an antecedent condition —while introspection can deal only with the immediate present, with the given now. This is not the place to detail the specific results accomplished through this application of experiment to the psychological sphere; but two illustrations may perhaps be permitted: one from the realm of sensation, showing how it has enabled us to analyze states of consciousness which were otherwise indecomposable; and the other from that of perception, showing how it has revealed processes which could be reached through no introspective method.

It is now well known that no sensation as it exists in consciousness is simple or ultimate. Every color sensation, for example, is made up by at least three fundamental sensory *quales*, probably those of red, green, and violet; while there is every reason to suppose that each of these qualities, far from being simple, is compounded of an indefinite number of homogeneous units. Thus the simplest musical sensation has also been experimentally proved to be in reality not simple, but doubly compound. First, there is the number of qualitatively like units constituting it which occasion the pitch of the note, according to the relations of time in which they stand to each other; and second, there is the relation which one order of these units bears to other secondary orders, which gives rise to the peculiar *timbre* or tone color of the sound; while in a succession of notes these relations are still further complicated by those which produce melody and harmony. And all this complexity occurs, be it remembered, in a state of consciousness which, to introspection, is homogeneous and ultimate. In these respects physiology has been to psychology what the microscope is to biology, or analysis to chemistry. But the experimental method has done more than reveal hidden parts, or analyze into simpler elements. It has aided explanation, as well as observation, by showing the processes which condition a psychical event. This is nowhere better illustrated than in visual perception. It is already almost a commonplace of knowledge that, for example, the most complex landscape which we can have before our eyes is, psychologically speaking, not a simple ultimate fact, nor an impression stamped upon us from without, but is built up from color and muscular sensations, with, perhaps, unlocalized feelings of extension, by means of the psychical laws of interest, attention, and interpretation. It is, in short, a complex judgment involving within itself emotional, volitional, and intellectual elements. The knowledge of the nature of these elements, and of the laws which govern their combination into the complex visual scene, we owe to physiological psychology, through the new means of research with which it has endowed us. The importance of such a discovery can hardly be overestimated. In fact, this doctrine that our perceptions are not immediate facts, but are mediated psychical processes, has been called by Helmholtz the most important psychological result yet reached.

But besides the debt we owe Physiology for the method of experiment, is that which is due her for an indirect means of investigation which she has put within our hands; and it is this aspect of the case which has led, probably, to such misconceptions of the relations of the two sciences as exist. For while no direct conclusions regarding the nature of mental activities or their causes can be drawn from the character of nervous structure or function, it is possible to reason indirectly from one to the other, to draw analogies and seek confirmation. That is to say, if a certain nervous arrangement can be made out to exist, there is always a strong presumption that there is a psychical process corresponding to it; or if the connection between two physiological nerve processes can be shown to be of a certain nature, one may surmise that the relation between corresponding psychical activities is somewhat analogous. In this way, by purely physiological discoveries, the mind may be led to suspect the existence of some mental activity hitherto overlooked, and attention directed to its workings, or light may be thrown on points hitherto obscure. Thus it was, no doubt, the physiological discovery of the time occupied in transmission of a nervous impulse that led the German psychologists to their epoch-making investigations regarding the time occupied in various mental activities; thus, too, the present psychological theories regarding the relation of the intellectual and volitional tracts of minds were undoubtedy suggested and largely developed in analogy with Bell's discovery of the distinct nature of the sensory and motor nerves. Again, the present theory that memory is not a chamber hall for storing up ideas and their traces or relics, but is lines of activity along which the mind habitually works, was certainly suggested from the growing physiological belief that the brain cells which form the physical basis of memory do not in any way store up past impressions or their traces, but have, by these impressions, their structure so modified as to give rise to a certain functional mode of activity. Thus many important generalizations might be mentioned which were suggested and developed in analogy with physiological discoveries.

The influence of biological science in general upon psychology has been very great. Every important development in science contributes to the popular consciousness, and indeed to philosophy, some new conception which serves for a time as a most valuable category of classification and explanation. To biology is due the conception of organism. Traces of the notion are found long before the great rise of biological science, and, in particular, Kant has given a complete and careful exposition of it; but the great role which the "organic" conception has played of late is doubtless due in largest measure to the growth of biology. In psychology this conception has led to the recognition of mental life as an organic unitary process developing according to the laws of all life, and not a theatre for the exhibition of independent autonomous faculties, or a *rendezvous* in which isolated, atomic sensations and ideas may gather, hold external converse, and then forever part. Along with this recognition of the solidarity of mental life has come that of the relation in which it stands to other lives organized in society. The idea of environment is a necessity to the idea of organism, and with the conception of environment comes the impossibility of considering psychical life as an individual, isolated thing developing in a vacuum.

This idea of the organic relation of the individual to that organized social life into which he is born, from which he draws his mental and spiritual sustenance, and in which he must perform his proper function or become a mental and moral wreck, forms the transition to the other great influence which I find to have been at work in developing the New Psychology. I refer to the growth of those vast and as yet undefined topics of inquiry which may be vaguely designated as the social and historical sciences—the sciences of the origin and development of the various spheres of man's activity. With the development of these sciences has come the general feeling that the scope of psychology has been cabined and cramped till it has lost all real vitality, and there is now the recognition of the fact that all these sciences possess their psychological sides, present psychological material, and demand treatment and explanation at the hands of psychology. Thus the material for the latter, as well as its scope, have been indefinitely extended. Take the matter of language. What a wealth of material and of problems it offers. How did it originate; was it contemporaneous with that of thought, or did it succeed it; how have they acted and reacted upon each other; what psychological laws have been at the basis of the development and differentiation of languages, of the development of their structures and syntax, of the meaning of words, of all the rhetorical devices of language? Anyone at all acquainted with modern discussions of language will recognize at a glance that the psychological presentation and discussion of such problems is almost enough of itself to revolutionize the old method of treating psychology. In the languages themselves, moreover, we have a mine of resources which, as a record of the development of intelligence, can be compared only to the importance of the paleontological record to the student of animal and vegetable life.

But this is only one aspect, and not comparatively a large one, of the whole field. Folklore and primitive culture, ethnology and anthropology, all render their contributions of matter, and press upon us the necessity of explanation. The origin and development of myth, with all which it includes, the relation to the nationality, to language, to ethical ideas, to social customs, to government and the state, is itself a psychological field wider than any known to the previous century. Closely connected with this is the growth of ethical ideas, their relations to the consciousness and activities of the nation in which they originate, to practical morality, and to art. Thus I could go through the various spheres of human activity, and point out how thoroughly they are permeated with psychological questions and material. But it suffices to say that history in its broadest aspect is itself a psychological problem, offering the richest resources of matter.

Closely connected with this, and also influential in the development of the New Psychology, is that movement which may be described as the commonest thoughts of everyday life in all its forms, whether normal or abnormal. The cradle and the asylum are becoming the laboratory of the psychologist of the latter half of the nineteenth century. The study of children's minds, the discovery of their actual thoughts and feelings from babyhood up, the order and nature of the development of their mental life and the laws governing it, promises to be a mine of greatest value. When it was recognized that insanities are neither supernatural interruptions nor utterly inexplicable "visitations," it gradually became evident that they were but exaggerations of certain of the normal workings of the mind, or lack of proper harmony and coordination among these workings; and thus another department of inquiries, of psychical experiments performed by nature, was opened to us, which has already yielded valuable results. Even the prison and the penitentiary have made their contributions.

If there be any need of generalizing the foregoing, we may say that the development of the New Psychology has been due to the growth, on the one hand, of the science of physiology, giving us the method of experiment, and, on the other, of the sciences of humanity in general, giving us the method of objective observation, both of which indefinitely supplement and correct the old method of subjective introspection.

So much for the occasioning causes and method of the New Psychology. Are its results asked for? It will be gathered, from what has already been said, that its results cannot be put down in black and white like those of a mathematical theory. It is a movement, no system. But as a movement it has certain general features.

The chief characteristic distinguishing it from the old psychology is undoubtedly the rejection of a formal logic as its model and test. The old psychologists almost without exception held to a nominalistic logic. This of itself were a matter of no great importance, were it not for the inevitable tendency and attempt to make living concrete facts of experience square with the supposed norms of an abstract, lifeless thought, and to interpret them in accordance with its formal conceptions. This tendency has nowhere been stronger than in those who proclaimed that "experience" was the sole source of all knowledge. They emasculated experience till their logical conceptions could deal with it; they sheared it down till it would fit their logical boxes; they pruned it till it presented a trimmed tameness which would shock none of their laws; they preyed upon its vitality till it would go into the coffin of their abstractions. And neither so-called "school" was free from this tendency. The two legacies of fundamental principles which Hume left, were: that every distinct idea is a separate existence, and that every idea must be definitely determined in quantity and quality. By the first he destroyed all relation but accident; by the second he denied all universality. But these principles are framed after purely logical models; they are rather the abstract logical principles of difference and identity, of A is A and A is not B, put in the guise of a psychological expression. And the logic of concrete experience, of growth and development, repudiates such abstractions. The logic of life transcends the logic of nominalistic thought. The reaction against Hume fell back on certain ultimate, indecomposable, necessary first truths immediately known through some mysterious simple faculty of the mind. Here again the logical model manifests itself. Such intuitions are not psychological; they are conceptions bodily imported from the logical sphere. Their origin, tests, and character are all logical. But the New Psychology would not have necessary truths about principles; it would have the touch of reality in the life of the soul. It rejects the formalistic intuitionalism for one which has been well termed dynamic. It believes that truth, that reality, not necessary *beliefs about* reality, is given in the living experience of the soul's development.

Experience is realistic, not abstract. Psychical life is the fullest, deepest, and richest manifestation of this experience. The New Psychology is content to get its logic from this experience, and not do violence to the sanctity and integrity of the latter by forcing it to conform to certain preconceived abstract ideas. It wants the logic of fact, of process, of life. It has within its departments of knowledge no psychostatics, for it can nowhere find spiritual life at rest. For this reason, it abandons all legal fiction of logical and mathematical analogies and rules; and is willing to throw itself upon experience, believing that the mother which has borne it will not betray it. But it makes no attempts to dictate to this experience, and tell it what it *must* be in order to square with a scholastic logic. Thus the New Psychology bears the realistic stamp of contact with life.

From this general characteristic result most of its features. It has already been noticed that it insists upon the unity and solidarity of psychical life against abstract theories which would break it up into atomic elements or independent powers. It lays large stress upon the will; not as an abstract power of unmotivated choice, nor as an executive power to obey the behests of the understanding, the legislative branch of the psychical government, but as a living bond connecting and conditioning *all* mental activity. It emphasizes the teleological element, not in any mechanical or external sense, but regarding life as an organism in which immanent ideas or purposes are realizing themselves through the development of experience. Thus modern psychology is intensely ethical in its tendencies. As it refuses to hypostatize abstractions into self-subsistent individuals, and as it insists upon the automatic spontaneous elements in man's life, it is making possible for the first time an adequate psychology of man's religious nature and experience. As it goes into the depths of man's nature it finds, as stone of its foundation, blood of its life, the instinctive tendencies of devotion, sacrifice, faith, and idealism which are the eternal substructure of all the struggles of the nations upon the altar stairs which slope up to God. It finds no insuperable problems in the relations of faith and reason, for it can discover in its investigations no reason which is not based upon faith, and no faith which is not rational in its origin and tendency. But to attempt to give any detailed account of these features of the New Psychology would be to go over much of the recent discussions of ethics and theology. We can conclude only by saying that, following the logic of life, it attempts to comprehend life.

4

SOUL AND BODY

LEST the reader trained in a school which holds that there
is nothing to be said of the relations of soul and body,
except that there is soul and there is body and that is the end
of it, should turn away at the outset in disgust from what
must seem to him an attempt to solve the insoluble—let me
say a word or two to avoid misapprehension. Lotze has somewhere called attention to the fact that the natural tendency of
an historical age, priding itself on its historical sense, and
working by an historical method, is to surrender the understanding to the imagination, and to demand pictures instead
of principles. We are not contented until we can *see* the object matter as a series of definite images. Instead of explanation we want a drama before our eyes. It is because of this
tendency, I believe, that it is assumed that there is some difficulty special in kind surrounding the question of the relations of soul and body which makes all attempts to consider
the subject necessarily futile. It seems to be assumed on the
one hand that nothing can be said about it unless we can see
into the bowels of the molecules constituting the brain, and
behold from their mutual attractions and repulsions, a sensation and a thought engendered. Or on the other hand, it is
assumed that to know anything about the relations of soul
and body, we must be able to contemplate the soul, seated as
on a throne in the body, thence sending forth her messengers
to lay hold of the nerves and cause them to bring her reports
of what is going on in the outlying regions of her domain, or

From *The Bibliotheca Sacra*, April, 1886; 239-263.

to execute her orders among refractory subjects. And if the only way of knowing anything about their relations were some such imaginative exploit, the question were well called insoluble. But questions, as science and philosophy can well testify, are more often insoluble by reason of some unnecessary and absurd assumption, than from the inherent nature of the case. And so the failure of all attempts on this line is rather, I conceive, testimony to the absurdity of the mode of search, than to the absurdity of the question itself. We have an understanding as well as an imagination; principles may be thought as well as pictures seen; laws exist as well as panoramas. We may well give up the attempt to imagine the neural and psychical processes so as to see a transition from one to another, and confine ourselves to the less picturesque, but more hopeful, task of inquiring what principles shall be employed in order to render intelligible the relations of the physical and psychical, so far as these relations have been actually made known. We have certain facts declared by physiology and psychology. The sole question is: what principles, conceptions, shall we use in order to explain these facts, *i.e.*, in order to render a consistent, intelligible account of them? To say that this cannot be done is simply to say that there are facts in the universe which are utterly irrational, which have no meaning. And the one who has the capacity of discovering by his reason that certain facts are non-rational to his reason, is not the one whom I address.

Therefore, if it is again stated that the object of this paper is to consider the relations of soul and body, I hope it will be understood that the object is not to get into the inside of nature and behold with mortal eyes what is going on there, but the less ambitious one of inquiring what principles must be used in order to give meaning to the facts of the case. How shall the facts of physiological psychology be interpreted?

What are these facts?

First. The nervous system, complex as it is, consists ultimately of fibers and cells. The fibers serve normally to conduct or transfer nervous stimuli either from the organ of sense to some collection of cells, or ganglion, or from this center back to the muscles and glands, or from one such center to another. The cells, on the other hand, receive the stimuli brought to them from the surface, and react upon them in such a way as either to neutralize them from their own supply of force, or so as to set free their own nervous energy. In short, the fibers conduct the nervous energy; the cells produce it and regulate its distribution. This distinction in the mode of work of the two elements exists. But it has been usual to regard this distinction in such a way as to make of it an actual separation of functions. This introduces a dualism into the action of the nervous system at the start. It has been held that the fibers are purely passive and receptive, while cells are active. This leads to this result: the cells alone are regarded as having psychical bearings, so that the brain is held to be the sole organ of the mind. The nerves and the peripheral organs are eliminated. Some even go so far as to hold that in the brain there must be some particular set of cells to which all stimuli must be conducted, and that this alone is the organ of the soul. We must avoid, at the outset, any such error. The truth is that the distinction between fiber and cell is a relative one. Fibers possess an activity of their own as well as the cells, and cells conduct. The fiber is not a string which, pulled at one end, rings a bell at the other, itself remaining the meantime indifferent to the process; it is a series of nervous elements each reacting upon the stimulus of the one before it, as the cell reacts to the whole, and each passing it on to the one after it, as the cell distributes its energy. It is, in effect, a connected series of cells. What makes it behave differently from the cell proper is the fact that its power of resistance is so small, and its stored-up energy relatively so slight. The cell, on the other hand, is something more than an explosive; it is a conductor. As there is no difference, chemically, between the firing of a gunpowder train and the resulting explosion of the magazine, so there is none, physiologically, between the processes of the nerve and cell. The difference of the result in both cases is due partly to the amount of energy at hand to be set free, and still more to the resistance offered. In the cell there are no tracks laid down for the carrying off of the energy introduced. It meets resistance, friction, and accumulates till either the cell energy inhibits that introduced, or reacts upon it so as to increase it, and send it forth through the nerve.[1]

I may seem to have dwelt needlessly upon so simple a point, but it is the foundation of any further approach to a correct theory of psychophysiological relations. The conclusion which it warrants in this respect is all-important. In brief it is this: The psychical is *homogeneously* related to the physiological. Whatever is the relation of the psychical to the neural, it is related in the same manner to all parts of the neural. The brain is no more the organ of mind than the spinal cord, the spinal cord no more than the peripheral endings of the nerve fibers. The brain is undoubtedly most closely and most influentially connected with the life of the soul, but its connection is of the same *kind* as that of every other part of the nervous system. Now this gives us but one alternative: either there is absolutely no connection between the body and soul at any point whatever, or else the soul is, through the nerves, present to all the body. This means that the psychical is immanent in the physical. To deny this is to go back to the Cartesian position, and make a miracle of the whole matter— to call in some utterly foreign power to make the transition which is actually found. This may cater to our love of pictures, but it is out of the line which we have laid down for ourselves. The nineteenth-century substitute of a double-faced substance is only another excursion into the land of fancy sketches. It makes the imagination the source of an ontology. But it fares even worse than the Cartesian scheme. A double-faced substance not only refuses to be thought, but, if one is in earnest, refuses to be imagined. It is the result of the decrepitude of the imagination as well as of the laziness of thought. Not colors for the imagination to see, but principles for the understanding to think, is the desideratum. That compromise which seemed to think that the problem of the relations of soul and body was simplified if the connection of the

[1] This is not theory, but physiological fact. The experimental data with the conclusions warranted will be found set forth in Wundt.

[66]

two could be reduced to as small a space as possible, and excluded it first from the fiber, then from the spinal cord, then from the basal ganglia, the cerebellum, all of the cerebrum except the cortex, then possibly one point of the cortex—that, too, must be abandoned. The fact is, that the action of the nervous tissue is the same in kind in the cortex and in the peripheral fiber, and hence if any part of the nervous system has any connection with the soul which is not supernatural in character, every part must have, in kind, the same. All, or none, is the disjunction forced upon us. The immanence of the psychical in the physical is, therefore, the foundation of our future inquiry. The nature of the immanence must now be inquired into. That there is unity of function in the cell and fiber is established. What this function is and what conclusion it warrants are the questions now to be asked.

Second. The fundamental nervous activity is a process of adjustment, consisting in a twofold contemporaneous process of stimulation and reaction or inhibition. If we turn to the same physiological authorities whence we learned of the homogeneous nature of the action of fiber and cell, we shall learn what this action is. Nervous tissue, in the first place, wherever found is a highly unstable chemical compound. Any excitation tends to set up such chemical change as will reduce it to relatively simpler and more stable compounds. There is thus set free an amount of energy equivalent to the amount which would be required to lift this lower compound up to its higher state again. The potential energy of the unstable compound has, in short, become kinetic. The first element in nervous action is, therefore, the excitatory or stimulating, which has the setting free of nervous energy for its result. But if this were all, the energy of the nervous system would be soon used up. Every stimulus would set free nervous force, and the result would be that the body would respond to every stimulus, however slight, and the process would end only with the complete exhaustion of the power. We would be physically in the condition of those having the Saint Vitus's dance; mentally, in the state of some of the insane, who, having no reserve power, react violently upon every impression, intel-

[67]

lectual or emotional, until they sink into a stupor, out of which they come only to repeat the process. In short, there must be something which gives control, which regulates the reaction, and which also ensures a reserve power. There must be opposed to the exciting activity one which resists, and thereby prevents the whole force at hand, the whole unstable compound, from being used, and which also restores it as it is expended. And so it is found that there is a complementary process. Not only is energy being constantly put forth, but energy is being constantly stored up or rendered latent. Not all the force which comes to a nervous element is employed in breaking down the unstable compounds and thereby losing energy; part—in some cases much the greater part—is used in building up these unstable compounds, thereby forming a reservoir of energy for future use, while the process itself acts as a restraint upon, a control over, the excitatory factor. Every nervous action is, therefore, a reciprocal function of stimulation, excitation, and inhibition; control through repression. Every nervous activity is essentially an adjustment. It is called forth through the stimulus, but the stimulus is not the sole factor; it does not wander at its own sweet will, but is checked and directed by the reacting activity, the inhibiting. This is true, of course, of every process, whether occurring in fiber or in cell; but because of the structural differences between the two, previously spoken of, the former mode of action greatly *predominates* over the other in the fiber; while in the cell the inhibitory activity exceeds at the expense of the stimulating. Since the fibers correspond, in a general way, to the peripheral nerve system and the cells to the central, it may truly enough be said that the stimulating or exciting is the peripheral, and the reacting and controlling is the central or ganglionic.

Looked at from this point of view, *the unitary nervous activity is evidently that known as reflex action.* In that, we have precisely these relations of excitement on the one hand, and adjusting activity on the other, of which we have just been speaking. Our conclusions are as follows: there is a fundamental mode of nervous activity; in this the psychical is immanent. This mode of activity is an adjusting activity; therefore the psychical is immanent in the physical as directing it toward a given end. It is not only immanent, but it is teleologically immanent. This teleological character is seen in the nature of the function itself as just described. The loss of the proper proportion of the stimulating and the inhibiting activity is a token of morbid disorder. It is pathological. If the centers react on feeble stimuli, they squander their force upon the little stimuli, which are constant, by playing upon them; if they react only upon very strong stimuli, the force they contain is never put forth when needed to perform the proper adjustment of the organism. But in normal life we find that exact proportion between the two activities which ensures that the force shall be used when its expenditure is for the good of the organism, and then alone. If we take the simplest case of nervous action, such a one as occurs in a cold-blooded animal deprived of all its nervous apparatus except the spinal cord, it will only render still more distinct the teleological character as objectively manifested. Read the following account of Wundt:

A decapitated frog moves its legs against the pincers with which it is irritated, or it wipes away with its foot the drop of acid applied to the skin. It sometimes tries to get away from a mechanical or electrical stimulation by a jump. If put into an unusual position (*e.g.,* on its back) it often returns to its normal position. The stimulus does not introduce merely a motion in general, which spreads from the irritated part with increasing intensity of the stimulus and growing irritability, but the movement is adapted *to the external impression.* It may be a movement of defence, or one to get rid of the stimulus, or a movement to remove the body from the sphere of irritation, or finally it may aim at restoration of the previous posture. *This purposive adaptation to the stimulus* stands out even more clearly in experiments by Pflüger and Auerbach in which the ordinary conditions of movement are somewhat changed. A frog, for example, whose leg has been cut off on the side on which it is irritated by acid, first makes some fruitless attempts with the amputated stump, and then, pretty regularly, chooses the other leg, which is wont to remain at rest when the animal is unmutilated. If the decapitated frog be fastened by its back, and the inner side of one of its thighs be sprinkled with acid, it tries to get rid of the latter by rubbing the two thighs against each other; but if the moved thigh be separated far from the other, after a few vain attempts it suddenly stretches this one out, and pretty accurately reaches the point which was irritated. Lastly, if one breaks the upper thighs of decapitated frogs and cauterizes, whilst they are stretched on their bellies the lower part of their backs, they correctly touch the cauterized spot with the feet of the broken limb, in spite of the disturbing nature of the treatment. These observations, which may be varied in diverse ways, show that the animal can adapt its movements to its changed conditions.

Of course what is true of this simplest form of nerve action is still more true of the higher forms, until we have a large number of nerve centers acting co-ordinately with each other, and all subordinated to the execution of a given act recognized as necessary for the preservation or development of the organism. But it is enough for our purpose to take our stand upon this elementary form of reflex action, and thus cut the very standing ground from under the feet of the materialist.

This, then, is our conclusion: the psychical is immanent in the physical; immanent as directing it toward an end, and for the sake of this end selecting some activities, inhibiting others, responding to some, controlling others, and adjusting and co-ordinating the complex whole, so as, in the simplest and least wasteful way, to reach the chosen end. We find, therefore, that in the simplest form of nervous action there are involved categories transcending the material; principles to which matter, as such, is an entire stranger. Matter *per se* knows no higher category than that of physical causality. Its highest law is that of the necessities of antecedent and consequent. In nervous action we find the category of teleology. The act is not determined by its immediate antecedents, but by the necessary end. We have gone from the sphere of physical to that of final causation, and thereby we recognize that we have gone from the purely physical to the immanence of the psychical in the physical, directing the latter for its own end and purpose.

The materialist, with his reversed logic, which attempts to get the higher from the lower, instead of accounting for the lower on the ground of the higher, utterly misses the nature of the case. To him, the fact of reflex action, the fact of purposive adjustment (if he be far enough advanced in the elements to recognize the fact at all) is evidence of the self-sufficiency of matter. He forthwith makes teleological action an attribute of matter, and intelligent purposiveness a function of the material. He does not recognize that in doing this he is giving up all that characterizes matter as matter, and is, in effect, recognizing the primacy of spirit. If teleology belong to the essence of matter, and purposive regulated action be the nature of the material, then matter and material cease to be what they are commonly regarded as being (*viz.*, matter and material), and become but the hiding places (which are the dwelling places) of spirit and the physical. The dispute is not, I suppose, about what words we shall use, but what principles. Nor is the question, again, about pictures, but about laws of explanation. If we cease to form a verbal or pictorial conception of matter we shall find that for scientific purposes it means the principle of physical causation; the constant and invariable relations of antecedent and consequent. To attempt to get more into the conception of matter is unscientific in that it is unwarranted; and unscientific in that, if it were accomplished, it would destroy the basis of all physical science and leave it the field for the play of imaginative fancies by whose side the highest flight of the science of the Greek, or of the Middle Ages, will sink into insignificance. The recognition of this one principle of physical causation, the invariableness of succession, is the theoretic basis of all physical science. To attempt to include more is to destroy the principle without reason, and to introduce unbounded confusion. Some foregleams of the depths of absurdity to which we may reach, once started on this course of surrendering principles to words or images, may be seen in the efforts of some German materialists, who, in their laudable efforts to be consistent, have found it necessary to supply the primordial atoms with sensations, and who hold that the laws of the universe are to be deduced from their primitive loves and hates, their desires and strivings. Such is the only consistent position for a materialist. But it is a consistency which looks marvelously like a *reductio ad absurdum*. And it is suicide as well, for it is to give up the very essence of the materialistic position, and to admit that the nature and laws of the material are constituted by the psychical, which is the determining and prior element in the case. To attempt to swallow up the psychical in the material is not only absurd, but it is useless, for the psychical always revenges itself by encroaching upon the material, and when we finally look for some independent speck of matter, there is none there. It has all been spiritualized. Or, if there be one speck there, it must be defined in terms of the conception of matter just laid down. It will be found to be matter because it acts according to the principles of physical causation and not of final causation; because it is determined by its antecedent, not by an end working itself out in it. So that after all there is no choice for the materialist. If he will but once open his eyes to the fact of purposive action he has no alternative. He may attempt to claim this function as an attribute of matter; if he does, as just seen, he dematerializes his matter. He may admit that there is matter whose principle and law is that of psychical causation. He will then recognize that whatever transcends this principle is essentially non-material, and that with the appearance of teleological action upon the scene, we have passed from the realm of the material into that of the psychical immanent in the material. This is rational, and this saves science from becoming the sport of every inflated and ill-balanced imagination.

There is another method of escaping the significance of purposive action, equally futile, but equally attractive to the mind that prefers panoramas to principles. It is, at present, the more fashionable method. In brief, it is to admit that the actions are at present teleological, but that they became such through a long series of accidental experiments (experiments which were not experiments, as they were not trying to reach any end) of which some happened to be advantageous to the organism, and, surviving, give us now the appearance of purpose. This theory attempts to make the teleological an accidental product of the mechanical. It generally hides itself behind imposing scientific terms connected with the theory of biological evolution. It uses its "variations" and "selection," and "survival of the fittest" and "heredity," and thinks that in the end it has got something out of nothing—purpose out of accident. But the argument is suicidal. It only changes the special case into a general law. It gets rid of the primitive purposiveness of, say, a given reflex act, only by importing purposiveness, and thus intelligence, into the very structure of nature. It simply says that nature is such that, by the observance of its own laws as ascertained by science, it gives rise to action for and by ends. Variation, selection, heredity, as *names,* do not, I suppose, accomplish the result. It is that there are embedded in the very constitution of things, forces and principles which as they work themselves out, by their action and reaction, give rise to activity for an end, to purposive action. In short, not only is the structure of the nervous system such that it gives rise to teleological action, but the structure of nature itself is such that it gives rise to this special kind of purposive action. He who has thought to get rid of teleology, and thereby intelligence, in this special case, has done it only by the recognition of teleology, and thereby intelligence, as a universal principle and acting force. Darwinism, far from overthrowing this principle, merely establishes it as a general law of the

[73]

universe, of the structure of things. Nature is made teleological all the way through.

From this digression, which has, I hope, developed the argument, as well as secured it from possible misconception, I return to the conclusion. The psychical is teleologically immanent in the physical. The simplest nerve action is not so simple as to exclude the adaptive, purposive factor. It is always an adjustment. It is never a mere mechanical result of a stimulus, but always involves selection, inhibition, and response. The stimulus favorable to the well-being of the organism is selected from the immense number playing upon the organism; others, especially those unserviceable, are inhibited, and then the action results according to the needs, that is, the purpose, of the organism itself. If we broaden our view and take in the consentaneous action of the whole organism, the conclusion appears only the more clearly. The various sensory and muscular stimuli, almost infinite in number, are always co-ordinated and harmoniously combined. The nerves of the cord, the cord itself, the special sense nerves, the cerebellum, the basal ganglia, the cerebral hemispheres, with their infinitude of fibers and cells, act as an adjusted unity for one purpose, and one alone—the welfare of the organism. At times it may seem as if one part were functioning alone, but it is always found (unless the action be pathological) that it is a relative independence. The end of the organism is best gained by allowing a certain amount of originative and self-executed action by the particular part. The apparent independence is but the evidence of the thoroughly teleological character of the whole. It signifies the division of labor in order that the whole task, the development of the organism, may be the more speedily and economically effected. There is no communistic level, but the due gradation and subordination of the various factors in the unity of the whole, as in a well-organized society. There is, in short, the co-ordination of all the nerve organs, and the further subordination of all to the end of the whole, self-realization.

Such is the conclusion we arrive at, without leaving the

purely physiological sphere. But such a conclusion is one-sided and narrow, until expanded to take in all the phenomena. The body, through the nervous system, is not only a *physiological,* but a *psycho*physiological organism. Expressed in its lowest terms, there is *sensation,* as well as adjustment of all the activities to one end. Those who have asserted the spirituality of the soul have often begun to build too high. They have taken as their fortress abstract thought, or the free will. Now these offer, indeed, an impregnable refuge, but, in opening the campaign from there, ground is abandoned which, by all territorial rights, is the eminent domain of the spiritual soul. To return to the former metaphor, we can finally build higher and more firmly, because on a broader foundation, on the basis of sensation. Too often is the claim of the materialist that sensation, at least, can be accounted for by material processes, admitted explicitly or tacitly. It seems to be thought that because the immediate and close connection of sensations with the nerve organs and the brain can be made out, that thereby their material character is established. At bottom, this is the survival of a metaphor, out of date at its very birth. The mischief that the term "impression" has played with psychology can never be measured. One of the greatest claims which physiological psychology has upon us is that it has forever outlawed the term and the conception. The only word which has any place in psychology as expressing the material antecedent of the psychical state, sensation, is *stimulus.* Our semimaterialists, like Mr. Huxley and Mr. Tyndall, always conclude their baldest assertions of the dependence of the mind upon the brain with some such statement as this: The passage from the physics of the brain, from a nervous irritation, from a change of motion and matter, to a fact of consciousness, to a psychical state, to a sensation, is unthinkable, is an inexplicable mystery, a gulf which imagination cannot span; and so on, *ad libitum.* One would think that if they would cease attempting to picture the transition and endeavor to *think* it, the explanation would be so patent as to stare them fairly out of countenance. The "mystery" would explode in its own fatuous vacuity. The unthinkable arises from the use of wrong categories, wrong principles. No better evidence that the physical and the psychical are not related as cause and effect, as producer and product, could be adduced than the utter "mysteriousness" hanging with "inexplicable" persistence over all attempts to get one out of the other. When it is recognized that "inexplicability" is not an ultimate fact to be supremely contented with, but a positive condemnation of the method and principles which have led to it, our scientific men will reflect twice before they thrust their uncomprehended physical categories into the psychical realm, thereby begging the whole question, and, themselves being witnesses, landing the whole affair in a mystery which cannot be discriminated from an absurdity. It was recognized some hundreds of years ago that in geometry a *reductio ad absurdum* is a perfect and beautiful demonstration of the untruth of the original hypothesis. Let us hope that the idea of the unity of all thought will finally dawn upon the scientific men who have taken the contract of philosophizing for the English-speaking portion of the nineteenth century, and that they will recognize that what holds in the basis of all scientific reasoning holds also in the rudiments of philosophical.

We will abandon, then, all attempts to picture the confessedly unimaginable, and those endeavors to explain which lead us into the confessedly inexplicable. We will begin with the facts, and inquire what principle they force upon us to explain them; we will not begin with a principle, and, after having in nine-tenths of the paper victoriously "explained" all facts by it, wind up with confessing that it is all inexplicable, and accordingly go on to revel in the unutterable bathos of the "mysterious." If we take the facts, they are simply these: (1) the constant sequence upon a certain nervous process of a psychical state known as a sensation; (2) the entire lack of any connection between the two by way of physical causation, *i.e.*, by way of identity of matter and motion involved. The principle which this leads us to is that the physical antecedent is a stimulus necessary for the production of a sensation; and that it is only a stimulus. The sensation does not come *from* it, although it would never come *without* it. The sensation has its *occasion* from the nervous process; it has its *cause* from within. The physical process awakens the mind, it incites it to action; the mind, thereupon, spontaneously and by its own laws develops from itself a sensation. The specific names given to the various factors involved is of no importance, as long as it is recognized that the principle concerned is that of stimulus and response; response, which, for its existence, depends upon the physical antecedent, but for its content and nature, upon something else. We must recognize that we have got to go beyond the principle of physical causation to the principle of self-developing activity, though an activity which is not infinite or self-produced, but dependent upon an occasioning impulse beyond it. In short, not only is the soul immanent in the body, as teleological, as subordinating and adjusting its various activities to an end, but the body is the stimulus to the soul. It is the condition of the calling forth of its activities. It is the spark which fires the mind to light its own inextinguishable flame. Sensation, and, *a fortiori,* all higher psychical activities, testify to the creative, self-determining power of the mind, with the proviso attached that this power has been called upon to act. There is just the same mystery about it that there is about every fact in the universe, the mystery that there should be such a fact at all. As to principles involved, there is no more mystery than in the explanation of any physical or chemical fact. In ultimate analysis, the spiritual principle is less mysterious, is lucidly transparent, in comparison with the mechanical; for it is only from the former that the latter gets its explanation and the guarantee of its validity.

If we include within our survey the psychophysiological facts as well as the purely physiological phenomena of nerve action, we come to the conclusion that the soul not only directs and focuses the activities of the organism, but that it transforms them into something which they are not. It realizes itself upon the hints, as it were, given by the body. The soul is not only immanent in the body, as constituting its

[77]

unity and end; it is transcendent to it, as transforming its activities for its own psychical ends. It uses it as material out of which to build its own structure, as food by which to nourish its own life. These two principles, of the immanence and the transcendence of the soul, to which we have been led by the study of the facts, cannot be left in this isolated way. They must be shown in their unity as necessarily involving each other. And again we turn to the facts of psychophysiological life with the assurance that the principle will be involved in them, and that we are not left to the logical manipulations of our conceptions.

They are the facts connected with the execution of definite psychophysiological functions. They may all be included under the phrase "localization of functions," if the phrase be understood in a broad sense to mean the performance of any definite act of psychical bearings by any specific, organized portion of the body. It would include, therefore, the performance of reflex acts by the spinal cord, as well as the supposed location of the "speech center" in the third frontal convolution of the central hemisphere. The ground for this extension of the term is the unity of all nervous action, as well as particular facts to be presently mentioned. The only difference between the regular and constant "localization" of reflex action in the spinal cord, and of speech in one part of the brain, is a difference of degree, not of kind. The difference is between a localization perfectly formed, and a localization in process of forming. Organization of function might be the better term.

If we turn again to our authorities we shall find the facts substantially as follows:

1. In some form or other localization or, to use the better term, organization of psychical function, is all but universal. The body is not a homogeneous mass which is indifferent, equally as a whole and in all its parts, to the soul. On the contrary, neither as a whole, nor in any of its parts, is it neutral to the soul. That it is not as a whole, we have seen when considering the immanence of the soul in the body; that it is not in any of its parts, is simply a detailed applica-

tion of the same principle. The soul is not only in the body, but it is in it in definite, particular ways. The body as a whole is not only the organ of the soul, but the various structures of the body are differentiated organs, of various capacities and tendencies, of the soul. That is the meaning of the localization of function, or of the fact that certain activities have certain, more or less defined, nervous centers in various portions of the spinal cord and brain.

To give the specific evidence of this localization would be but to repeat the whole of the morphology and physiology of the nervous system. The nervous system itself is but a differentiation of the ectoderm; the special sense organs are only so many continuations of the brain and spinal cord. If we take the various movements, we find that, in going from the simplest to the most complex, from the mere reflex action to the most consciously purposive movement, nowhere does the will act without a structure already formed for it. Learning the higher movements, like walking, talking, etc., is but the formation of the organized structures of the body. If these be wanting, no matter how completely the end and the proper means of reaching it are present to consciousness, the volition cannot be performed. If we leave the motor and sensory spheres and come to the higher ideal operations, the evidence for the localization of functions is much less complete and forcible. But we need only to recognize the dependence of thought upon sense for its materials, and largely upon language for its form, to be aware that the same principles must, in some degree at least, hold here also. The fact that in thinking we never deal with the ultimate psychical elements, but with symbolic wholes, with processes already integrated, is still more striking psychological evidence of the same fact. Just as it would take hours to perform a simple act like dressing, if the motor functions did not become organized in the bodily structure, if the will were obliged to go into detail of the act, instead of simply setting the whole mechanism into operation to work itself out, so in the intellectual sphere. If the various sensations and ideas remained isolated, if they were not organized into wholes, if they were not changed

[79]

from material into structure, the mind would require hours to take in the meaning of a single sentence, or to reason out a simple inference. But the fact is that the mind does not deal with ultimate elements; it always has integral wholes which it may grasp and use without endeavoring or needing to resolve them. And that there is some similar physiological grouping and integration, some corresponding organization of function in the brain, all artificial experiments upon animals, and all natural experiments, performed by disease upon man, go to show.

2. But there must be explicitly stated, what has already been suggested; *viz.*, that the degree of this localization, both as to definiteness and completeness, varies very greatly. The lower the function, the more perfectly and narrowly is it localized. The wider its scope, and the greater its consequent necessity, the more complete and spatial, so to speak, its localization. Thus the functions of breathing, digesting, swallowing, etc., which are necessary to life, and which have only indirect psychical bearings, have very definite and thoroughly localized centers: while the higher activities, like walking, talking, reading, and writing, involving more and more activities and of a more complex kind, have less and less definite local centers. In the higher activities there is no perfect mapping out at all, but all sorts of shadings-off and variations. So if we consider the sensory sphere, we find that, while the sense centers may for some of the lower animals be made out pretty certainly, there is no such certainty and agreement in the case of man. And the reason is evident; in the animals, the sensations remain mostly what they are— pure sense-feelings, while in man these sensations have been so related and interpreted that they have become for the most part perceptions, and even higher ideal relations. Consequently we find that *ideas* as such have no localization whatever. *There is not the slightest evidence whatever that any special idea, whether a percept, an image, or a concept, has any definite specific center. There are all kinds of evidence that it has not.* The elaborate calculations of Mr. Bain in his work upon Mind and Body going to show that there

are as many fibers and cells in the brain as the mind has
separate ideas and associations, is based upon an utterly
unfounded *a priori* assumption; *viz.,* that cells in the brain
correspond to ideas, and fibers to associations. It cannot be
stated too strongly, or insisted upon too often, that there is
not the slightest fragment of experimental evidence for the
theory. There is much experimental evidence to show that
the case cannot possibly stand thus. This evidence may be
summed up in the statement that all lines of inquiry, morpho-
logical, anatomical, and physiological, converge to one result: the psychical function or bearing of the cell is dependent, not on its own structure, but upon its connections by
means of the fibers. An "idea," however simple it may seem,
has not its physical basis in a cell, but in a group of cells,
connected and interconnected by multitudinous fibers. If
the idea be very complex it may possibly have relations to all
the cells in the brain. This may be an extreme statement,
but, beside the statement that any idea may be localized in
a given cell, it is truth itself. Hence we see the entire failure
of all attempts definitely to localize the higher intellectual
functions. The evidence does not warrant the statement that,
upon the whole, they have no physical connection; it does
warrant the statement that the relations involved are so
many, so far reaching, and so complex, that any attempt to
find a sharply marked-out center must be forever in vain.

3. The two statements already made, that localization is
practically universal and yet that the higher intellectual
powers cannot be definitely localized at all, do not contradict each other. They find their reconciliation in the statement that *localization is not original, but acquired.* It has
already been stated that the localization is no quality originally inherent in the cell; but that it depends upon the cell's
connections through its fibers. As Wundt says, "No element
executes specific functions, but the form of the latter depends
upon the connections and relations of the cell." And this
dependence of localized function upon connection is the
same as to say that given elements of the brain act in a certain way only because they have been associated in the per-

formance of the act. The localization is dependent upon use and exercise. Thus it is that Wundt goes on to state the two following principles: "Every definite function has, under given conditions of connection, a definite place in the central organ from which it proceeds: that is to say, whose elements stand in relations fitted for the execution of the function," and "Every element is the more fitted to the performance of a definite function, the more often it has been occasioned by external conditions to its performance." Localization of function is, in short, only the physiological way of saying habit. The organization of function is not indwelling in the brain as so much matter: it has been *learned* by the brain and learned through the tuition and care of the soul. By no twisting can the phenomena of localization of function be twisted into the support of materialism. The very fibers and cells cry out against such treatment. They all assert that the powers they have, they possess, not of their own original and indefeasible right, but by means of the activity, and under the authority of the soul. This accounts for the various degrees of localization found. The acts most necessary for the soul's ends, and therefore oftenest performed, have, through heredity, become definitely and completely organized, and, like reflex actions, go on without consciousness, or, like instinctive actions, involve others which in complexity and far-reaching influence are beyond the immediate consciousness of the moment. But the soul, for its own ends, requires again that its higher activities be not thus mechanized. There must be a constant growth, adjustment to new relations, intellectual and moral, and this requires plasticity, variability. In the higher activities complete organization would mean stagnation, death. Thus it is that the higher we come, both in the range of animal life and in the range of intellectual function, the less the localization. But in each case the evidence all goes to show that the localization is not original, but is acquired because the soul has repeatedly employed the given elements for the performance of a given act. The soul does not write in water, but in the plastic brain and spinal cord. *Litera scripta manet.* By the performance of its acts the soul gains a mechanism by which to perform them again the more readily, economically, and perfectly.

Thus we see how the phenomena of localization of function give us a standpoint whence to view the nature of the immanence and transcendence of the soul. The soul is immanent in the body just so far as it has made the body its organic instrument. The common saying that the "body is the organ of the soul" is literally much truer and more significant than is usually thought or meant. The term "organ" expresses a much more intimate and internal relation than is commonly understood. Organ presupposes function, and soul and body are related indeed as function and organ, activity and instrument. As Aristotle said so long ago, the body is the organ of the soul, as the eye is the organ of seeing. The body is not an external instrument which the soul has happened upon, and consequently uses, as a musician might happen upon a piano. The body is the organ of the soul because by the body the soul expresses and realizes its own nature. It is the outward form and living manifestation of the soul. To quote from one of the most original and deeply spiritual thinkers whom America has yet produced: "It is the outward man, in and through which the inward powers of the soul express their form and character. It is the necessary mode of our existence in the world of sense, without the intervention of which we have no knowledge, either objective or subjective, no existence in nature, either in space or in time. It is not merely an organ to be conceived as distinct from our personal self, but *it is our proper self as existent in space,* in the order and under the laws of nature." [2]

But this is only one-half the tale. The soul is immanent in the body only because, and in so far as, it has realized itself in the body. The body is its organ only because the soul has *made* the body its organ. The immanence is shown by the localization; the transcendence, by the fact that this localization has come about through the soul's own activities. The body as an organ of the soul is the result of the informing, creating activity of the soul itself. In short, the soul is im-

[2] President James Marsh, *Remains,* p. 257.

[83]

manent in the body, not by virtue of the body as mere body, but because, being transcendent, it has expressed and manifested its nature in the body.

The soul, accordingly, is not a powerless, impotent something, so transcendent that it cannot be brought into relation with matter. It is a living and acting force which has formed, and is constantly forming, the body as its own mechanism. This assures, on the one hand that no act or deed of the mind is ever lost, that it finds its registration and record, and that not alone in some supralunary sphere, but down here in the world of matter; and, on the other hand, it forms a mechanism by which the soul can immediately know, can grasp the fragments of its knowledge into one symbolic whole without laboriously gathering them and piecing them together, and by which it can immediately act. It is, as it were, the mind's automaton, ceaselessly and tirelessly executing the demands responding to the needs of the soul. All the phenomena which the materialist parades forth as "proofs" —the unconscious cerebration, the automatic, yet apparently intelligent, action in many states of unconsciousness; the dependence of perception and memory upon the proper condition and integrity of the brain; the accompaniment of brain disease with unconsciousness and insanity; the ratio between mental power and weight and complexity of the brain, etc., are the farthest removed from evidence of materialism. They are but the conclusive evidence of the thoroughness with which the soul has done its work, has formed its mechanism. They are all evidence that the soul is not hanging helpless in the air, but has made the body its home, and has realized itself so effectually in this body as its mechanism, can now act all but automatically, while disturbance of the mechanism of the organ excludes the execution of the corresponding activity, until the soul by its power form the organ again. The materialist but looks at the body after the soul has done its work in making the body what it is, and cries, "Lo, see what the body can do." Every one of the phenomena mentioned, as well as all which the materialist can mention, concern the formed body, the body in which the soul has already organized its functions. The true cry is, "Lo, see what the soul *has* done. It has tabernacled in the flesh and transformed that flesh into its own manifestation. The body is the bodying forth of the soul."

It was the "master of those who know" that said that the soul was the perfect realization or expression of a natural body, and at the same time, not the product of body, but its very life, its essence, its truth and reality—at once its final and efficient cause. (Aristotle, *De Anima,* ii. 1.) And it was the Teacher of all who know, the Light which lighteth every man that cometh into the world, who said: "Except a corn of wheat fall into the ground and die it abideth alone: but if it die it bringeth forth much fruit." And it was the great disciple of the great Teacher who wrote: "That which thou sowest is not quickened except it die; and that which thou sowest, thou sowest not the body that shall be, but bare grain, it may chance of wheat or of some other grain; but God giveth it a body as it has pleased Him, and to every seed his own body. . . . It is sown a natural body, it is raised a spiritual body. There is a natural body and there is a spiritual body."

Christianity has no sympathy with those who have such a superfine fear of materialism that they aetherialize the soul past all contact with the body. It knows that in the body the soul is incarnate; that through the soul the natural body comes to be a spiritual body, as the soul works itself out, and realizes itself in it. The soul does apparently die in the body; it hides itself so effectually that the materialist says there is no soul; but it has died as dies the seed, to quicken and transform the body. It is by no accident or meaningless chance that we read in the Apostles' Creed those sublime words: "I believe in the Resurrection of the Body." Catholic historic Christianity, having such a confession on its lips, has no alliance with the metaphysical dualism of spirit and matter, and no fear of the exactest demonstrations of physiology regarding the closest connections of body and soul. It takes its stand upon the words of St. Paul, to which these demonstrations can only add more weight: "There is a natural body and there is a spiritual body. . . . Howbeit that was not first which is spiritual, but that which is natural; and afterwards that which is spiritual." There is the body, the natural body, first. Spirit indwells within the body, and manifesting itself, realizing its own nature, it makes that body its own organ and servant. It thus makes it the spiritual body. Let it be no surprise that physiological psychology has revealed no new truth concerning the relations of soul and body. It can only confirm and deepen our insight into the truth divined by Aristotle and declared by St. Paul, and with good reason. *Das Wahre war schon längst gefunden.*

5

THE PSYCHOLOGICAL STANDPOINT

I

IT is a good omen for the future of philosophy that there is now a disposition to avoid discussion of particular cases in dispute, and to examine instead the fundamental presuppositions and method. This is the sole condition of discussion which shall be fruitful, and not word-bandying. It is the sole way of discovering whatever of fundamental agreement there is between different tendencies of thought, as well as of showing on what grounds the radical differences are based. It is therefore a most auspicious sign that, instead of eagerly clamoring forth our views on various subjects, we are now trying to show *why* we hold them and *why* we reject others. It is hardly too much to say that it is only within the past ten years that what is vaguely called Transcendentalism has shown to the English reading world just why it holds what it does, and just what are its objections to the method most characteristically associated with English thinking. Assertion of its results, accompanied with attacks upon the results of Empiricism, and *vice versa*, we had before; but it is only recently that the grounds, the reasons, the method, have been stated. And no one can deny that the work has been done well, clearly, conscientiously, and thoroughly. English philosophy cannot now be what it would have been, if (to name only one of the writers) the late Professor Green had not written. And now that the differences and the grounds for them have been so definitely and clearly stated, we are in a

From *Mind*, January, 1886; 1-19.

condition, I think, to see a fundamental agreement, and that just where the difference has been most insisted upon, *viz.*, in the standpoint. It is the *psychological* standpoint which is the root of all the difference, as Professor Green has shown with such admirable lucidity and force. Yet I hope to be able to suggest, if not to show, that after all the psychological standpoint is what both sides have in common. In this present paper, I wish to point out that the defects and contradictions so powerfully urged against the characteristic tendency of British Philosophy are due—not to its psychological standpoint but—to its *desertion* of it. In short, the psychological basis of English philosophy has been its strength: its weakness has been that it has left this basis—that it has not been psychological enough.

In stating what is the psychological standpoint, care has to be taken that it be not so stated as to prejudge at the outset the whole matter. This can be avoided only by stating it in a very general manner. Let Locke do it. "I thought that the first step towards satisfying several inquiries the mind of man was very apt to run into was to take a view of our own understandings, examine our own powers, and see to what things they were adapted." This, with the further statement that "Whatsoever is the object of the understanding when a man thinks" is an Idea, fixed the method of philosophy. We are not to determine the nature of reality or of any object of philosophical inquiry by examining it as it is in itself, but only as it is an element in our knowledge, in our experience, only as it is related to our mind, or is an "idea." As Professor Fraser well puts it, Locke's way of stating the question "involves the fundamental assumption of philosophy, that real things as well as imaginary things, whatever their absolute existence may involve, exist for us only through becoming involved in what we mentally experience in the course of our self-conscious lives." Or, in the ordinary way of putting it, the nature of all objects of philosophical inquiry is to be fixed by finding out what experience says about them. And psychology is the scientific and systematic account of this experience. This and this only do I understand to be essential

to the psychological standpoint, and, to avoid misunderstanding from the start, I shall ask the reader not to think
any more into it, and especially to avoid reading into it any
assumption regarding its "individual" and "introspective"
character. The further development of the standpoint can
come only in the course of the article.

Now that Locke, having stated his method, immediately
deserted it will, I suppose, be admitted by all. Instead of
determining the nature of objects of experience by an account of our knowledge, he proceeded to explain our knowledge by reference to certain unknowable substances, called
by the name of matter, making impressions on an unknowable substance, called mind. While, by his method, he should
explain the nature of "matter" and of "mind"—two "inquiries the mind of man is very apt to run into"—from our
own understandings, from "ideas," he actually explains the
nature of our ideas, of our consciousness, whether sensitive
or reflective, from that whose characteristic, whether mind
or matter, is to be *not* ideas nor consciousness nor in any
possible relation thereto, because utterly unknowable. Berkeley, in effect, though not necessarily, as it seems to me, in
intention, deserted the method in his reference of ideas to a
purely transcendent spirit. Whether or not he conceived it as
purely transcendent, yet at all events, he did not show its
necessary immanence *in* our conscious experience. But
Hume? Hume, it must be confessed, is generally thought to
stand on purely psychological ground. This is asserted as his
merit by those who regard the theory of the association of
ideas as the basis of all philosophy; it is asserted as his defect
by those who look at his skeptical mocking of knowledge as
following necessarily from his method. But according to
both, he, at least, was consistently psychological. Now the
psychological standpoint is this: nothing shall be admitted
into philosophy which does not show itself in experience,
and its nature, that is, its place in experience, shall be fixed
by an account of the process of knowledge—by Psychology.
Hume reversed this. He started with a theory as to the nature
of reality and determined experience from that. The only

reals for him were certain irrelated sensations and out of these knowledge arises or becomes. But if knowledge or experience becomes from them, then *they* are never known and never can be. If experience *originates from* them, they never were and never can be elements *in* experience. Sensations as known or experienced are always related, classified sensations. That which is known as existing only in experience, which has its existence only as an element of knowledge, cannot be the same when transported out of knowledge, and made its origin. A known sensation has its sole existence *as* known; and to suppose that it can be regarded as *not* known, as prior to knowledge, and still be what it is *as* known, is a logical feat which it is hoped few are capable of. Hume, just as much as Locke, assumes that something exists out of relation to knowledge or consciousness, and that this something is ultimately the only real, and that from it knowledge, consciousness, experience, come to be. If this is not giving up the psychological standpoint, it would be difficult to tell what is. Hume's "distinct perceptions which are distinct existences," and which give rise to knowledge only as they are related to each other, are so many things-in-themselves. They existed prior to knowledge, and therefore are not for or within it.

But it will be objected that all this is a total misapprehension. Hume did not assume them *because* they were prior to and beyond knowledge. He examined experience and found, as any one does who analyzes it, that it is made up of sensations; that, however complex or immediate it appears to be, on analysis it is always found to be but an aggregate of grouped sensations. Having found this by analysis, it was his business, as it is that of every psychologist, to show *how* by composition these sensations produce knowledge and experience. To call them things-in-themselves is absurd—they are the simplest and best-known things in all our experience. Now this answer, natural as it is, and conclusive as it seems, only brings out the radical defect of the procedure. The dependence of our knowledge upon sensations—or rather that knowledge is nothing but sensations as related to each other —is not denied. What is denied is the correctness of the procedure which, discovering a certain element *in* knowledge to be necessary for knowledge, therefore concludes that this element has an existence prior to or apart from knowledge. The alternative is not complex. Either these sensations are the sensations which are known—sensations which are elements in knowledge—and then they cannot be employed to account for its origin; or they can be employed to account for its origin, and then are not sensations as they are known. In this case, they must be something of which nothing can be said except that they are *not* known, *are* not in consciousness—that they are things-in-themselves. If, in short, these sensations are not to be made "ontological," they must be sensations known, sensations which are elements in experience; and if they exist only for knowledge, then knowledge is wherever they are, and they cannot account for its origin. The supposed objection rests upon a distinction between sensations as they are known, and sensations as they exist. And this means simply that existence—the only real existence—is not for consciousness, but that consciousness comes about from it; it makes no difference that one calls it sensations, and another the "real existence" of mind or matter. If one is anxious for a thing-in-itself in one's philosophy, this will be no objection. But we who are psychological, who believe in the relativity of knowledge, should we not make a halt before we declare a fundamental disparity between a thing as it is and a thing as it is known—whether that thing be sensation or what not?

As this point is fundamental, let me dwell upon it a little. All our knowledge originates from sensations. Very good. But what are these sensations? Are they the sensations which we know: the classified related sensations; *this* smell, or *this* color? No, these are the results of knowledge. They too presuppose sensations as their origin. What about these original sensations? They existed before knowledge, and knowledge originated and was developed by their grouping themselves together. Now, waiving the point that knowledge *is* precisely this grouping together and that therefore to tell us that it originated from grouping sensations is a good deal like telling us that knowledge originated knowledge, that experience is the result of experience—I must inquire again what these sensations are. And I can see but this simple alternative: either they are known, are, from the first, elements in knowledge, and hence cannot be used to account for the origin of knowledge; or they are not, and, what is more to the point, they never can be. As soon as they are known, they cease to be the pure sensation we are after and become an element *in* experience, *of* knowledge. The conclusion of the matter is, that sensations which can be used to account for the *origin* of knowledge or experience, are sensations which cannot be known, are things-in-themselves which are not relative to consciousness. I do not here say that there are not such: I only say that, if there are, we have given up our psychological standpoint and have become "ontologists" of the most pronounced character.

But the confusion is deeply rooted, and I cannot hope that I have yet shown that any attempt to show the *origin* of knowledge or of conscious experience presupposes a division between things as they are for knowledge or experience and as they are in themselves, and is therefore non-psychological in character. I shall be told that I am making the whole difficulty for myself; that I persist in taking the standpoint of an adult whose experience is already formed; that I must become as an infant to enter the true psychological kingdom. If I will only go back to that stage, I shall find a point where knowledge has not yet begun, but where sensations must be supposed to exist. Owing to our different standing, since these sensations have to us been covered with the residues of thousands of others and have become symbolic of them, we cannot tell what these sensations are; though in all probability they are to be conceived in some analogy to nervous shocks. But the truth of our psychological analysis does not depend upon this. The fact that sensations exist before knowledge and that knowledge comes about by their organic registration and integration is undisputed. And I can imagine that I am told that if I would but confine myself to the analysis of given facts, I should find this whole matter per-

fectly simple—that the sensations have not the remotest connection with any sort of "metaphysics" or analogy with
things-in-themselves, and that we are all the time on positive
scientific ground. I hope so. We are certainly approaching
some degree of definiteness in our conception of what constitutes a sensation. But I am afraid that in thus defining the
nature of a sensation, in taking it out of the region of vagueness, my objector has taken from it all those qualities which
would enable it to serve as the origin of knowledge or of
conscious experience. It is no longer a thing-in-itself, but
neither is it, I fear, capable of accounting for experience.
For, alas, we have to use experience to account for it. An infant, whether I think myself back to my early days or select
some other baby, is, I suppose, a known object existing in the
world of experience; and his nervous organism and the objects which affect it, these too, I suppose, are known objects
which exist for consciousness. Surely it is not a baby thing-
in-itself which is affected, nor a world thing-in-itself which
calls forth the sensation. It is the known baby and a known
world in definite action and reaction upon each other, and
this definite relation is precisely a sensation. Yes, we are on
positive scientific ground, and for that very reason we are on
ground where the origin of knowledge and experience cannot be accounted for. Such a sensation I can easily form some
conception of. I can even imagine how such sensations may
by their organic registration and integration bring about
that knowledge which I may myself possess. But such a sensation is not prior to consciousness or knowledge. It is but an
element in the world of conscious experience. Far from being
that from which all relations spring, it is itself but one relation—the relation between an organic body, and one acting
upon it. Such a sensation, a sensation which exists only
within and for experience, is not one which can be used to
account for experience. It is but one element in an organic
whole, and can no more account for the whole, that a given
digestive act can account for the existence of a living body,
although this digestive act and others similar to it may no
doubt be shown to be all-important in the formation of a

given living body. In short, we have finally arrived at the root of the difficulty. Our objector has been supposing that he could account for the origin of consciousness or knowledge because he could account for the process by which the given knowledge of a given individual came about. But if he accounts for this by something which is not known, which does not exist for consciousness, he is leaving the psychological standpoint to take the ontological; if he accounts for it by a known something, as a sensation produced by the reaction of a nervous organism upon a stimulus, he is accounting for its origin from something which exists only for and within consciousness. Consequently he is not accounting for the origin of consciousness or knowledge as such at all. He is simply accounting for the origin of an individual consciousness, or a specific group of known facts, by reference to the larger group of known facts or universal consciousness. Hence also the historic impotency of all forms of materialism. For either this matter is unknown, is a thing-in-itself, and hence may be called anything else as well as matter; or it is known, and then becomes but one set of the relations which in their completeness constitute mind—when to account for mind from it is to assume as ultimate reality that which has existence only as substantiated by mind. To the relations of the individual to the universal consciousness, I shall return later. At present, I am concerned only to point out that, if a man comes to the conclusion that *all* knowledge is relative, that existence means existence for consciousness, he is bound to apply this conclusion to his starting point and to his process. If he does this, he sees that the starting point (in this case, sensations) and the process (in this case, integration of sensations) exist for consciousness also—in short, that the *becoming* of consciousness exists for consciousness only, and hence that consciousness can never have become at all. That for which all origin and change exists, can never have originated or changed.

I hope that my objector and myself have now got within sight of each other so that we can see our common ground, and the cause of our difference. We both admit that the becoming of certain definite forms of knowledge, say Space, Time, Body, External World, etc., etc., may (in deal, at least, if not yet as matter of actual fact) be accounted for as the product of a series of events. Now he supposes that, because the origin of some or all of our knowledge or conscious experience, knowledge of all particular things and of all general relations, can be thus accounted for, he has thereby accounted for the origin of consciousness or knowledge itself. All I desire to point out is that he is always accounting for their origin *within* knowledge or conscious experience, and that he cannot take his first step or develop this into the next, cannot have either beginning or process, without presupposing known elements—the whole sphere of consciousness, in fact. In short, what he has been doing is not to show the origin of consciousness or knowledge, but simply how consciousness or knowledge has differentiated itself into various forms. It is indeed the business of the psychologist to show how (not the *ideas of* space and time, etc., but) space, time, etc., arise, but since this origin is only within or for consciousness, it is but the showing of how knowledge develops *itself;* it is but the showing of how consciousness specifies itself into various given forms. He has not been telling us how knowledge became, but how it came to be in a certain way, that is, in a certain set of relations. In making out the origin of any or all particular knowledges (if I may be allowed the word), he is but showing the elements of knowledge. And in doing this, he is performing a twofold task. He is showing on the one hand what place they hold within experience, *i.e.,* he is showing their special adequacy or validity, and on the other he is explicating the nature of consciousness or experience. He is showing that it is not a bare form, but that, since these different elements arise necessarily within it, it is an infinite richness of relations. Let not the psychologist imagine then that he is showing the *origin* of consciousness, or of experience. There is nothing but themselves from which they can originate. He is but showing *what they are,* and, since they *are,* what they always have been.

I hope that it has now been made plain that the polemic

against the attempt of the psychologist to account for the origin of conscious experience does not originate in any desire to limit his sphere but simply to call him away from a meaningless and self-contradictory conception of the psychological standpoint to an infinitely fruitful one. The psychological standpoint as it has developed itself is this: all that is, is for consciousness or knowledge. The business of the psychologist is to give a genetic account of the various elements within this consciousness, and thereby fix their place, determine their validity, and at the same time show definitely what the real and eternal nature of this consciousness is. If we actually believe in experience, let us be in earnest with it, and believe also that if we only ask, instead of assuming at the outset, we shall find what the infinite content of experience is. How experience became we shall never find out, for the reason that experience always is. We shall never account for it by referring it to something else, for "something else" always is only for and in experience. *Why* it is, we shall never discover, for it is a whole. But how the elements within the whole become we may find out, and thereby account for them by referring them to each other and to the whole, and thereby also discover why they are.

We have now reached positive ground, and, in the remainder of the paper, I wish to consider the relations, within this whole, of various specific elements which have always been "inquiries into which the mind of man was very apt to run," *viz.*: the relations of Subject and Object, and the relations of Universal and Individual, or Absolute and Finite.

II

From the psychological standpoint the relation of Subject and Object is one which exists within consciousness. And its nature or meaning must be determined by an examination of consciousness itself. The duty of the psychologist is to show how it arises for consciousness. Put from the positive side, he must point out how consciousness differentiates itself so as to give rise to the existence within, that is for, itself of subject and object. This operation fixes the nature of the two (for they have no nature aside from their relation in consciousness), and at the same time explicates or develops the nature of consciousness itself. In this case, it reveals that consciousness is precisely the unity of subject and object.

Now psychology has never been so false to itself as to utterly forget that this is its task. From Locke downwards we find it dealing with the problems of the origin of space, time, the "ideas" of the external world, of matter, of body, of the *Ego,* etc., etc. But it has interpreted its results so as to deprive them of all their meaning. It has most successfully avoided seeing the necessary implications of its own procedure. There are in particular two interpretations by which it has evaded the necessary meaning of its own work.

The first of these I may now deal with shortly, as it is nothing but our old friend *x,* the thing-in-itself in a new guise. It is Reasoned or Transfigured Realism. It sees clearly enough that everything which we know is relative to our consciousness, and it sees also clearly enough that *our* consciousness is also relative. All that we can know exists for our consciousness; but when we come to account for our consciousness we find that this too is dependent. It is dependent on a nervous organism; it is dependent upon objects which affect this organism. It is dependent upon a whole series of past events formulated by the doctrine of evolution. But this body, these objects, this series of events, they too exist but for our consciousness. Now there is no *"metaphysics"* about all this. It is positive science. Still there is a contradiction. Consciousness at once depends upon objects and events, and these depend upon, or are relative to consciousness. Hence the fact of the case must be this: The nervous organism, the objects, the series of events *as known,* are relative to our consciousness, but since this itself is dependent, is a product, there is a reality behind the processes, behind our consciousness, which has produced them both. Subject and object as known *are* relative to consciousness, but there is a larger circle, a real object from which both of them emerge, but which can never be known, since to know is to relate to our consciousness. This

[97]

is the problem: on one hand, the relativity of all knowledge to our consciousness; on the other, the dependence of our consciousness on something not itself. And this is the solution: a real not related to consciousness, but which has produced both consciousness itself, and the objects which as known are relative to consciousness. Now all that has been said in the first part of this article has gone for naught if it is not seen that such an argument is not a solution of the contradiction, but a statement of it. The problem is to reconcile the undoubted relativity of all existence as known, to consciousness, and the undoubted dependence of our own consciousness. And it ought to be evident that the only way to reconcile the apparent contradiction, to give each its rights without denying the truth of the other, is to think them together. If this is done, it will be seen that the solution is that the consciousness to which all existence is relative is not our consciousness, and that our consciousness is itself relative to consciousness in general. But Reasoned Realism attempts to solve the problem not by bringing the elements together, but by holding them apart. It does not seek the higher unity which enables each to be seen as indeed true, but it attempts to divide. It attributes one element of the contradiction to our consciousness, and another to a thing-in-itself—the unknown reality. But this is only an express statement of the contradiction. If all *be* relative to consciousness, there is no thing-in-itself, just consciousness itself. If there be a thing-in-itself then all is not relative to consciousness. Let a man hold the latter if he will, but let him expressly recognize that thereby he has put himself on "ontological" ground and adopted an "ontological" method. Psychology he has forever abandoned.

The other evasion is much more subtle and "reasoned." It is a genuine attempt to untie the Gordian knot, as the other was a slashing attempt to cut it with the sword of a thing-in-itself. It is Subjective Idealism. And I wish now to show that Subjective Idealism is *not* the meaning of the psychological standpoint applied to the relation of subject and object. It is rather a misinterpretation of it based upon the same refusal to think two undoubted facts in their unity, the same attempt to divide the contradiction instead of solving it, which we have seen in the case of attempts to determine the origin of knowledge, and of Transfigured Realism. The position is this: The necessary relation of the world of existences to consciousness is recognized. [Thus Bain:] "There is no possible knowledge of a world except in reference to our minds —knowledge is a state of mind. The notion of material things is a mental fact. We are incapable even of discussing the existence of an independent material world; the very fact is a contradiction. We can speak only of a world presented to our own minds." But this being stated, consciousness is now separated into two parts—one of which is the subject, which is identified with mind, *Ego,* the Internal; while the other is the object, which is identified with the External, the *Non-Ego,* Matter. "Mind is definable, in the first instance, by the *method of contrast,* or as a remainder arising from *subtracting the object world from the totality of conscious experience.*" "The totality of our mental life is made up of *two kinds* of consciousness—the object consciousness and the subject consciousness. The first is the external world, or *Non-Ego;* the second is our *Ego,* or mind proper." Consciousness "includes our object states as well as our subject states. The object and subject are *both parts* of our being, as I conceive, and hence we have a subject consciousness, which is in a special sense Mind (*the scope of mental science*), and an object consciousness in which all other sentient beings participate, and which gives us the extended and material universe." It is, of course, still kept in view (which constitutes the logical superiority of Subjective Idealism over Realism) that "the object consciousness, which we call Externality, is still a mode of self in the most comprehensive sense." "Object experience is still conscious experience, that is Mind." I have quoted at this length because the above passages seem to me an admirable statement of a representative type of Subjective Idealism.

The logic of the process seems to be as follows. It is recognized that all existence with which philosophy or anything else has to do must be known existence—that is, that all existence is for consciousness. If we examine this consciousness, we shall find it testifying to "two kinds of consciousness"— one, a series of sensations, emotions, and ideas, etc., the other, objects determined by spatial relations. We have to recognize then two parts in consciousness, a subject part, mind more strictly speaking, and an object part, commonly called the external world or matter. But it must not be forgotten that this after all is a part of my own being, my consciousness. The subject swallows up the object. But this subject, again, "segregates" itself into "two antithetical halves," into "two parts," the subject and the object. Then again the object vanishes into the subject, and again the subject divides itself. And forever the process is kept up. Now the point I wish to make is that consciousness is here used in two entirely different senses, and that the apparent plausibility of the argument rests upon their confusion. There is consciousness in the broad sense, consciousness which includes subject and object; and there is consciousness in the narrow sense, in which it is equivalent to "mind," *"Ego,"* that is, to the series of conscious states. The whole validity of the argument rests, of course, upon the supposition that ultimately these two are just the same—that it is the individual consciousness, the *"Ego,"* which differentiates itself into the "two kinds of consciousness," subject and object. If not, "mind," as well as "matter"—the series of psychical states or events which constitute the *Ego* and are "the scope of mental science," as well as that in which all "sentient beings participate"—is but an element *in* consciousness. If this be so, Subjective Idealism is abandoned and Absolute Idealism (to which I hardly need say this article has been constantly pointing) is assumed. The essence of Subjective Idealism is that the subject consciousness or mind, which remains after the "object world has been subtracted," is that for which after all this object world exists. Were this not so— were it admitted that this subject, mind, and the object, matter, are both but *elements within,* and both exist only *for,* consciousness—we should be in the sphere of an eternal absolute consciousness, whose partial realization both the individual "subject" and the "external world" are. And I wish to

[100]

show that this is the only meaning of the facts of the case; that Subjective Idealism is but the bald statement of a contradiction.

This brief digression is for the purpose of showing that, to Subjective Idealism, the consciousness for which all exists is the consciousness which is called mind, *Ego,* "my being." The point which I wished to make was that this identification is self-contradictory, although it is absolutely necessary to this form of Idealism. I shall be brief here in order not to make a simple matter appear complicated. How can consciousness which gives rise to the "two kinds" of consciousness be identified with either of them? How can the consciousness which in its primary aspect exists in time as a series of psychical events or states be the consciousness for which a permanent world of spatially related objects, in which "all sentient beings participate," exists? How can the "mind" which is defined by way of "contrast," which exists after the object world has been "subtracted," be the mind which is the whole, of which subject and object are alike elements? To state that the mind, in the first instance, is but the remainder from the totality of conscious experience "minus the object world, and to state also that this object world is itself a part of mind"—what is that but to state in terms a self-contradiction? Unless it be to state that this way of looking at mind, "in the first instance," is but a partial and unreal way of looking at it, and that mind in truth is the unity of subject and object, one of which cannot be subtracted from the other, because it has absolutely no existence without the other. Is it not a self-contradiction to declare that the "scope of mental science" is subject consciousness or mind, and at the same time to declare that "both subject and object are parts of our being," are but "two kinds" of consciousness? Surely Psychology ought to be the science of our whole being, and of the whole consciousness. But no words can make the contradiction clearer than the mere statement of it. The only possible hypothesis upon which to reconcile the two statements that mind is consciousness with the object world subtracted, and that it is the whole of our conscious experience, including both subject and object world, is that the term Mind is used in two entirely different senses in the two cases. In the first it must be individual mind, or consciousness, and in the second it must be absolute mind or consciousness, for and in which alone the individual or subject consciousness and the external world or object consciousness exist and get their reality.

The root of the whole difficulty is this. It is the business of Psychology to take the whole of conscious experience for its scope. It is its business to determine within this whole what the nature of subject and object are. Now Subjective Idealism identifies at the outset, as may be seen in the passages quoted, subject with "Mind," "*Ego*," and object with "Matter," "*Non-Ego*," "External World," and then goes on to hold that the "scope" of Psychology is the former only. In short, the psychological standpoint, according to which the nature of subject and object was to be determined from the nature of conscious experience, was abandoned at the outset. It is presumed that we already know what the "subject" is, and Psychology is confined to treatment of that. It is assumed that we know already what the "object" is, and Psychology is defined by its elimination. This method, as psychology, has two vices. It is "ontological," for it sets up some external test to fix upon the nature of subject and object; and it is arbitrary, for it dogmatically presupposes the limitation of Psychology to a series of subjective states. It assumes that Psychology instead of being the criterion of all, has some outside criterion from which its own place and subject matter is determined, and more specifically, *it assumes that the standpoint of Psychology is necessarily individual or subjective.* Why should we be told that the scope of Psychology is subject consciousness, and subject consciousness be defined as the totality of conscious experience *minus* the object world, unless there is presupposed a knowledge of what subject and object are? How different is the method of the true psychological standpoint! It shows how subject and object arise within conscious experience, and thereby develops the nature of consciousness. It shows it to be the unity of subject and object. It shows therefore that there cannot be "two kinds" of consciousness, one subject, the other object, but that all consciousness whether of "Mind," or of "Matter," is, *since* consciousness, the unity of subject and object. Consciousness may, and undoubtedly does, have two aspects—one aspect in which it appears as an individual, and another in which it appears as an external world over against the individual. But there are not two kinds of consciousness, one of which may be subtracted from the whole and leave the other. They are but consciousness in one phase, and how it is that consciousness assumes this phase, how it is that this division into the individual and the external world arises for consciousness (in short, how consciousness in one stage appears as perception)—that is precisely the business of Psychology to determine. But it does not determine it by assuming at the outset that the subject is "me," and the object is the world. And if this be not assumed at the outset it certainly will not be reached at the conclusion. The conclusion will show that the distinction of consciousness into the individual and the world is but one form in which the *relation* of subject and object, which everywhere constitutes consciousness, appears. This brings us definitely to the relation of the individual and the universal consciousness.

III

We have seen that the attempt to account for the origin of knowledge, at bottom, rests on the undoubted fact that the individual consciousness does become, but also that the only way to account for this becoming, without self-contradiction, is by the postulate of a universal consciousness. We have seen again that the truth at the bottom of subjective idealism is the undoubted fact that all existence is relative to our consciousness, but also that the only consistent meaning of this fact is that our consciousness as individual is itself relative to a universal consciousness. And now I am sure that my objector, for some time silent, will meet me with renewed vigor. He will turn one of these arguments against the other and say: "After all, this consciousness for which all exists is your individual consciousness. The universal consciousness itself exists only for it. You may say indeed that this individual consciousness, which has now absorbed the universal again, shows the universal as necessary to its own existence, but this is only to fall into the contradiction which you have already urged against a similar view on the part of Subjective Idealism. Your objection in that case was that consciousness divided into subject consciousness and object consciousness, of which the former immediately absorbed the latter, and again subdivided itself into the subject and object consciousness. You objected that this was the express statement of a contradiction—the statement that the subject consciousness was and was not the whole of conscious experience. It was only as it was asserted to be the whole that any ground was found for subjective idealism; but only as it was regarded as a remainder left over from subtraction of the object world does it correspond to actual experience. Now you have yourself fallen into precisely this contradiction. You do but state that the individual consciousness is and is not the universal consciousness. Only so far as it is not, do you escape subjective idealism; only so far as it is, do you escape the thing-in-itself. If this universal consciousness is not for our individual consciousness, if it is not a part of our conscious experience, it is unknowable, a thing-in-itself. But if it be a part of our individual consciousness, then after all the individual consciousness is the ultimate. By your own argument you have no choice except between the acceptance of an unknowable unrelated reality or of subjective idealism."

This objection amounts to the following disjunction: Either the universal consciousness is the individual and we have subjective idealism; or, it is something beyond the individual consciousness, and we have a thing-in-itself. Now this dilemma looks somewhat formidable, yet its statement shows that the objector has not yet put himself upon the psychological ground: there is something of the old "ontological" man left in him yet, for it assumes that he has, prior to its determination by Psychology, an adequate idea of what "individual" is and means. If he will take the psychological standpoint, he will see that the nature of the individual as well as of the universal must be determined within and through conscious experience. And if this is so, all ground for the disjunction falls away at once. This disjunction rests upon the supposition that the individual and the universal consciousness are something opposed to each other. If one were to assert that the meaning of the individual consciousness is that it is universal, the whole objection loses not only its ground but its meaning; it becomes nonsense. But I am not concerned just at present to state this; I am concerned only to point out that, if one starts with a presupposition regarding the nature of the individual consciousness, one is leaving the psychological standpoint. In forming the parallel between the position attributed to the writer and that of subjective idealism, the supposed objector was building wiser than perhaps he knew. The trouble with the latter view is that it supposes that consciousness may be divided into "two kinds," one subjective, the other objective; that it presupposes, at the start, the nature of subject and object. The fact of the case is that, since consciousness is the unity of subject and object, there is no purely subjective or purely objective. So here. It is presupposed that there are "two kinds" of consciousness, one individual, the other universal. And the fact will be found to be, I imagine, that consciousness is the unity of the individual and the universal; that there is no purely individual or purely universal. So the disjunction made is meaningless. But however that may be, at all events it leaves the psychological basis, for it assumes that the nature of the individual is already known.

This has been said that it may be borne in mind from the outset that Psychology must determine within consciousness the nature of the individual and the universal consciousness, thereby determining at once their place within experience, and explicating the nature of consciousness itself. And this, stated in plain terms, means simply that, since consciousness does show the origin of individual and universal consciousness *within itself,* consciousness is therefore both universal and individual. *How* this is, the present article, of course, does not undertake to say. Its more modest function is simply to point out that it is the business of psychology to show the nature of the individual and the universal and of the relation existing between them. These must not be presupposed, and then imported bodily to determine the nature of psychologic experience. There has now been rendered explicit what was implied concerning the psychological standpoint from the first, *viz.*, that it is a universal standpoint. If the nature of all objects of philosophical inquiry is to be determined from fixing their place within conscious experience, then there is no criterion outside of or beyond or behind just consciousness itself. To adopt the psychological standpoint is to assume that consciousness itself is the only possible absolute. And this is tacitly assumed all the while by subjective idealism. The most obvious objection to subjective idealism is, of course, that it presupposes that, if "mind were to become extinct, the an-nihilation of matter, space, time would result." And the equally obvious reply of subjective idealism is: "My conception of the universe even though death may have over-taken all its inhabitants, would not be an independent reality, I should merely take on the object-consciousness of a sup-posed mind then present" (Bain). In short, the reality of the external world, though I should imagine all finite minds destroyed, would be that I cannot imagine consciousness de-stroyed. As soon as I imagine an external world, I imagine a consciousness in relation to which it exists. One may put the objection from a side which gets added force with every advance of physical science. The simplest physiology teaches that all our sensations originate from bodily states—that they are conditioned upon a nervous organism. The science of biology teaches that this nervous organism is not ultimate but had its origin; that its origin lies back in indefinite time, and that as it now exists it is a result of an almost infinite series of processes; all these events, through no one knows how much time, having been precedent to your and my mind, and being the condition of their existence. Now is all this an illu-sion, as it must be, if its only existence is for a consciousness which is "but a transition from one state to another"? The usual answer to this argument is that it is an *ignoratio elenchi:* that it has presupposed a consciousness for which these events existed; and that they have no meaning except when stated in terms of consciousness. This answer I have no call to rebut. But it must be pointed out that this is to suppose the individual consciousness capable of transcending itself and assuming a universal standpoint—a standpoint whence it can see its own becoming, as individual. It is this *implication* of the universal nature of the individual consciousness which has constituted the strength of English philosophy; it is its lack of *explication* which has constituted its weakness. Subjective idealism has "admitted of no answer and produced no conviction" because of just this confusion. That which has admitted of no answer is the existence of all *for* consciousness; that which has produced no conviction is the existence of all for our consciousness as merely individual. English philosophy can assume its rightful position only when it has become fully aware of its own presuppositions; only when it has become conscious of that which constitutes its essential characteristic. It must see that the psychological standpoint is necessarily a universal standpoint and consciousness necessarily the only absolute, before it can go on to develop the nature of consciousness and of experience. It must see that the individual consciousness, the consciousness which is but "transition," but a process of becoming, which, in its primary aspect, has to be defined by way of "contrast," which is but a "part" of conscious experience, nevertheless is when viewed in its finality, in a perfectly concrete way, the universal consciousness, the consciousness which has never become and which *is* the totality; and that it is only because the individual consciousness is, in its ultimate reality, the universal consciousness that it affords any basis whatever for philosophy.

The case stands thus: We are to determine the nature of everything, subject and object, individual and universal, as it is found within conscious experience. Conscious experience testifies, in the primary aspect, my individual self is a "transition," is a process of becoming. But it testifies also that this individual self is conscious of the transition, that it knows the process by which it has become. In short, the individual self can take the universal self as its standpoint, and thence know its own origin. In so doing, it knows that it has its origin in processes which exist for the universal self, and that therefore the universal self never has become. Consciousness testifies that consciousness is a result, but that it is the result of consciousness. Consciousness is the self-related. Stated from the positive side, consciousness has shown that it involves *within* itself a process of becoming, and that this process becomes conscious of itself. This process is the individual consciousness; but, since it is conscious of itself, it is consciousness of the universal consciousness. All consciousness, in short, is self-consciousness, and the self is the universal consciousness, for which all process is and which, therefore, always is. The individual consciousness is but the process of realization of the universal consciousness through itself. Looked at as process, as realizing, it is individual consciousness; looked at as produced or realized, as conscious of the process, that is, of itself, it is universal consciousness.

It must not be forgotten that the object of this paper is simply to develop the presuppositions which have always been latent or implicit in the psychological standpoint. What has been said in the way of positive result has been said, therefore, only as it seemed necessary to develop the meaning of the standpoint. It must also be remembered that it is the work of Psychology itself to determine the exact and concrete relations of subject and object, individual and universal, within consciousness. What has been said here, if said only for the development of the standpoint, is therefore exceedingly formal. To some of the more concrete problems I hope to be able to return at another time.

6

PSYCHOLOGY AS PHILOSOPHIC METHOD

IN "The Psychological Standpoint," I endeavored to point out that the characteristic English development in philosophy—the psychological movement since Locke—had been neither a "threshing of old straw," nor a movement of purely negative meaning, whose significance for us was exhausted when we had learned how it necessarily led to the movement in Germany—the so-called "transcendental" movement. Its positive significance was found to consist in the fact that it declared consciousness to be the sole content, account and criterion of all reality; and psychology, as the science of this consciousness, to be the explicit and accurate determination of the nature of reality in its wholeness, as well as the determination of the value and validity of the various elements or factors of this whole. It is the ultimate science of reality, because it declares what experience in its totality is; it fixes the worth and meaning of its various elements by showing their development and place within this whole. It is, in short, *philosophic method*. But that paper was necessarily largely negative, for it was necessary to point out that as matter of fact the movement had not been successful in presenting psychology as the method of philosophy, for it had not been true to its own basis and ideal. Instead of determining all, both in its totality and its factors, through consciousness, it had endeavored to determine consciousness from something out of and beyond necessary relation to consciousness. It had determined its psychology from a dogmatically presupposed on-

From *Mind*, April, 1886; 153-173.

tology, instead of getting at its ontology from a critical examination of the nature and contents of consciousness, as its standpoint required. It had a thing-in-itself, something whose very existence was to be opposed to consciousness, as in the unknowable "substances" of Locke, the transcendent Deity of Berkeley, the sensations or impressions of Hume and Mill, the "transfigured real" of Spencer; and it used this thing-in-itself as the cause and criterion of conscious experience. Thus it contradicted itself; for, if psychology as method of philosophy means anything, it means that nothing shall be assumed except just conscious experience itself, and that the nature of all shall be ascertained from and within this.

It is to the positive significance of psychology as philosophic method—its significance when it is allowed to develop itself free from self-contradictory assumptions—that this present paper is directed. It was suggested in the previous paper that this method, taken in its purity, would show substantial identity with the presuppositions and results of the "transcendental" movement. And as the principal attacks upon the pretensions of psychology to be method for philosophy, or anything more than one of the special sciences, have come from representatives of this movement, this paper must be occupied with treating psychology in reference to what we may call German philosophy, as the other treated it in reference to English philosophy. In so far as the criticisms from this side have been occupied with pointing out the failure of the actual English psychology to be philosophy, there is of course no difference of opinion. That arises only in so far as these criticisms have seemed (*seemed*, I repeat) to imply that the same objections must hold against every *possible* psychology; while it seems to the writer that psychology is the only *possible* method.

It is held, or seems to be held, by representatives of the post-Kantian movement, that man may be regarded in two aspects, in one of which he is an object of experience like other objects: he is a finite thing among other finite things; with these things he is in relations of action and reaction, but possesses the additional characteristic that he is a knowing, feeling, willing *phenomenon*. As such, he forms the object of a special science, psychology, which, like every other special science, deals with its material as pure object, abstracting from that creative synthesis *of subject and object,* self-consciousness, through which all things are and are known. It is therefore, like all the special sciences, partial and utterly inadequate to determining the nature and meaning of that whole with which philosophy has to deal. Nay more, it is itself ultimately dependent upon philosophy for the determination of the meaning, validity, and limits of the principles, categories, and method which it unconsciously assumes. To regard psychology therefore as philosophic method is to be guilty of the same error as it would be to regard the highest generalizations of, say, physics as adequate to determining the problems of philosophy. It is an attempt to determine the unconditioned whole, self-consciousness, by that which has no existence except as a conditioned part of this very whole.

> Metaphysics [says Professor Caird] has to deal with conditions of the knowable, and hence with self-consciousness or that unity which is implied in all that is and is known. Psychology has to inquire how this self-consciousness is realized or developed in man, in whom the consciousness of self grows with the consciousness of a world in time and space, of which he individually is only a part, and to parts of which only he stands an immediate relation. In considering the former question we are considering the sphere within which all knowledge and all objects of knowledge are contained. In considering the latter, we are selecting one particular object or class of objects within this sphere. . . . It is possible to have a *purely objective* anthropology or psychology—which abstracts from the relation of man to the mind that knows him—just as it is possible to have a purely objective science of nature.[1]

[1] Art. "Metaphysic," *Ency. Britt.*, xvi, 89. Cp. Professor Adamson, *Philosophy of Kant,* pp. 22 ff., *Fichte,* pp. 109 ff.; *Essays in Philosophical Criticism,* pp. 44 ff.; Professor A. Seth, *Ency. Britt.*, art. "Philosophy."

The other aspect of man is that in which he, as self-conscious, has manifested in him the unity of all being and knowing, and is not finite, *i.e.,* an object or event, but is, in virtue of his self-conscious nature, infinite, the bond, the living union of all objects and events. With this infinite, universal self-consciousness, philosophy deals; with man as the object of experience, psychology deals.

In stating the position of the post-Kantian movement, I used the word *seemed,* and used it advisedly, as I do not conceive that at bottom there is any difference of opinion. But it seems to me that there are invariably involved in the reasonings of this school certain presuppositions regarding the real science of psychology which, probably for the reason that the writers have seen such misuse made of a false psychology, are not distinctly stated, and which, accordingly, not only lessen the convincing force with which their reasonings are received by those unacquainted with the necessity and rationality of these presuppositions, but which also, as not distinctly thought out, tend at times to involve these reasonings in unnecessary obscurity and even contradictions. It is these presuppositions regarding the nature of a real psychology, lying at the basis of all the work of the post-Kantian school, conditioning it and giving it its worth, which it is the object of this paper to examine.

The start is made accordingly from the supposed distinction of aspects in man's nature, according to one of which he is an object of experience and the subject of psychology, and according to the other of which, he, as self-consciousness, is the universal condition and unity of all experience, and hence not an object of experience. As I have already referred to Professor Adamson's treatment of this distinction, let me refer to a later writing of his which seems to retract all that gave validity to this distinction. After pointing out that the subject matter of psychology *cannot* be *pure* objects but must always be the reference of an individual subject to a content which is universal, he goes on with the following most admirable statement:

[112]

It is in and through the conscious life of the individual that all the thinking and acting which form the material for other treatment is realised. When we isolate the content and treat it as having a *quasi*-existence *per se*, we are in the attitude of objective or natural science. When we endeavour to interpret the significance of the whole, to determine the meaning of the connective links that bind it together, we are in the attitude of philosophy. But when we regard the modes through which knowledge and acting are realised in the life of an individual subject, we are in the position of the psychological inquirer.

Now, when psychology is defined as the science of the realization of the universe in and through the individual, all pretense of regarding psychology as merely one of the special sciences, whose subject matter by necessity is simply some one department of the universe, considered out of relation to the individual, is, of course, abandoned. With this falls, as a matter of course, the supposed twofold character of man's nature. If the essence of his nature is to be the realization of the universe, there is no aspect in which, *as man*, it appears as a mere object or event in the universe. The distinction is now transferred to the two ways of looking at the same material, and no longer concerns two distinct materials. Is this distinction, however, any more valid? Is there any reason for distinguishing between the modes through which the universe is realized in an individual, and the significance of this universe as a whole? At first sight there may appear to be, but let us consider the following questions. Does the whole have any significance beyond itself? If we consider experience in its absolute totality so far as realized in the individual, can the "significance of the whole" be determined beyond what itself testifies to as a whole; and do the "connective links which bind together" have any "meaning" except just as they do bind together? And since this whole and these connective links are given to us by the science of psychology, what is this except completed philosophic method, and what more has philosophy

[113]

to do except to abstract from this totality, and regard it, on its material side, as philosophy of nature, and on its formal as real logic? Psychology, as science of the realization through the individual of the universe, answers the question as to the significance of the whole, by giving that whole, and at the same time gives the meaning of the parts and of their connection by showing just their place within this whole.

It would be fatal to the existence of philosophy as well as of psychology to make any distinction here. Were not the universe realized in the individual, it would be impossible for the individual to rise to a universal point of view, and hence to philosophize. That the universe has not been completely realized in man is no more an objection to the employment of psychology as the determination of the nature of this universe, than it is to any treatment of philosophy whatever. In no way can the individual philosophize about a universe which has not been realized in his conscious experience. The universe, except as realized in an individual, has no existence. In man it is partially realized, and man has a partial science; in the absolute it is completely realized, and God has a complete science. Self-consciousness means simply an individualized universe; and if this universe has *not* been realized in man, if man be not self-conscious, then no philosophy whatever is possible. If it *has* been realized, it is in and through psychological experience that this realization has occurred. Psychology is the scientific account of this realization, of this individualized universe, of this self-consciousness. What other account can be given? It is the object of this paper to show that no other account can be given. Not only is any final distinction or dualism, even of aspects, in man's nature utterly untenable, but no distinction even of aspects can be made in the *treatment* of man's nature. Psychology has to do with just the consciousness which constitutes man's experience, and all further determinations of experience fall within this psychological determination of it, and are hence abstract. More definitely, Psychology, and not Logic, is the method of Philosophy. Let us deal *seriatim* with these two questions.

I

No such distinction in the nature of man, as that in one aspect he is "part of the partial world," and hence the subject of a purely natural science, psychology, and in another the conscious subject for which all exists, the subject of philosophy, can be maintained. This is our first assertion. Let us turn again to that most lucid and comprehensive statement of philosophic doctrine by Professor Caird, from which extract has already been made. The distinction to be upheld is that between the "sphere in which all knowledge and all objects of knowledge are contained" and "one particular object within this sphere." The question which at once arises is, How does this distinction come about? Granted that it is valid, how is man known as requiring in his nature this distinction for his proper comprehension? There is but one possible answer: it is a distinction which has arisen within and from conscious experience itself. In the course of man's realization of the universe there is necessitated this distinction. This distinction therefore falls within the sphere of psychology, and cannot be used to fix the position of psychology. Much less can psychology be identified with some one aspect of experience which has its origin only within that experience which in its wholeness constitutes the material of psychology. The distinction, as we shall immediately see, cannot be an absolute one: by no possibility or contingency can man be regarded as *merely* one of objects of experience; but so far as the distinction has relative validity it is a purely psychological one, originating because man in his experience, at different *stages* of it, finds it necessary to regard himself in two lights—in one of which he is a particular space- and time-conditioned being (we cannot say object or event) or activity, and in the other the unconditioned eternal synthesis of all. At most the distinction is only one of various stages in one and the same experience, both of which, as stages of experience—one, indeed, of experience in its partiality and the other of experience in its totality—fall within the science of experience, *viz.*, psychology.

We will see how the question stands if we state it otherwise. Does or does not the self-consciousness of man fall within the science of psychology? What reason can be given for excluding it? Certainly few would be found so thoroughgoing as to deny that perception is a matter which that science must treat; those however who admit perception would find themselves hard put to it to give a reason for excluding memory, imagination, conception, judgment, reasoning. Why having reached the stage of reasoning, where the original implicit individual with which we began has been broken up into the greatest possible number of explicit relations, shall we rule out self-consciousness where these relations are again seen united into an individual unity? There is no possible break: either we must deny the possibility of treating perception in psychology, and then our "purely objective science of psychology" can be nothing more than a physiology; or, admitting it, we must admit what follows directly from and upon it—self-consciousness. Self-consciousness is indeed a *fact* (I do not fear the word) of experience, and must therefore find its treatment in psychology.

But this is not all. Not only does self-consciousness appear as one of the stages of psychological experience, but the explanation of the simplest psychological fact—say one of perception, or feeling, or impulse—involves necessary reference to self-consciousness. Self-consciousness is involved in every simpler process, and no one of them can be scientifically described or comprehended except as this involution is brought out. In fact, their comprehension or explanation is simply bringing to light this implication of self-consciousness within them. This would be the last thing that the upholders of self-consciousness as the final unity and synthesis, the absolute meaning of experience, could deny. The organic nature of self-consciousness being their thesis, it must indeed reveal itself in, or rather constitute, each of its members and phases. The very *existence* of any idea or feeling being ultimately its relation to self-consciousness, what other account of it can be given except its organic placing in the system? If there be such an act as perception, a candid, careful examination of it, *not of its logical conditions,* but of itself as *matter of experienced fact,* will reveal what it is; and this revelation will be the declaration of its relation to that organic system which in its wholeness is self-consciousness. We may then abstract from this relation, which constitutes its very being, and consider it as an *object of perception,* and, generalizing the case, produce a philosophy of nature; or, considering it as conditioned by thought, we may thus produce a logic. But both of these proceedings go on in abstraction from its real being, and cannot give the real method of philosophy. In short, the real *esse* of things is neither their *percipi,* nor their *intelligi* alone; it is their *experiri.* Logic may give us the science of the *intelligi,* the philosophy of nature of the *percipi,* but only psychology can give us the systematic connected account of the *experiri,* which is also in its wholeness just the *experior—* self-consciousness itself.

We may see how the matter stands by inquiring what would be the effect upon philosophy if self-consciousness were not an *experienced fact, i.e.,* if it were not one actual stage in that realization of the universe by an individual which is defined as constituting the sphere of psychology. The result would be again, precisely, that no such thing as philosophy, under any theory of its nature whatever, is possible. Philosophy, it cannot be too often repeated, consists simply in viewing things *sub specie aeternitatis* or *in ordine ad universum.* If man, as matter of fact, does not realize the nature of the eternal and the universal *within* himself, as the essence of his own being; if he does not at one stage of his experience consciously, and in all stages implicitly, lay hold of this universal and eternal, then it is mere matter of words to say that he can give no account of things as they universally and eternally are. To deny, therefore, that self-consciousness is a matter of psychological experience is to deny the possibility of any philosophy.

What the denial comes to we have had historically demonstrated in Kant. He admits perception and conception as matters of experience, but he draws the line at self-consciousness. It is worth noticing that his reason for denying it is not psychological at all, but logical. It is not because self-consciousness *is* not a fact, but because it *cannot* be a fact according to his logical presuppositions. The results following the denial are worthy of notice as corresponding exactly to what we might be led to expect: first, with the denial of the fact of self-consciousness comes the impossibility of solving the problem of philosophy, expressed in the setting up of an unknown thing-in-itself as the ultimate ground and condition of experience; and, secondly, comes the failure to bring perception and conception into any organic connection with experience, that is, the failure to really comprehend and explain them, manifested in the limitation of both perception, through the forms of space and time, and thinking, through the categories, to phenomena which are in no demonstrable connection with reality. The failure to recognize self-consciousness as a stage of psychological experience leads not only to a failure to reach the alternate synthesis of experience, but renders it impossible to explain the simpler forms of psychological experience. This failure of Kant teaches us another lesson also, in that, as already stated, it was due to abandoning his real method, which was *psychological*, consisting in the self-knowledge of reason as an organic system by reason itself, and setting up a *logical* standard (in this latter case the principles of non-contradiction and identity), by which to determine the totality of experience. The work of Hegel consisted essentially in showing that Kant's *logical* standard was erroneous, and that, as matter of logic, the only true criterion or standard was the organic notion, or *Begriff,* which is a systematic totality, and accordingly able to explain both itself and also the simpler processes and principles. That Hegel accomplished this work successfully and thoroughly there can be to the writer no doubt; but it seems equally clear that the work of Kant is in need of another complement, following more closely his own conception of method and of philosophy, which shall consist in showing self-consciousness as a fact of experience, as well as perception through organic forms and thinking through organic principles. And it seems further that, only when this has been done, will, for the first time, the presuppositions latent in the work of Hegel, which give it its convincing force and validity, be brought out.

Again, it seems worthy of note that the late Professor Green (of whom the writer would not speak without expressing his deep, almost reverential gratitude), when following out Kant's work from its logical side, hardly escaped Kant's negative results. (By Kant's logical method we mean the inquiry into the *necessary conditions* of experience; by his psychological method the inquiry into the *actual nature* of experience.) After his complete demonstration of consciousness as the final condition, synthesis and unity of all that is or is knowable, he finds himself obliged to state: "As to what that consciousness in itself or in its completeness is, we can only make negative statements. *That* there is such a consciousness is implied in the existence of the world; but *what* it is we can only know through its so far acting in us as to enable us, however partially and interruptedly, to have knowledge of a world or an intelligent experience." Had he begun from the latter statement, and shown as matter of fact that this universal consciousness *had* realized itself, though only partially and interruptedly, in us, he certainly would have been able to make very positive statements regarding it, and would also have furnished a basis in fact for his logical method, which now seems to hang upon nothing but a unity of which all that can be said is that it *is* a unity, and that it *is not* anything in particular. When one reflects that it is not only upon the existence of this unity, but upon its working in and through us, that all philosophy and philosophizing depend, one cannot conceal the apprehension that too great a load of philosophy has been hung upon too feeble a peg.

So, too, after his victorious demonstration that upon the existence of this spiritual unity depends the possibility of all moral experience, he finds himself obliged to state, with that candor so characteristic of all his thinking: "Of a life of completed development, of activity with the end attained, we can only speak or think in negatives, and thus only can we speak

[119]

or think of that state of being in which, according to our theory, the ultimate moral good must consist." Once more, had he started from the fact that as matter of actual realization this absolute good has been reproduced in our lives and the end attained (for surely the good is a matter of quality and not of quantity, and the end a power, not a sum), he would not have found himself in this difficulty. But with a purely logical method, one can end only with the *must be* or the *ought:* the *is* vanishes, because it has been abstracted from. The psychological method starts from the *is,* and thereby also gives the basis *and* the ideal for the *ought* and *must be.*

But it is time that we returned to our thesis, which, in brief, was that no distinction which maintains that psychology is the science of man as "part of this partial world" can be maintained. The following reasons for this denial have been given: it was pointed out that the relative validity which this distinction in man's nature undoubtedly possesses is itself the product and manifestation of psychological experience; that man as man, or as the conscious experience whose science is psychology, is self-conscious, and that therefore self-consciousness as the unity of subject and object, not as "purely objective," as the totality, not as a "part," must be included in the science of psychology; and that furthermore this treatment of self-consciousness is necessary for the explanation and comprehension of any partial fact of conscious experience. And finally, it was pointed out that the denial of self-consciousness as constituting matter of experience, and hence of psychology, was the denial of the possibility of philosophy itself; and this was illustrated by historic examples. Before passing on to the second topic, I wish briefly to return to Professor Caird's exposition, and shelter myself somewhat beneath the wings of his authority. In the article already referred to, he goes on to state that the natural objective science of man after all "omits the distinctive characteristic of man's being"; that while we may treat inorganic nature and even organic with purely natural objective methods and principles, because "they are not unities for *themselves,* but only *for us,*" such treatment cannot be applied to man, for man *is for himself, i.e.,* is not a pure object, but is self-consciousness. Thus, he continues:

> In man, in so far as he is self-conscious—*and it is self-consciousness that makes him man*—the unity through which all things are and are known is manifested. . . . Therefore to treat him as a simply natural being is *even more inaccurate and misleading* than to forget or deny his relation to nature altogether. A true psychology must avoid both errors: it must conceive man as at once spiritual and natural; it must find a reconciliation of freedom and necessity. It must face *all the difficulties involved in the conception of the absolute principle of self-consciousness*—through which all things are and are known—*as manifesting itself in the life of a being like man,* who "comes to himself" only by a long process of development out of the unconsciousness of a merely animal existence.

When it is stated, later on, that the natural science of man "is necessarily abstract and imperfect, as it omits from its view the central fact in the life of the object of which it treats," it is hardly worth while discussing whether there be any such science or not. But there is suggested for us in the quotation just made our second problem—the final relation of psychology, which confessedly must deal with self-consciousness, to philosophy. For there the problem of psychology was stated to be the question of the "absolute principle of self-consciousness, manifesting itself in the life of a being like man." That is, it is here suggested that psychology does not deal with the absolute principle in itself, but only with the modes by which this is manifested or realized in the life of man. Psychology no longer appears as an objective science; it now comes before us as a phenomenology, presupposing a science of the absolute reality itself. It is to this question that I now turn. Is psychology the science *merely* of the manifestation of the Absolute, or is it the science of the Absolute itself?

II

The relation of Psychology to Philosophy now stands, I suppose, something like this: There is an absolute self-consciousness. The science of this is philosophy. This absolute self-consciousness manifests itself in the knowing and acting of individual men. The science of this manifestation, a phenomenology, is psychology. The distinction is no longer concerned with man's being itself; it is a distinction of treatment, of ways of looking at the same material. Before going to its positive consideration the following questions may suggest the result we desire to reach. How does there come about this distinction between the "spiritual" and the "natural," between "freedom" and "necessity"? How does there come into our knowledge the notion of a distinction between the "absolute principle of self-consciousness" and "man coming to himself only by a long process of development out of the unconsciousness of a merely animal existence"? Is this a distinction which falls outside the subject matter of psychology, and which may therefore be used to determine it; or is it one which has originated *within* psychological experience, and whose nature therefore, instead of being capable of fixing the character of psychology, must itself be determined *by* psychology? Furthermore, what *is* this distinction between the absolute self-consciousness and its manifestation in a being like man? Is the absolute self-consciousness complete in itself, or does it involve this realization and manifestation in a being like man? If it is complete in itself, how can any philosophy which is limited to "this absolute principle of self-consciousness" face and solve the difficulties involved in its going beyond itself to manifest itself in self-consciousness? This cannot be what is meant. The absolute self-consciousness must involve within itself, as organic member of its very being and activity, this manifestation and revelation. Its being must be this realization and manifestation. Granted that this realization and manifestation is an act not occurring in time, but eternally completed in the nature of the Absolute, and that it occurs only "partially" and "interruptedly" *through* (not *in*) time, in a being like man—the fact none the less remains that philosophy, under any theory of its nature, can deal with this absolute self-consciousness only so far as it has partially and interruptedly realized itself in man. For man, as object of his philosophy, this Absolute has existence only so far as it has manifested itself in his conscious experience. To return to our questions: If the material of philosophy be the absolute self-consciousness, and this absolute self-consciousness *is* the realization and manifestation of itself, and as material for philosophy exists only in so far as it has realized and manifested itself in man's conscious experience, and if psychology be the science of this realization in man, what else can philosophy in its fullness be but psychology, and psychology but philosophy?

These questions are stated only to suggest the end which we shall endeavor to reach. I shall not attempt to answer them directly, but to consider first the relations of Psychology to Science, and hence to Philosophy; and secondly to Logic.

(1) *The Relation of Psychology to Science.* Psychology is the completed method of philosophy, because in it science and philosophy, fact and reason, are one. Philosophy seems to stand in a double relation to Science. In its first aspect it is *a* science—the highest of all sciences. We take one sphere of reality and ask certain questions regarding it, and the answers give us some one science; we find in the process that this sphere of reality can only artificially be thus isolated, and we broaden and deepen our question, until finally, led by the organic connection of science with science, we ask after the nature of all reality, as one connected system. The answer to this question constitutes philosophy as one science amid the circle of sciences. But to continue to regard it in this way is to fail to grasp the meaning of the process which has forced us into philosophy. At the same time that philosophy is seen as the completion of the sciences, it is seen as their basis. It is no longer *a* science; it is Science. That is to say, the same movement of thought and reality which forces upon us the conception of a science which shall deal with the totality of reality

forces us to recognize that no one of our previous sciences was in strict truth science. Each abstracted from certain larger aspects of reality, and was hence hypothetical. Its truth was conditioned upon the truth of its relations to that whole which that science, as special science, could not investigate without giving up its own independent existence. Only in this whole is categorical truth to be found, and only as categorical truth is found in this whole is the basis found for the special sciences. Philosophy as the science of this whole appears no longer therefore as *a* science, but as all science taken in its organic systematic wholeness—not merely to which every so-called special science is something subordinate, but of which it constitutes an organic member. Philosophy has no existence except as the organic living unity and bond of these sciences; they have no existence except through their position in this living synthesis.

Now the question is, where does psychology stand within this organism? On the one hand, psychology is certainly a positive science. It finds its materials in certain facts and events. As to systematic observation, experiment, conclusion and verification, it can differ in no essential way from any one of them. It is based upon and deals with fact, and aims at the ordered comprehension and explanation of fact as any special science does. Yet the whole drift of this paper has been to show that in some way psychology does differ very essentially from any one of them. Where shall we find this difference? In one word, its relation to them is precisely that which we have discovered philosophy to bear: it is not only *a* science, but it turns out to be science as an organic system, in which every special science has its life, and from which it must abstract when it sets up for an independent existence of its own. We begin with any special science. That turns out to be not only some one department or sphere of reality, but also some one department of conscious experience. From one science to another we go, asking for some explanation of conscious experience, until we come to psychology, which gives us an account of it, in its own behalf, as neither mathematics, nor physics, nor biology does. So far we have only *a* special science,

[124]

though the highest and most concrete of all. But the very process that has made necessary this new science reveals also that each of the former sciences existed only in abstraction from it. Each dealt with some one phase of conscious experience, and for that very reason could not deal with the totality which gave it its being, consciousness. But in psychology we have the manifestation and explication of this consciousness. It gives in its wholeness what each of them would give in part, *viz.*, the nature of experience, and hence is related to them as the whole is to the part. It appears no longer, therefore, as the highest *of* sciences: it appears as Science itself, that is, as systematic account and comprehension of the nature of conscious experience. Mathematics, physics, biology, exist, because conscious experience reveals itself to be of such a nature, that one may make virtual abstraction from the whole, and consider a part by itself, without damage, so long as the treatment is purely scientific, that is, so long as the implicit connection with the whole is left undisturbed, and the attempt is not made to present this partial science as metaphysic, or as an explanation of the whole, as is the usual fashion of our uncritical so-called "scientific philosophies." Nay more, this abstraction of some one sphere is itself a living function of the psychologic experience. It is not merely something which it allows: it is something which it *does*. It is the analytic aspect of its own activity, whereby it deepens and renders explicit, realizes its own nature; just as their connection with each other is the synthetic aspect of the same self-realizing movement, whereby it returns to itself: while psychology in its completeness is the whole self-developing activity itself, which shows itself as the organic unity of both synthetic and analytic movements, and thus the condition of their possibility and ground of their validity. The analytic movement constitutes the special sciences; the synthetic constitutes the philosophy of nature; the self-developing activity itself, as psychology, constitutes philosophy.

What other position can be given psychology, so soon as we recognize the absurdity and impossibility of considering it a purely objective science? It is the science of the modes by which, in and through the individual, the universe is realized, it is said. But that the universe has no existence except as absolutely realized in an individual, *i.e.*, except as self-consciousness, is precisely the result of philosophy, and can therefore be no objection to such a consideration of the universe: in fact, such a statement only amounts to saying that psychology considers the universe as it really is. If the assertion is varied again, to read that philosophy treats of this individualized universe as it eternally *is,* while psychology can treat of it only as it partially and interruptedly *becomes,* this loses sight of two very important facts. First, philosophy can treat of absolute self-consciousness only in so far as it *has become* in a being like man, for otherwise it is not material for philosophy at all; and, secondly, it falls into the error of regarding this realization in man as a time-conditioned product, which it is not. Time is not something outside of the process of conscious experience; it is a form within it, one of the functions by which it organically constitutes its own being. In fact, psychology as philosophic method has an immense advantage at just this point over any other method of treating this problem. To any philosophy attempting to consider the absolute self-consciousness by itself, it must remain forever an insoluble problem why the *is* should ever appear as *becoming,* why the eternal should ever appear through the temporal. Psychology solves the problem by avoiding the assumption which makes it a problem. For, dealing with an individualized universe, one of whose functions of realization *is* time, it knows nothing about any consciousness which is out of relation to time. The case is just here: if philosophy will deal with the absolute consciousness conceived as purely eternal, out of relation to time, then the existence of that which constitutes the actual content of man's experience is utterly inexplicable; it is not only a mystery, but a mystery which contradicts the very nature of that which is, *ex hypothesi,* the absolute. If philosophy does deal with the eternal absolute consciousness as forever realized, yet as forever having time as one of its organic functions, it is not open to anyone to bring charges

[126]

against psychology as philosophy, for this and no more psychology does.

The question just comes to this: If we start from reason alone we shall never reach fact. If we start with fact, we shall find it revealing itself as reason. The objection to an account of fact or experience as philosophy is but a prejudice, though historically considered a well-grounded one. On the one hand, it has arisen because some partial account of experience, or rather account of partial experience, has been put forth as the totality, and just because thus put forth as absolute, has lost even the relative validity which it possessed as partial. Such is the procedure of Empiricism. On the other hand, we have had put forth as matter of fact certain truths declared to be immediate and necessary and intuitive, coming no one knows whence and meaning no one knows what. The aversion to immediacy, to "undeduced" fact, as given us by the Intuitionalists, is certainly a well-grounded one. But neither of these objections lies against psychology as account of the facts of experience. Men are mortal, and every actual account of experience will suffer from the defects of mortals, and be but partial, no doubt; unfortunately we are none of us omniscient yet. But the very essence of psychology as method is that it treats of experience in its absolute totality, not setting up some one aspect of it to account for the whole, as, for example, our physical evolutionists do, nor yet attempting to determine its nature from something outside of and beyond itself, as, for example, our so-called empirical psychologists have done. The vice of the procedure of both is at bottom precisely the same —the abstracting of some one element from the organism which gives it meaning, and setting it up as absolute. It is no wonder that the organism always has its revenge by pronouncing this abstracted element "unknowable." The only wonder is that men should still bow in spirit before this creation of their own abstracting thought, and reverence it as the cause and ground of all reality and knowledge. There is indeed an anthropomorphism which is degrading, but it is the anthropomorphism which sets up the feeblest element of its own thinking, pure being, as Mr. Spencer does, or the poorest element of its own feeling, a sensation, and reverences that as its own and the universe's cause. That is the anthropomorphism of the enslaved thought which has not yet awakened to the consciousness of its own totality and spiritual freedom.

Nor does the account of fact given by psychology have anything in common with the "ultimate, inexplicable, necessary" mental facts called intuitions. The fact of psychology reveals itself as precisely reason, which thereby accounts for itself, and in accounting for itself accounts for all its members. The fact of psychology is not isolated "truths," but the organic system of self-consciousness. This fact is indeed "immediate," but it is immediate only in and through a process, hence of mediation. It is indeed self-evidencing, but what it evidences is simply, of the parts, relation to and dependence upon the whole, and of the whole, that it is self-conditioned and self-related. Of the whole fact it may be said indeed that it is inexplicable. "It is true that we cannot explain the spiritual principle which is implied in all experience by reference to anything else than itself." [2] "Because all we can experience is included in this one world, and all our inferences and explanations relate only to its details, neither it as a whole, nor the one consciousness which constitutes it, can be accounted for in the ordinary sense of the word. They cannot be accounted for by what they include; and being all-inclusive, there remains nothing else by which they can be accounted for." [3] In short, any system of philosophy must ultimately fall back on the fact for which no reason can be given except precisely just that it is what it is. This implication of fact[4] is latent in all philosophy whatever, and all that psychology as philosophic method does is to render this necessary implication explicit. It alone starts from the completed fact, and it alone is therefore completed philosophy.

If it may have seemed at times in the course of the discus-

[2] Professor E. Caird, *Mind*, viii, 560.

[3] Green, *Prolegomena to Ethics*, p. 52.

[4] The insistence upon this seems to have been Lotze's great work as a philosopher.

sion that the nominal subject—the relation of psychology to science—had been left, it will now appear, I think, that we have all the time been dealing with just that subject. Science is the systematic account, or *reason* of *fact;* Psychology is the completed systematic account of the ultimate fact, which, as fact, reveals itself as reason, and hence accounts for itself, and gives the "reasons" of all sciences. The other point, the relation of psychology to logic, has already been dealt with by implication, and need not detain us long again.

(2) *The Relation of Psychology to Logic.* The whole course of philosophic thought, so far as the writer can comprehend it, has consisted in showing that any distinction between the form and the matter of philosophic truth, between the content and the method, is fatal to the reaching of truth. Self-consciousness is the final truth, and in self-consciousness the form as organic system and the content as organized system are exactly equal to each other. It is a process which, as form, has produced itself as matter. Psychology as the account of this self-consciousness must necessarily fulfill all the conditions of true method. Logic, since it necessarily abstracts from the ultimate fact, cannot reach in matter what it points to in form. While its content, if it be true philosophy, must be the whole content of self-consciousness or spirit, its form is only one process within this content, that of thought-conditions, the *Idee.* While the content is the eternal nature of the universe, its form is adequate only to "thinking what God thought and was before the creation of the world," that is, the universe in its unreality, in its abstraction. It is this contradiction between content and form in logic which makes it not philosophic method, but only one moment within that method. No contradiction results as soon as logic is given its proper place *within* the system. The contradiction occurs when, at the same moment that it is said that logic is "abstract," the logical method is still said to be the method of philosophy.

Such contradictions certainly appear to exist, for example, in the philosophy of Hegel. They have been often pointed out, and I shall only summarize them, following for the most

part a recent writer.[5] There is no way of getting from logic
to the philosophy of nature *logically*. The only way is to fall
back upon the fact; "we know from experience" that we have
nature as well as the *Idee*. In truth we do not go from logic to
nature at all. The movement is a reverse movement. "In
reality, the necessity for any such transition is purely facti-
tious, because *the notions never existed otherwise than in
nature and spirit*. . . . They were got by abstraction from
the concrete. . . . We owe, therefore, no apology for a return
to the reality from which we took them." In short, it is
necessity of fact, a necessity of conscious experience, which
takes us from the realm of the *Idee* to the realm of nature,
from the sphere of thought-conditions to the sphere of existent relations. "The same is true when we pass to the philosophy of spirit. The general *form* of personality is deducible,
but not a living human spirit with its individual thoughts,
feelings and actions." This remains "the incomprehensible
and inexplicable point in philosophy." And so it does undoubtedly while we regard logic as method of philosophy.
But this "inexplicability" is but the express condemnation of
the method, not a fact to be contented with. If we go deeper
and inquire not how is the transition from logic to the philosophy of nature or to the philosophy of spirit made, but how
is any transition whatever possible, we find the same difficulty.
It exists only by reason of the presupposed fact. "We cannot
in strictness say that the result has been independently
proved, because it has been reached in this fashion by the
method. It was presupposed *in* the method all along." In a
definite case, how is the transition, say from the category of
quality to that of quantity, made? It occurs not by virtue of
the category of quality in itself, but by virtue of the fact that
the whole *Idee* is implicitly contained in the principle of
quality, and must manifest itself, which it does by forcing
quality, as an inadequate expression of its own nature, into
quantity, which expresses its being more fully. And thus the
process continues until the *Idee* has manifested itself as the
whole organic system, which has expressed explicitly all that

[5] Professor A. Seth, "Hegel: an Exposition and Criticism," *Mind*, 24.

which in *Idee* it is. But this movement itself depends on spirit, and on the manifestation of spirit in nature, as already seen. Every purely logical transition therefore occurs at bottom because of fact, *i.e.*, seen in its wholeness it is not a logical transition but a factual. Psychology, as philosophic method, merely starts from this everywhere presupposed fact, and by so doing, for the first time, gives logic its basis and validity.

There can be no escape from this result by saying that after all in the philosophy of spirit, spirit is shown to be the *prius* and condition of the whole, as it undoubtedly is by Hegel himself. This merely brings the contradiction itself into clearer light. For logic, being thus confessedly determined as abstract, is still retained to determine the nature of the concrete. Logic, while it is thus declared to be only one moment of spirit, is still used to determine the nature of the whole. Thus is revealed the contradiction between form and content involved in the use of logic as the method of philosophy. Spirit is reached by a *logical* process, and the *logical* result is that as fact it is not reached at all. As concrete, it is beyond the reach of any abstract process. Either one must call in the aid of the presupposed but suppressed Fact, and recognize that after all the process has been going on within a further and higher determination; or, failing to see this, must recognize Spirit as only one factor or moment of the logical movement, that is, give up the notion of self-consciousness as subject, and fall back into Spinozistic pantheism. The logical movement, considered by itself, is always balancing in unstable equilibrium between dualism and pantheism. Set up as absolute method, it either recognizes the fact, but being unable to comprehend it, has to regard this fact, as foreign element over against it, as the matter of Plato and Aristotle, the thing-in-itself of Kant, and *Anstoss* of Fichte,[6] or endeavors to absorb the Fact as a mere element in its own logical being, and falls into Pantheism.

[6] The inability to go from the "because" of reason to the "cause" of fact, from logic to reality, when logic is not taken simply as one movement *within* reality, is clearly set forth in the closing chapters of Mr. Bradley's *Principles of Logic*.

This is the reason why Hegel, although the very center of his system is self-conditioned spirit, lends himself so easily to pantheistic treatment. Logic cannot reach, however much it may point to, an actual individual. The gathering up of the universe into the one self-conscious individuality it may assert as *necessary,* it cannot give it as *reality.* It is only as logic contradicts itself and faces back on the constant presupposition of this reality that it can demonstrate what it asserts. Taken purely by itself it must issue in a pantheism where the only real is the *Idee,* and where all its factors and moments, including spirit and nature, are real only at different stages or phases of the *Idee,* but vanish as imperfect ways of looking at things, or as illusions, when we reach the *Idee.* And thus the *Idee* itself vanishes, as an organic system, as a unity which lives through its distinctions, and becomes a dead identity, in no way distinguishable from the substance of Spinoza. Logic set up as absolute method reveals its self-contradiction by destroying itself. In a purely logical method the distinctions, the process, must disappear in the final unity, the product. Only a living actual Fact can preserve within its unity that organic system of differences in virtue of which it lives and moves and has its being. It is with this fact, conscious experience in its entirety, that psychology as method begins. It thus brings to clear light of day the presupposition implicit in every philosophy, and thereby affords logic, as well as the philosophy of nature, its basis, ideal and surety. If we have determined the nature of reality, by a process whose content equals its form, we can show the meaning, worth and limits of any one moment of this reality.

The conclusion of the whole matter is that a "being like man," since self-conscious, is an individualized universe, and hence that his nature is the proper material of philosophy, and in its wholeness the only material. Psychology is the science of this nature, and no dualism in it, or in ways of regarding it, is tenable. Whatever the dualism may be, it is only relative, and one which occurs within, not without, psychological experience. Psychology, as the complete systematic account of man, at the same time shows the value and meaning, and affords the condition, of the special sciences, the philosophy of nature and of logic. Or, in a word, if the reality of spirit be the presupposition, the *prius* and the goal, the condition and the end of all reality, the science of spirit must occupy a corresponding position with relation to all science. Surely then, as the Editor of *Mind* formerly urged, "the method of phychological approach is not philosophically valueless," and we have "ground for the belief that it has only to be more systematically followed out for the attaining of as great results as have been claimed for another way, while in this way the results are more likely to secure general acceptance" [7]—because, we may add, it simply expresses in a scientific way that which lies at the basis of all that has been otherwise secured.

[7] "Psychology and Philosophy," *Mind,* Vol. viii, 20.

7

"ILLUSORY PSYCHOLOGY"

THE fact that so acute and experienced a philosophical thinker as Mr. Shadworth Hodgson has misapprehended the bearing of ["The Psychological Standpoint" and "Psychology as Philosophic Method"] must be my excuse for again troubling the readers with reference to the matters discussed there. Mr. Hodgson seems to think that it was the object of one to explain the nature of the individual and the universal consciousness, and of the other to give some definite directions regarding the application of method to philosophy and psychology. Thus apprehending them, he quite naturally complains of the "blanks" in the argument; and, if I may judge from the tone of his remarks, thinks, indeed, that there is not so much an argument as an assumption, while my lack of logic is to him lamentable. May I be allowed to state that I had no such ends in view, and that what seems to Mr. Hodgson a lack of logic on my part seems to me a misunderstanding of logical *bearing* on his part? The logical purpose of the first article was as follows: Granted the general truth of that way of looking at philosophical questions which is specifically English (and which, following the usual custom, I called psychological), (1) to determine whether some important factor has not been overlooked; (2) to show that it is involved in this standpoint that all questions must be decided from their place in conscious experience; (3) to show that this general statement applies to particular questions, like the nature of subject and object, universal and individual; and (4) to show

From *Mind*, January, 1887; 83-88. A reply to Hodgson's criticism entitled "Illusory Psychology" in *Mind*, October, 1886; 478-494.

that this in turn implies that the psychological standpoint is one which transcends and underlies the distinction of subject and object, etc. Now it was open to Mr. Hodgson, or anyone else, to reply that I misinterpreted the standpoint of British philosophy; or that, while its standpoint was correctly stated, it involved no such implications as I thought it did; or that while it did involve such implications, this fact is, at bottom, only a *reductio ad absurdum* of the standpoint. But objections like those of Mr. Hodgson, with all due deference, seem to me a huge *ignoratio elenchi*.

And his misunderstanding of the logical bearing of the whole has influenced his treatment of details. Mr. Hodgson's aversion to some expressions is so acute that he seems hardly to have asked himself in what connection these phrases are used. If he will reread certain pages of the article referred to, I think he will see that the terms "postulate" and "presupposition," whose use seems to him to involve a contradiction on my part, are used not generally, nor with reference to my own standpoint, but in connection with this examination of British philosophy, and that the contention of the article is, rather, that what has been an unconscious presupposition ought to be given a psychological examination and position.

So the logical bearing of the second article was not to give recommendations regarding specific methods, but to suggest to those whom Mr. Hodgson calls my "Germanising friends" that their results will never have a firm basis until they are reached by a psychological method. The article was entitled "Psychology as Philosophic Method," just as Mr. Hodgson might call a portion of his article "Metaphysic as Philosophic Method."

It thus appears to me that the mass of Mr. Hodgson's direct specific criticism is so beside the mark that it is needless to undertake a detailed review of it. But one may always learn much from Mr. Hodgson when he is positively propounding his own views; and certain discussions, as, *e.g.*, regarding the nature of the universal and the individual, and the mutual connections of science, philosophy and psychology, are never beside the mark. I should like briefly to discuss the attempts which Mr. Hodgson kindly makes to fill the "blanks" in my argument.

I

First, then, as to the relation of the individual and the universal consciousness, or, more properly speaking, of the individual and the universal in consciousness. The position of Mr. Hodgson, as I understand it, is that I have not duly distinguished between perceptual processes, which give us the individual, and conceptual processes, which generalize it and give us a result more or less abstract, and that consequently I have erected a generalized notion of my individual consciousness—a logical abstraction into an actual *ens,* which I call universal consciousness. The real state of the case, we are to believe, is as follows: There is a "stream of states and changes" which comes to every individual; this is an individualized stream, and occurs in perceptual order. Out of it the world of ordinary experience is built. But the individual can think as well as perceive, and he comes gradually to generalize. This process of generalization he extends even to his own consciousness; he generalizes conscious experience itself. But the generalization does not give, either in knowledge or belief, a universal consciousness different in any way from his own. It is merely the logical or conceptual way of representing individuality of what in actual experience is perceptual. A universal self can only be represented in thought as an individual self indefinitely or infinitely magnified. The result is that, while we may speak of universal knowledge, the content of consciousness, it is fallacious and self-contradictory to speak of a universal knower, the agent or bearer of consciousness. The gist of the whole controversy is that, while we may and must assume individuality as given to us, universality is the result of a logical process. As to this I have to say:

1. Mr. Hodgson is misled by an ambiguity in the use of the term "individual." In one sense (in which it cannot be the subject matter of any science) it is given to us; in another (in the sense in which it is an object of scientific knowledge) it is

not given to us, but is a product of psychological experience. Every experience is given to us as a unique experience, a fact of absolute and immediate interest. Individuality in this sense is indeed an assumption which we need not care to avoid. But this assumption is only the assumption that a fact exists; it tells us nothing of the *meaning* of the fact. And it is the assumption that we know at the outset what individuality *means,* and that the immediate fact of experience is the same as an interpretation of the fact, which plays such havoc with Mr. Hodgson's ideas. It is this assumption which enables him to slide unconsciously from the immediate unique interest which accompanies every experience, and which makes it mine or thine, to the fact of individuality, as one being among others, limited in space and time, and whose ideas occur as a "stream." Individuality in this sense is not "given," is not "immediate," and is an assumption which we must avoid making until we see what it *means*—until, in short, it is not an assumption. Individuality in this sense may be provisionally opposed to universality, but this sense is not an original or immediate *dictum.* It is a product which has come about through experience, through psychological experience. The process of its coming about, the way in which this gets to be a fact of our conscious experience, is something to be examined by psychology. The psychological standpoint is prior, so to speak, to this result. It is confusion enough to substitute this psychological product for the immediate individuality which is a matter of feeling, but to substitute a philosophical interpretation of the fact is to carry the confusion a step further. And this Mr. Hodgson does in giving individuality a meaning—that is, an interpretation—which opposes it absolutely to universality. One thing which Mr. Hodgson would have learned by going to psychology rather than to metaphysics would be to avoid this threefold confusion of the individuality of immediate feeling, of constructed fact of experience, and of philosophical interpretation of the fact.

2. The substitution appears, however, in a still worse plight when we consider that this view of individuality which op-

poses it absolutely to universality is an *incorrect* interpretation. I speak, not as a Germanizing transcendentalist, but according to my humble lights as a psychologist, when I say that I know nothing of a perceptual order apart from a conceptual, and nothing of an agent or bearer apart from the content which it bears. As a psychologist, I see the possibility of abstractly analyzing each from the other, and, if I were as fond of erecting the results of an analysis into real entities as Mr. Hodgson believes me to be, I should suppose that they were actually distinct as concrete existences. But, sticking fast to what Psychology teaches me, I must hold that they are aspects, analytically arrived at, of the one existing reality—conscious experience. Mr. Hodgson finds no difficulty in making the separation. He assumes—and speaking from the metaphysical standpoint would naturally assume—that there is "a stream of changes and states" which "come to an individual," and "out of this as data is built up ordinary experience." So he regards this "stream" as in some way individual, while the world built up out of it—the content—may be distinguished from it. To me it seems that this "stream" is built up along with, and mostly out of, the experiences of the everyday world. Stream and world are equally psychological constructions, built up by psychological processes. It must be from Metaphysic (it cannot be from Psychology) that Mr. Hodgson gets a "stream" which is given ready made. Psychology would tell us that the "stream" is essentially due to projections out from the present by a psychological mechanism in the form of memory and expectation. Consciousness is not a moving body which, flying through time, leaves a trail behind it, as does a rocket in space. When the idea of an absent person is suggested to an infant, the child does not conceive this as an idea, but looks about him to localize the person. His life is a present one, and it is only through a psychological development that he comes to have experiences placed as past and anticipated as future. The experiences of time and of "streams" are due to psychological dynamics. The process by which the individual comes to connect certain experiences with himself as a being continuous in time, and to separate

them from others which he refers to existences in space, is one
of the problems of psychology. What is the bearing of all this?
Simply, that we have no ready-made distinction between the
individual agent and the world of experience over against
him, but that each is built up out of a common material by
contemporaneous processes. A correct psychology would teach
Mr. Hodgson, it seems to me, not only that the *ordo ad indi-
viduum* and the *ordo ad universum* are built out of a common
stock, but that the process is a reciprocal one, so that our ideas
of ourselves as individuals, nay ourselves as individuals, are
made up out of our experiences of the world, and *vice versa.*
The agent is not the agent which it is without the content,
not only in the sense that it bears that content and no other,
but in the sense that this content reacts upon it and is organized into it to make it what it specifically is. If Mr. Hodgson
will make an absolute separation between the individual as
agent and the content of consciousness as general, he will find
that all that is left to the agent is: x is experienced and is interesting, where it is impossible to give x any definite values.
Its analogies we may hypothetically find in the consciousness
of an oyster.

3. And finally upon this point, I know of no perception
which is not made what it is by conceptual elements within it.
Mr. Hodgson well says that "every act of attention to a percept is the commencement of a generalization." But it cannot
be possible that Mr. Hodgson supposes that perceptions are
given to us prior to attention, and that this is an activity
which supervenes, the perception once formed. Correct psychology seems to teach that the attention—the active connection between the mind and a given psychical complex—
is necessary to interpret, to make it a percept. And unless
there are two utterly different kinds of attention, generalization must be thus introduced, and a universal element be
present in the percept. I cannot believe accordingly that Mr.
Hodgson's attempt to set up individuality of consciousness
as opposed to universality is successful, whether it proceeds by
distinguishing the perceptual order from the conceptual, or
by distinguishing the stream of consciousness as given from

the content of that consciousness as interpreted. At all events, I hope it is clear that this conception of universality of consciousness is not that of an individual indefinitely magnified. I should still be compelled to ask, What is this individual which is magnified? and if I deal with facts and not with analytic abstractions, I find it to be bound up through and through with universal factors, nay constituted by its relation to the universal factor. One word more, and I have done with this point. The universality of consciousness stands just where its individuality does. An individuality is "given" in the sense that every consciousness has a unique interest; so universality is "given" in the sense that *every* consciousness has a *meaning*. But the experience of the world as a fact, like the experience of the individual stream as a fact, is a constructed product. And the philosophical interpretation of the fact that there is a world of experience is still more remote from being immediate or given. In each of these three stages it stands just where individuality does.

II

I can treat but briefly of the other point: the relation between Psychology and what Mr. Hodgson calls Metaphysic and what I called Logic. Mr. Hodgson seems to think that upon my theory no place can be left for physiological psychology, for race psychology, etc., etc. They would, however, be left just where they are now—as special *methods* for determining the conditions and genesis of various factors in conscious experience.

When Mr. Hodgson says that Metaphysic abstracts from the fact that consciousness is individually conditioned he simply suggests the point which was uppermost in my mind when I wrote "Psychology as Philosophic Method." Metaphysic or Logic does abstract from the individual, which conditions the content. As thus abstract, it cannot furnish the final method of philosophy, for as abstract it makes an assumption and is incomplete. It is incomplete; for is this unique and yet absolutely universal fact that the content of consciousness is known only in and to an individual—is this fact to be left out of account? The play of *Hamlet* with Hamlet left out seems to me nothing in comparison. It makes an assumption, for to make assumptions is simply to see how facts look when some integral factor is omitted.

English thought, according to Mr. Hodgson, has commonly ignored the universal or all-embracing character of the consciousness, and has identified it with individual being. So it seems to me, and "The Psychological Standpoint" was written to show that psychology could not be even psychology, much less philosophy, until the universal factor in consciousness was attended to. Transcendentalism, he says, inclines to identify consciousness with universal being, and if this be interpreted to mean that it inclines to neglect the individual agent, without which the universality of the content is naught, I heartily agree with him. "Psychology as Philosophic Method" was written to show that transcendentalism was incomplete till it recognized that the universal content can be realized only in an individual bearer. And I make bold to add that Mr. Hodgson thinks the two sides may be split, one surrendered to Psychology, the other reserved for Metaphysic; while to me it seems that we shall never get the surest footing and the completest results until we recognize that such halves —the individual without the universal content, and the universal content without the individual bearer—are *disjecta membra*. The science which unites them, and considers the content as realized in and by an individual, and the individual as realized through and by the content, seems to me to be Psychology. A psychology which should attempt to occupy the position Mr. Hodgson gives to it would have nothing to say except—Here is a consciousness which interests me, but about which I can say nothing.

8

KNOWLEDGE AS IDEALIZATION

THAT the word "idea," as commonly used, is about as ambiguous a term as could well be invented, is an old story. I need here to call attention only to two connotations. It implies *existence,* and it implies *meaning* or the content of the psychical existence. When we speak of the idea of virtue, we may mean either the "idea conveyed" by the term, its significance, or we may mean the particular psychical existence, which occurs now and here in experience, and stands for the meaning. But this double connotation is not confined to abstract terms. It holds equally of the most definite perception —say, mine of my pen as I write. There is the idea "in my mind," an existence coming after many ideas, and before many others; a psychical existence which is a unique, unshareable, irrecoverable experience. What constitutes it we need not here inquire, though our psychological research goes to show that it is a clustering of sensations, visual, muscular and tactile, due to the immediate stimulation of my nervous system. *Similar* stimuli may occur again doubtless, but the present existence endures only while the given stimulus is actually there. How stands it with the other connotation of the term? It is evident that here we are dealing with meaning or significance—all that would be included in the definition, say, of pen, plus the fact that it is now present, which is, after all, part of the meaning, and not of the existence. To state the whole matter simply, every psychical state or "idea," in Locke's sense, is at once sensation and interpretation of that sensation or meaning conveyed. It is sign and significa-

From *Mind*, July, 1887; 382-396.

tion. We do not go here into the theoretical justification of the latter element. We do not ask whether there *is* any pen really there, or whether, if there is, our idea of it corresponds to reality. We merely state the fact that in every psychical experience there is the psychical existence, and there is what this existence stands for to the mind. It is an undoubted fact that the meaning *seems* to be objective, permanent and universal; that the idea of existence, in other words, seems to us to report a reality which is there, aside from our particular mental state, one which is equally there for my intelligence at all times under the same conditions and for all intelligences. This apparent report is part of the complete psychical fact, but we do not now ask whether it has any right to be, or whether it is an allusion unconsciously superadded to the legitimate content of the fact. Recognizing that every psychical fact does have these two aspects, we shall, for the present, confine ourselves to asking the nature, function and origin of the aspect of meaning or significance—the content of the idea as opposed to its existence.[1]

To develop what is meant let us take Locke's favorite example—a perception of gold. If we ask what is psychically present, by way of immediate existence, we shall find that it is only a group of sensuous feelings—some strong, some faint. If we inquire further, we find that the stronger ones are due to a direct stimulation of some organ of sense, while the fainter are due to the indirect stimulation of some central organ. If we simply look at the piece of gold, there are the vivid sensations of color and muscular tension only; clustered about these may be less vivid feelings of contact, perhaps of slight metallic taste and odor. But it is a mistake to call these latter feelings ideal, and the former real. One class is just as real as the other; the only distinction is one of strength. It is quite true that the weaker feelings may be found upon examination to be due to previous stimulations, and to be due to connections in the brain previously established, so that

[1] In thus calling attention to the distinction of the two senses of the term "idea," I am, of course, but repeating what many others have said—among them most clearly Mr. F. H. Bradley, in his *Principles of Logic*, pp. 5 and 6.

now a direct peripheral excitation serves to set up a change in some connected part of the brain and awaken sensation. But as existences, there is no difference in the feelings, whether peripherally set up or centrally excited. The stronger one, as existence, does not report that it is due to present direct stimulation; the weaker one does not report that it is ultimately due to past stimulations. This is a matter of interpretation, and even as interpretation it does not enter into the *perception* of the gold. I repeat, as existence, we have only a clustering of sensuous feelings, stronger and weaker.

But what is perceived is *not* a clustering of feelings of any sort. It has taken centuries of scientific psychological observation even to ascertain that sensations of these kinds are involved at all: so far is their presence from being an element of the content of perception. What is perceived is the thing gold, with its various properties, which the sensations stand for. And in our anxiety to get at meaning, to find out what is symbolized, we actually neglect utterly that which is the symbol, the psychical existence. What is perceived is, in short, significance, meaning. The amount of perception one has, whether as a babe or adult, as layman, or as chemist, is precisely the meaning that one finds signified by one's sensations: the *sensations*, as such, may be precisely alike in the four cases. Perceiving, to restate a psychological commonplace, is interpreting. The content of the perception is what is signified.

Now, it is to be noted that the meaning constitutes for us the whole value of the experience. As a physiological fact, the occurrence of nerve tremors of some sort may be the important thing. But as a fact of human experience, the important thing is that the experience has significance. It means something to us. It reports something to our intelligence. Absolute nonsense and nonentity are synonymous as matters of conscious experience. It is true enough that without the idea *as existence* there would be no experience; the sensuous clustering is a condition *sine qua non* of all, even the highest spiritual, consciousness. But it is none the less true that if we could strip any psychical existence of all its qualities except bare existence, there would be nothing left, not even existence, for our intelligence. Even the fact that there *is* an experience, aside from *what* it is, is not the sensation itself; it is the interpretation of the sensation. It is part of the meaning. If we take out of an experience all that it *means,* as distinguished from what it *is*—a particular occurrence at a certain time, there is no psychical experience. The barest fragment of consciousness that can be hit upon has meaning as well as being. Take away the meaning, and consciousness vanishes.

We may seem to be dwelling needlessly upon the veriest truism of psychology—that its subject matter is conscious experience, for that is all that is really meant when we say that significance constitutes the worth of an idea. But, perhaps because it is such a truism, there is no fact so often overlooked. The fundamental distinction between physical facts and psychical facts is not that the former exist in space, the latter in time, or any other specific distinction of mode of occurrence. It is that physical facts as such are facts of existence; psychical facts are facts of meaning. Physical facts have meaning, but they have it as psychical, in relation to intelligence; psychical facts have existence, but the existence does not constitute their express value in human experience. An idiot has as many ideas, *qua* existences, as Shakespeare; the delirious patient has, in all probability, more in a given time than his physician.

What then is the nature of meaning, of significance, of that which is conveyed by every fact of consciousness, and which constitutes the value of that fact? It is, of course, a mediate factor; it is due to inference. In passing, I must commend this statement to those who are telling us that the only realities which we can ultimately admit are those which are immediately present in some state of consciousness, and that we must reject all inference if we are to get the fact. For my part, it seems that when the mediate element is gone, meaning is gone, and consciousness itself disappears. If someone takes away from me all the inference contained in a fact, hunt as hard as I will, I cannot find but that he has taken with him the fact also. He may have left me with nervous tremors in my brain, but all significance, *i.e.*, conscious experience, is gone. So far is it from being true that we know only what is *immediately* present in consciousness, that it should rather be said that what is *immediately* present is never known.

But we must leave these general statements and come to particulars. That which is immediately present is the sensuous existence; that which is known is the content conveyed by this existence. The sensuous material is of worth only as it is a sign; it is a sign only as it signifies or points out meaning. This meaning is present as mediated. It is not there as existence; it is there as pointed toward, as symbolized. If we owe nothing else to what is called physiological psychology, the experimental result reached by Helmholtz, that we always neglect sensations, or pay no attention to them as existence, in behalf of the meaning conveyed by them, gives physiological psychology a higher scientific stand than introspective psychology has yet attained; for introspective psychology is always descriptive, while Helmholtz's generalization explains. It is true, for example, that every experience of tone is complex, containing the fundamental and the partials. Yet we are entirely unconscious of this complexity, which as matter of sensuous existence is the all-important thing. Why? Because this complexity is taken solely as a sign of the instrument to which the tone is referred—human voice, violin, piano. We interpret the various combinations of sensations as signifying this or that object. We are equally unconscious of the nature of the sensations in themselves, and of the process we go through. Psychical result or significance is all intelligence cares for. Starting point and way to this result are swallowed up in what they symbolize. This explains "unconscious cerebration" on its psychical side. Processes, whether of perception or of reasoning, are of no account to intelligence except as they lead to meaning. Perception is well defined as unconscious reasoning. And as such it illustrates the way in which the process loses itself in the result. The process is nothing *as* a process, or psychical existence; it is everything in what it means or symbolizes. In reasoning proper, the processes are of some account to us, because we know that upon variations in the process depend variations in result. The matter is more complex, and we go through it step by step; but even here we do not pay attention to the process as an existence. We simply take one *meaning* at a time, and then go on to the next meaning. Reasoning is the way in which we separate and unite meanings into one complex meaning. As our power to reason becomes developed, and the subject matter becomes familiar, we cease considering the various subordinate meanings in their relation to each other. We grasp the meaning as a whole, as we do in perception, and reasoning becomes, as we say, automatic or intuitive. Conversely, when we are in doubt in perception as to whether the result is genuine or is an illusion, we do pay attention to the process. We repeat the process, analyzing it into its steps, to see if we have drawn a correct inference. So, when we wish to decide whether that red color is really on the wall or is due to a purely organic affection, we move the body or head, and observe results, and draw our inference accordingly. We often separate the various steps in perception, just as we often consolidate them in reasoning; but the separation and the consolidation are always of meaning, and never of the psychical process as an existence.

But let us consider another example or two of the fact that we neglect sensuous *basis* and regard meaning alone. Everyone knows that we have two retinal images of an object in every case of binocular vision; that is to say, we have two complete sensuous outfits. In the vast majority of cases, these two sensuous bases are slightly different; in one case in a thousand they may be alike. Yet we are ordinarily conscious of but one object; in some cases, those where the retinal images are similar, we can be conscious of but one, do what we will. I know of no more striking illustration of the fact that sensations, as existences, are nothing for us, while sensations in their symbolic function are for us everything. The sensations *mean* but one object, and, do what we will, we *see* but one object. The duality of the sensation is nothing for us. But we neglect the greater part of the case, when we speak of the matter as if it were confined to a few special cases of eye and ear, and as if in these cases the sensations, as existences, were only double, or triple or quadruple. In fact, as existences, they are indefinitely multiple in every case. As I touch the table, how many distinct sensations do I have? As the ray of light affects my retina, consider what a chaos of sensations is stimulated. I may remark incidentally that a large number of the psychologists who have occupied themselves with the problem of space perception do not seem to have realized the elements of the problem. They first talk as if the problem were: How to get space relations out of sensations, as existences? and secondly, as if the problem were: Given isolated sensations as equivalent to isolated points in space, to tell how these come to be connected with each other in complex space forms? But the problem in the first place is: How do we *interpret* sensations into spatial meanings? and secondly: How do we interpret *some* sensations as isolated points and *others* as connected bodies? We do not start with separate points which are to be combined through the medium of motion, or in any other way. The separate point is as much an inference, an interpretation of the sensation, as the connected line, surface, or solid. Our experience of one is built up along with that of the other. Sensations, as existences, in spatial perceptions as in all perceptions, are naught; sensations, in their symbolic quality, as inference is put into them and they become meaning, are all.

Our fundamental position is that sensation, as existence, and the process, as psychical occurrence, by which sensations are connected, never enter into knowledge. Knowledge is both the sensation and the process in their significant or sign-bearing quality.

But what is the sense in calling the sign-borne content inferential, and in separating it from the sensational basis as immediate? The general ground is the fact that the sensuous clustering is all that is present by way of immediate existence, and it is convenient to have a term to express that which is present by way of being signified or symbolized. The sensuous basis stands for, conveys to intelligence, the content of the experience, and the meaning is present only as thus represented. The sensations, as immediate existences, have no more meaning than letters of the alphabet or than vocal noises. The meaning is read into them or out of them, as one may prefer to state it. But more specifically, this element may be called mediate or inferential because it is present as the result of a process of reasoning. There is no need at this time, I suppose, to do more than state the fact that every perception is a judgment based on an inference. It is indifferent to the sensation whether it is interpreted as a cloud or as a mountain; a danger signal, or a signal of open passage. The auditory sensation remains unchanged whether it is interpreted as an evil spirit urging one to murder, or as intraorganic, due to disordered blood pressure. The result is arrived at by a process of inference. It is not the sensation in and of itself that means this or that object; it is the sensation as associated, composed, identified, or discriminated with other experiences; the sensation, in short, as mediated. The whole worth of the sensation for intelligence is the meaning it has by virtue of its relation to the rest of experience. Since the rest of experience is not and cannot be present as so much immediate existence, we may well call the element which gives any psychical fact its value mediate.

We have just been introduced to some terms which, indeed, it has long been difficult to keep in the background; terms like "identification," "discrimination," "relation." For this mediate element is precisely what we mean by relation, and the processes by which it is got at, and read into the sensation, are those of association and comparison. It has long seemed to me a remarkable fact that the later writers of the specifically British school of psychology, led by Mr. Spencer, recognize this truth and yet do not think it necessary to revise their fundamental notions of intelligence. I can account for it only on the supposition that they do not attend to the double sense of the term "idea." Their general theory of intelligence, as at bottom sensational, requires that it be the sensations as existences which are compared and related. Their theory, as it actually works, is that the sensations in their intellectual quality, as significances, are compared and identified. Their theory as they employ it for purposes of explanation is in direct contradiction to their theory in its fundamental presuppositions. If all intelligence is a product of psychical existences, called sensations, plus their association and comparison, no amount of association and comparison will ever give a result which has meaning for consciousness. Strictly speaking, it is impossible for such processes to occur. But if the comparison of sensations does result in significant experience, there must be a certain intellectual quality in the sensations not due to their properties as bare existences. A relation of identity is not a sensuous skeleton which runs through psychical occurrences and ribs them together. It is identity of meaning; permanence, in short, of intelligence.

And discrimination is not the introduction of unlikeness between ideas as occurrences in the psychical life. They are already as unlike as they can be, each being already a unique distinct existence: as Hume says, every distinct idea is a separate existence. Nor can it mean recognition of this unlikeness of existence, except in the sense that it is recognized that the two psychical occurrences do not mean the same. They may *be* unlike, but we should never know they were did we not discover that they did not point to or symbolize the same intellectual content. They must mean difference of times at least, and conscious experience of difference of times is just as much a matter of interpretation of sensations as recognition of spatial differences is.

Wundt has shown clearly enough, as it seems to me, that association is finally a function of attention; but, not to confuse ourselves with terms, let us take a simple example. Of all the sensations which, as existences, are presented to us at any one time, how many come into consciousness together? To put it in the old-fashioned way, how many ideas can we be conscious of at once? To answer the question in this form: Of idea in the sense of meaning, we can be conscious of but one; of idea in the sense of existence, or psychical occurrence due to separate stimulation, we may be conscious of an indefinite, limitless number. Just as many as can be made to convey one meaning, just so many may be comprehended in one idea. If we make, for the sake of example, the assumption that the universe is a unity, it is theoretically possible to grasp every detail of the universe in one idea. In fact, it must be so grasped, for the unity of the world can only mean that it ultimately possesses oneness of meaning.

In any given complex of presentations, therefore, just as much will be selected and united into a conscious experience as harmonizes in meaning. The astronomer cannot attend to the ticking of the clock and to the passage of a star at the same time, because they are *interpreted* in two different ways. Were they interpreted in the same content of significance, they would be, *ipso facto,* members of the same experience. To borrow Wundt's illustration, if the eye sees a falling rod at one place, and there is a noise made at a slight distance, and if the noise occurs regularly after the rod falls, although there is no connection between them, the sight of the rod and the sound will be united in the same idea. So ineradicable is the mind's bent after meaning, that it will force it if it be possible. In case, however, the noise is not harmoniously related to the fall of the rod, the mind will have to alternate between the two facts. They cannot both be present in the same consciousness. Their unlike significance makes them, by necessity, two distinct consciousnesses.

Unity and difference, relation in short, is always a matter of significance, of content for intelligence, and not of psychical existence. When we say then, as Mr. Spencer and all the later English writers do say, that a sensation is nothing until it is identified and discriminated—that is, brought into relations of unity and difference—it is necessary to remember that the identification and the discrimination are elements of meaning, of relation to intelligence. The sensations, or existences, never unite themselves, and never differentiate themselves. But sensations, as they exist in conscious experience, are always united and differentiated. What is this but to say that intelligence is necessarily involved in every sensation as known, and, therefore, that it is impossible to derive intelligence from any combination of sensations? Let us remember two things: first, a sensation is not knowledge until united and differentiated; secondly, these processes have absolutely no reference to the existence of the sensations, but only to their significance, to the meaning conveyed by them. Can we avoid drawing the conclusions: negatively, that relations —that is, connections of unity and difference of meaning— can never be produced by sensations as psychical existences; and, positively, that the factor of relation—or ideal significance—is necessarily required to make sensations elements of conscious experience?

This brings us to the fact that relations are thoroughly *ideal*. Lewes frequently noted that science is a process of idealization, but he seems never to have realized either the true import of idealization, or the fact that all knowledge, perception included, requires the ideal element. Idealization is not a process of departure from the material presented in perception, for this material is itself ideal. The idealization of science is simply a further development of this ideal element. It is, in short, only rendering explicit and definite the meaning, the idea, already contained in perception. In the act of perception we do not realize anything like the whole meaning of what the sensations convey; our interpretation is fragmentary and inadequate. The other processes of knowledge, the so-called faculties of memory, conception, judgment, self-consciousness, etc., are only progressively fuller interpretations, as each introduces some ideal factor—that is, relation —neglected by the previous. Memory, for example, simply makes explicit that ideal relation of our present experience to past experiences, which is involved in every perception, and which indeed makes it what it is, although in the stage of perception we are not conscious of this relation. Self-consciousness, again, is simply the conscious recognition that the ideal element *is* involved in all knowledge together with what is implied in this statement. Self-consciousness is the idealizing process of all knowledge continued till it becomes conscious of itself. But these are aspects of the question that must now be deferred.

We have to ask what is the especial ground for calling the

element which makes knowledge significant an *ideal* element? The answer in general is that this factor is ideal, because it is not present by way of immediate psychical occurrence, but as meaning. It is significance; and this is *significance*, presence as symbolized. It is convenient to have a term to denote what is present in the way of meaning rather than in the way of existence, and the term "ideal" just meets the demand. It meets it negatively in suggesting that this factor is not one of space- and time-existence and occurrence; it meets it positively in suggesting that it is due to intelligence.

This is the point which has now to be shown, and shown not through an examination of the logical *conditions* of experience, but through a psychological inquiry into its *facts*. Whence come the ideal elements which give to experience its meaning? By what process do we interpret sensations so that they become significant to us of objects and events in space and time? These questions are simply the fundamental questions of psychology, and can be answered only by a complete treatise on psychology. Nothing but very general considerations may be expected of me here. The answer which is ordinarily given to the question, the one we have just seen given, is undoubtedly the correct answer. Sensations get meaning by being interpreted through their relations to the rest of experience; through the processes of identification and discrimination. But the sensation is not identified with nor discriminated from another sensation. This would add no whit to its significance, besides being a process psychologically impossible. Previous sensations, as existences, are gone forever; gone as much as the time in which they occurred. It is true, doubtless, that they have left organic traces of their occurrence in the brain; it may be true that these organic traces may, by indirect stimulation, reawaken sensations like to the previous ones. But in this process there is, as such, no aid. There is so much sensuous material indirectly stimulated added to the sensuous material directly stimulated, and that is all. If sensations before were multiple, chaotic, needing interpretation, there has been added more multiple chaotic material, equally in need of interpretation. Multiplication of sensations is not interpretation of sensations previously existent.

The identification is of the meaning of the present sensation with some meaning previously experienced, but which, although previously experienced, still exists because it *is* meaning, and not occurrence. This identification gives the present sensation all the meaning possessed by those experiences with which it is identified. It renders it symbolic of whatever these other experiences signified. If I attribute any meaning to the idea gold, all that meaning is transferred into the present sensation as soon as this sensation is seen to have the same symbolism. And it is seen to have the same symbolism just because the mind brings this meaning to bear upon the given sensation. There is undoubtedly a mechanism, conveniently termed the association of ideas, which ensures that the mind brings a certain set, as it were, of its interpreting activities to bear rather than another, but the final result of meaning is wholly dependent upon the group of ideal significances which is brought to bear. The interpreting activity may bring itself to bear in such a way that it shall regard the sensations as iron pyrites or as the talisman of life; but upon this way depends the meaning of the experience. In short, the sole way of accounting for the fact that we have significant experience, or that sensations, in addition to being psychical occurrences, are also psychical meanings, is that the mind conserves permanently out of every experience the meaning of that experience, and, when it sees fit, reads this conserved meaning into a given sensation, thereby completing the transfer of significance. The experience, as an existence at a given time, has forever vanished. Its meaning, as an ideal quality, remains as long as the mind does. Indeed, its remaining *is* the remaining of the mind; the conservation of the ideal quality of experience is what makes the mind a permanence.

If it be asked, then, how psychical experience can begin, the answer is, indifferently, either that it does not begin, or that it begins as the beginning of the development—the manifestation—of internal content of intelligence. It does not begin in the sense that meaning arises out of that which has no meaning. It does not begin in the sense that sensations as mere occurrences ever group themselves so that they have in addition meaning. For meaning is mediate, being through relation; it is ideal, being what is symbolized to intelligence. If intelligence were not present with a minimum of intelligent or ideal quality to read into sensations, these sensations would never get significance, or presence in conscious experience. The mind must possess at the very outset the idea that there is meaning there. It must project into sensations the conception *that* they are significant, even if it does not develop the measure of this significance. A mind which does not come to sensations with an ineradicable prejudgment that the sensations are interpretable, that is, possible bearers of an ideal quality, does not have the starting point for any interpretation, and its sensation could not ever get a beginning on the road of meaning. The sensations might conceivably revive each other and fuse with each other indefinitely, but meaning is absent until they symbolize each other; and they fail to symbolize each other until the *meaning* of one is represented by another. But, after all, the conception of the recalling and fusing of sensations is not one to be allowed, except upon the supposition of the interpreting activity of intelligence. The very fact that sensations are so connected that the peripheral stimulation of one kind will set up the central stimulation of another is due to the unification of meaning which has some time made them fractional members of one whole, so that one cannot recur, even as existence, without the other. Attention has at some time laid its delaying hand upon them and conjoined them; it has selected them for and excluded others from its connecting grasp; and this is to say that they have been given a unity in that which they symbolize. Sensations cannot revive each other except as members of one whole of meaning; and even if they could, we should have no beginning of significant experience. Significance, meaning, must be already there. Intelligence, in short, is the one indispensable condition of intelligent experience.

This seen and stated, it becomes a question of simple fact

how far developed in any case the necessary intelligence may be. For our general considerations, it is enough that the minimum requirement of an intelligence which recognizes that its sensations have meaning be met; whether any definite meanings, and, if so, what, are projected into sensations, is at present a matter of indifference. We do not care whether they are interpreted as in space and time; as possessing necessarily quantity, quality, relation and modality or not. It is enough to know that they become experience only as interpreting intelligence projects into them something of its own being; they are what they are through this relation to intelligence. There is therefore no beginning of intelligent experience, except such as involves intelligence.

This leads us to recognize that intelligence has a necessary internal permanent content; and that it is only because it has, and because it supplies it to its sense stimuli, that there ever arises significant experience, and that this occurs just in the degree in which intelligence possesses a synthetic content which it can project into its stimuli. In other words, whether we inquire after the origin or growth of mental experience we find involved a synthetic intelligence, that is to say, an intelligence which possesses a content as opposed to one which is purely formal. Recent Empirical Psychology shows that it has run the circuit and returned to the position of Locke. Locke fitted the mind out with sensations on the one side, and associating comparing activities on the other. These latter were purely formal. They merely operated from without *upon* the material of sense, dividing and combining. Then Psychology attempted to get along with the sensations only. But it was driven to reintroduce the associating activity, and now we see it driven to bring back the comparing relating activity. We have complaints that the Empirical School has neglected the native relating capacity of the mind, and that we must recognize that it is endowed with the ability to identify and discriminate. But this relating capacity is still conceived as formal, although the conception involves a contradiction. The relations are conceived as superinduced, as it were, upon the material of sensation, introducing *ab extra* order into them; instead of as necessary to constitute their entire being as members of conscious experience. When Psychology recognizes that the relating activity of mind is one not exercised *upon* sensations, but one which supplies relations and thereby makes meaning (makes experience, as Kant said), Psychology will be in a position to explain, and thus to become Philosophy.

The mention of Kant's name suggests that both his strength and his weakness lie in the line just mentioned. It is his strength that he recognizes that an apperceptive unity interpreting sensations through categories which constitute the synthetic content of self-consciousness is indispensable to experience. It is his weakness that he conceives this content as purely logical and hence as formal. Self-consciousness has a material, a psychological content. Kant was never able to bridge the dualism between his *a priori* form and his *a posteriori* content, because he conceived of sensations as furnishing meaning provided only they were unified by the forms of intuition and the categories of understanding. In truth, the sensations supply no meaning. It is the sensations, however, with the ideal content given them by the self, which are meaning. The self does not work with *a priori* forms upon an *a posteriori* material, but intelligence as ideal (or *a priori*) constitutes experience (or the *a posteriori*) as having meaning.

But I must return from this digression. Experience begins when intelligence projects something of itself into sensations. We have now to recognize that experience grows, or gets more meaning, just in the degree in which intelligence reads more ideal content into it. The adult has more experience than the child—the Englishman than the Bushman—because he has more ideas in his intellect to bring to bear upon his sensations and thus make them significant. Were the theory of our recent writers of the Empirical School correct, the difference must be (1) that the English adult has his formal capacity of relating more sharpened, and (2) that he has a greater number of revived sensations which he combines with his present. But it ought to be evident by this time that (to take the latter point first) the addition of revived sensations would in itself make the experience more confused, make it less significant. It is the addition of sensations selected because they possess the same meaning, it is their unification with the present as same content to intelligence, it is their discrimination as suggesting here and there a new and different shade of meaning—it is, in short, the supplying of *meaning through sensations,* and not of sensations, that makes the experience more significant. And this is to say that experience grows as intelligence adds out of its own ideal content ideal quality. So we may see (to take up the other point) that any amount of sharpening of the mere power of identification and discrimination, of comparison as a formal power, would add no whit to the experience. The experience as an existence, as a clustering of sensations, is already there. The sole thing is to find out what it means, and this can be done only as there is supplied the mediate relational ideal factor. The growth of the power of comparison implies not a formal growth, but a synthetic internal growth. It implies that when the mind is stimulated to an act of comparison, it has a more varied, complex, better organized system of ideas or meanings to bring to bear upon its sensations, and thus to transfer to these its own content of significance.

This transference evidently incorporates the given experience into the system of meanings or of intelligence, and thereby the better prepares the latter for future apperceptive acts; its incorporation adds to the synthetic content of intelligence, and thereby to the meaning of possible future experiences. The process of the growth of experience is accordingly a reciprocal one. Any experience has meaning as the self projects this meaning into it from its own ideal store; this projection appropriates the given experience, as to *its* meaning, into the ideal store of the self, thereby further developing it. Knowledge might be indifferently described, therefore, as a process of idealization of experience, or of realization of intelligence. It is each through the other. Ultimately the growth of experience must consist in the development out of itself by intelligence of its own implicit ideal content upon occasion of the solicitation of sensation. But this is again a thought to be elaborated at another time.

We may sum up our results as follows: meaning constitutes the worth of every psychical experience; meaning is not bare existence, but is an inferential mediate factor; it is relation and is ideal; as ideal it is supplied by intelligence out of its own content; this content constitutes, indeed, the reality of intelligence. I think we may have reason now to congratulate ourselves that we did not, at the beginning, make any inquiry into the connection between this ideal quality or the meaning of experience and objective reality. For, it seems to me, that would have been to begin at the wrong end, and imply that there was somehow, somewhere present to consciousness, a conception of what reality is by which we could measure the significance of our experience. And I have become convinced by the inquiry set forth in the preceding pages that if reality is itself an element in conscious experience, it must as such come under the scope of the significance, the meaning of experience, and hence cannot be used as an external standard to measure this meaning. The reality of experience is, in short, an element of its interpretation, of its ideal quality or relation to intelligence. We do not have externally given to us some fixed conception of reality which we can compare with our ideas, and thereby see how much agreement with reality the latter have. Reality, like everything else that has meaning, is a function of our ideas. To find out what it is we must look within these ideas. It is the great merit of English Psychology that in attempt, at least, it has recognized this. It is its defect that it has tried to find this reality in the ideas, as existences, where naught can be found. We have now to see whether better fortune may meet an attempt to discover the nature of reality, where all is ultimately contained and must be found in the ideas as significances, as meanings. I hope, accordingly, at some future time, to ask after this relation of idea to reality.

9

ON SOME CURRENT CONCEPTIONS
OF THE TERM "SELF"

I

IT is the aim of this paper to analyze certain conceptions involved in the terms Self and Self-consciousness as currently used. No attempt will be made to judge of the value of the ideas themselves. Indeed, there is such confusion in the use of the conceptions that an independent analysis of them would seem to be a necessary preliminary to any decision upon their validity. Whether or not philosophy is exhausted in the clearing up of conceptions, it is certain that without an occasional clearing up, philosophy will get so entangled in the *impedimenta* of its own notions as to be hindered in its onward march. Unless this analysis is confined to ideas having or claiming to have some community of meaning, it will include ideas wholly incomparable with one another, and thus end in a mere account of the way in which various writers use the same word. A study of the terminology of philosophy is, no doubt, helpful; but, as that is not intended in this paper, I shall confine my analysis to the conception of the "transcendental self"—to the idea of self which has affiliations with the movement set going by Kant, however divergent its various developments.

For a starting point, and to a certain extent for a basis, Professor Seth's recent work, *Hegelianism and Personality*, presents itself as convenient, occupied, as it so largely is, with just this notion of the self. In that work, three separate con-

From *Mind*, January, 1890; 58-74.

ceptions—used, however, interchangeably—may be discriminated. In the first place, we have it laid down that "the self *is* the world, and the world is the self. The self and the world are only two sides of the same reality: they are the same intelligible world looked at from two opposite points of view. . . . The mind and the world, subject and object, are convertible terms; we may talk indifferently of the one or the other: the content of our notion remains the same in both cases." This result is based upon an examination of Kant's transcendental inquiry and method which is, so far as quoted above, accepted, to all appearances, by Seth. The meaning of this view of the self may stand out more plainly if we call attention to another feature of it. This is that the "ultimate fact of knowledge is neither pure subject nor pure object." These are both abstractions: to separate them, to make independent existences of them, is to "substantiate abstractions." In truth, the self is a synthetic unity. "It binds together, as related members of one whole, what would otherwise fall apart as unrelated particulars; and, moreover, it is only through this synthesis that the unity of the Self or Ego exists. It is the unity *of* the synthesis, and, apart from its synthetic activity, would no more be real than the particulars of sense would be real without its action." It cannot be identified, in other words, with the mere act of uniting: it includes within itself what is united, just as, on the other hand, what is united has no existence outside of its being united. Because this is so—because, as Seth expresses it, "the form is the form *of* the matter, and the matter is, as it were, simply the exhibition of the form"—the self and the world are correlative, and have the same content.

This, then, is the first notion conveyed by the term self— the self is the correlative of the intelligible world. Its content is that of the intelligible world. It even *is* the intelligible world in one of its aspects. And since Seth has expounded with great force the notion that the intelligible world is the only real world, that the unknowable to intelligence is "nonsense," we may say that, according to this notion, the self is one with the real world, when this is considered in its ultimate unity. This view is clear and self-consistent; with its truth we have

[161]

nothing to do. But we find that the question as to the nature of the transcendental self has not been sufficiently answered. The question is again raised: What is the transcendental self? And the question is answered in a way which seems to me the exact opposite of the answer just given. It now turns out that the transcendental Ego represents *merely* the *formal* unity of the universe. Although the self was shown to be a single self, its singularity is simply that which belongs to every abstract notion—a logical identity of type. It is the "notion of knowledge in general." And, finally, Kant's characterizations of it are quoted. It is "a merely logical qualitative unity of self-consciousness in thought generally." It is a "logical exposition of thought in general." It is, finally, the "mere form of self-consciousness in general."

I confess that, to me, this second position, that the self is merely the formal unity of thought, appears to be the contrary of the first position taken by Seth. There the self was not formal; the form was an abstraction apart from matter. Kant was then rebuked for making the self formal. The necessity of correlating matter and form was the fundamental feature of the transcendental method. So far was the self from being merely formal that it was the world. Instead of being merely logical, the self was the unified universe; it was a synthetic unity which had no existence apart from the particulars unified in the synthesis. But in this second and revised view, Kant is praised for his superior consistency in holding that the self arrived at by his investigation is an abstract condition and not a metaphysical reality or concrete fact. The subject which "exists only as the unity of the manifold whose central principle of connection it is" becomes transformed in ten short pages into a *"focus imaginarius* into which the multiple relations which constitute the intelligible world return"—a *"principle* of unity." To cut short this comparison of contradictory statements, the language first used regarding the self conveys, as clearly as language can convey anything, that the self is objective and real, is ontological; while the second view taken is that the self is merely formal and logical. The first view is that the self and the real cannot be separated

[162]

without "substantiating abstractions"; the second view is that to unite them is to "hypostatize an abstraction."

But, as we advance further, it appears that the outcome of the transcendental view of the self is not in reality either that the self is the real world, or that the self is a mere logical form or abstract unity of thought. The view which finally emerges is that self is the "ultimate category of thought." So far as the varying expressions permit us to judge, this is Seth's real thought in the matter. It is, at least, the view which [he has] unambiguously reiterated [elsewhere]. It is stated once in connection with passages which have been quoted as belonging to the first interpretation: "The transcendental self, as an implicate of all experience, is for a theory of knowledge simply the necessary point of view from which the universe can be unified, that is, from which it becomes a universe." It is elsewhere stated that the transcendental theory of knowledge resolves itself into an immanent criticism of categories, or of the conceptions by which we express and unify our experience. This criticism shows that self-consciousness is the highest category—the most adequate to determine existence. We are thus "justified in using the conception of self-consciousness as our best key to the ultimate nature of existence as a whole." In fine, "self-consciousness is the ultimate category of thought —that through which we think everything else, and through which alone the universe is intelligible to us."

I cannot persuade myself that this third conception of self-consciousness is identical with either of the other two. It means less than the first, which identifies the self with the world; it means more than the second, which makes self-consciousness a merely formal or abstract unity of thought. For it must be remembered that Kant would no more have accepted self-consciousness as the ultimate category of experience, or as a category of experience at all, than he would have accepted it as identical with the real world. In fact, the various expressions which Seth has quoted with approval from Kant are directed as much against making self-consciousness a category of experience as against making it a real self-existent being. How can the "poorest of all our ideas" be the richest and most comprehensive principle of philosophic explanation? The very reason for holding that the self is merely a logical unity of thought is that the self cannot be employed to determine experience at all. But perhaps it may be said that it was just the result of the Hegelian development of the Kantian method and presuppositions to demonstrate that the self, instead of being the emptiest of categories, a conception the sole use of which is to show that all our thoughts are accompanied by consciousness, is the organic system, the reality of all categories. I am not in the least concerned to deny such a contention. But this contention only shows the inadequacy of defining the self as a "merely logical qualitative unity of self-consciousness in thought generally," and not that it is consistent to unite such a view with a view that the self is our ultimate principle of verifying and explaining experience. Indeed, the purpose of Kant in calling the self merely logical was to oppose it to experience; but, when it is said from the point of view of the Hegelian development of Kant that the self is the highest logical category, the idea conveyed is that of the complete correlativity of thought in general, and this thought in particular, to experience. When Kant speaks of a logical unity of thought he means that thought is formal, not real; Hegel in speaking of a logical unity means that thought is real and not formal. The relation between thought and knowledge is not at all the same in the two cases. With Hegel, to say that self is the highest type of thought is to say that self-consciousness is the ultimate principle of knowledge. The object of Kant is to show that the self, since merely a principle of *thought,* is not a principle of *knowledge* at all. While both therefore might call the self "the logical exposition of thought in general," the phrase would have absolutely opposed meanings in the case of the two writers.

No relation of opposition exists between the transcendental self as equal to the real world and as equal to the ultimate category—between, that is, the first interpretation and the third which Seth gives. But although not opposed, they are not the same. To pass directly from the one to the other *would* be to hypostatize an abstraction. The transition may be justifiable, but it cannot, of course, be assumed without justification. The transcendental self may be the highest thought of the world, but it cannot be said to be the correlative of the world, unless the content of the world can be shown to be exhausted in thinking it—or unless the transcendental self is more than a principle of thought. Because thought is objective, it does not follow that it is all there is of objectivity. The world as thought—and thus brought under the principle of self-consciousness—may be real as far as it goes, and yet not be identical with the world as known—with the whole meaning of the real world. The known world may be, for example, a world thought and felt, and not thought alone. Thus while self-consciousness—if it equaled only the ultimate category of thinking—would be an adequate determination of the world as thought, it would, after all, be only a partial determination of the whole as it really exists, and could not thus be called, as Seth at first calls it, a term convertible with the world and having the same content.

These may appear distinctions so notorious that it is trifling to spend so much time upon them; but the fact that so experienced a writer as Seth has presented all three interpretations as explications of the meaning of the "transcendental self" is my excuse for dwelling upon them. There is a certain kinship, indeed, between the three interpretations which would render it easy to pass unwittingly from one to another. The idea of the self as the ultimate category of philosophic explanation stands between the other two. Its content is logical, or thought; and thus when one is arguing against a writer who seems to transform this category into an existence by itself, it is easy to go to the extent of saying that it is *merely* logical, and approve an author who held to the view that it was wholly abstract, even though that author meant by that expression that self was not a category of explanation at all. But, on the other hand, having in mind the fact that self-consciousness is a notion for explaining the world in a sense in which mere "being" or "quantity" or "mechanism" is not—that it exhausts the meaning of the universe as an object of thought—it is easy to go to the other extreme, and hold that self-consciousness *is* the intelligible world seen from one of its sides. But none the less the conception of self as merely formal and abstract contradicts the other two conceptions; and these other two, while not mutually incompatible, are so far from being identical with each other that to pass from one to the other without more ado is to "erect an abstraction into a concrete existence."

II

As the object of this paper is not to convict Seth of either verbal or real inconsistencies, but to help to clear up certain ambiguities in the current use of the conception of "transcendental self" (these ambiguities finding an unusually clear expression, as it were, in Seth's book), I wish now to pass to the historical origin of these various meanings, chiefly as found in Kant, incidentally in Hegel as related to Kant.

Kant's theory is brought out in his "Transcendental Deduction." This is so familiar that it may be given summarily. Its gist is the proof that the identity of self-consciousness involves the synthesis of the manifold of feelings through rules or principles which render this manifold objective, and that, therefore, the analytic identity of self-consciousness involves an objective synthetic unity of consciousness. That self-consciousness is identical is, in itself, a merely analytic proposition. It means nothing more than that I am I—that what *I* am conscious of is in *my* consciousness, and that what belongs to your consciousness I am not conscious of. It finds its empirical application in the fact that, unless the consciousness which has ideas today is identical with that which was conscious yesterday or a year ago, it can no more now be conscious of what it was conscious of then than it can now be conscious of what is in your consciousness. But this does not prove the existence of any real self or substantial mind. It is still an analytic proposition and means that the same consciousness is the same consciousness. But if we ask how we know this sameness or identity of consciousness, the barren principle becomes wonderfully fruitful. For we do not know this sameness through the various successive ideas; they are not the same, but *ex hypothesi* various. And, furthermore, instead of knowledge of the identity of self depending upon them, I should not know them even as various, unless they were already mine. The identity of self-consciousness cannot be derived from knowledge of them, for this knowledge pre-supposes that identity. But perhaps we may go behind the apparent variety and disparateness of our ideas, and say that one consciousness *accompanies* all these different ideas, and that knowledge of this common element is the knowledge we are in search of. This does not suffice. The mere fact that consciousness accompanies every idea gives no identity unless these ideas are already conceived as *mine*—unless identity is presupposed. Otherwise, I should "have as various and many-colored a self as I have different ideas." If we say that the *common* element gives us that knowledge of the identity of self which we are in search for, we doubly beg the question. A common element means an identity present in the midst of difference, and thus presupposes the sameness of conscious-ness through different ideas; and knowledge of this common element could be attained only if it were possible to compare many and various ideas in *one* consciousness, and thus see that they had a common element. These methods of knowing the sameness of consciousness thus presuppose what they would account for.

The sole way of accounting for this analytic identity of consciousness is through the activity of consciousness in con-necting or "putting together" the manifold of sense. Since this putting together occurs according to fixed rules and prin-ciples, it is an objective synthesis. Knowledge of the identity of self presupposes, therefore, a self which acts synthetically, regularly so, upon sense-material. "The original and necessary consciousness of the identity of one's self is, at the same time, a consciousness of the equally necessary unity of the synthesis of all phenomena according to conceptions. . . . The mind

would never conceive the identity of itself in the manifoldness of its ideas, if it did not perceive the *identity of the action by which it subjects this manifoldness to unity.*"

The "Deduction," instead of beginning with the consciousness of self-identity, begins with the consciousness of objects,
and asks what is involved in *that*. The answer is the same.
Consciousness of *objectivity* means unity of self-consciousness,
and this not a formal or analytic activity, but one which connects the manifold of sense according to rules or conceptions.
Whether, then, we inquire what is involved in mere sameness of consciousness, or what is involved in an objective
world, we get the same answer: a consciousness which is not
formal or analytic, but which is synthetic of sense, and which
acts universally (according to principles) in this synthesis.

Apparently we have here a conception of the transcendental self like the first one laid down by Seth. This self, since
its existence is its synthetic activity upon the particular manifold of sense, is thoroughly objective. It has precisely the same
content as the real world. And the objective world, since it
turns out to be the synthesis of particulars of sense through
the action of self according to conceptions, is subjective; it
has the same content as the transcendental self. It is the transcendental self looked at as "there," as a product, instead of
as an activity or process.

The next step in the analysis is to see why Kant, after having attained to the conception of an objective self, should
shift his ground. Kant, in reaching this result, or in his transcendental deduction, has proceeded as if the synthetic action
of self and the manifold of sense were wholly constituted
through their mutual relations to each other—as if each had
no existence excepting as a factor in the self, or in the world,
determined by the other. The conceptions exist only as synthetic activity upon the manifold of sense; the manifold of
sense exists only as connected by these conceptions. But while
Kant has chosen in the deduction to consider them as
mutually related to each other, they have a meaning entirely
apart from this mutual qualification, which, having been

abstracted from in the transcendental deduction, must now be brought in that we may see how it affects the result.

The final meaning of the manifold of sense is found, not in its relation to the synthetic notions of the understanding, but in its relation to a thing-in-itself which produces it. In order to be known by us, this manifold must, indeed, be subjected to synthesis, and enter into relation to the self. But it has its own being entirely apart from such qualification. And, on the other hand, the conceptions of the understanding are not exhaustively determined by their synthetic action upon sense. They have a nature of their own, entirely independent of this synthetic action. The transcendental deduction does not give us, therefore, an analysis of the self, or of knowledge, or of the world as such; but simply of the conditions under which a manifold of sense (having a nature outside its relations to self) is knowable by us, or of the conditions under which conceptions of the understanding become categories of experience, these conceptions having their real and essential meaning, all the while, in a purely logical character which belongs to them apart from knowledge or experience. The transcendental self is thus a name for the incident under which our knowledge occurs, instead of giving the analysis of knowledge itself. It cannot be identified, therefore, as at first it seemed it might be, with either the real object (the thing-in-itself) or with the real subject. Just as the synthetic principles of experience are in themselves logical forms of analytic thought, so the self, in its own nature, is known only as the bare unity of these logical forms, the simple "I think" that must accompany all thought. The introduction of the thing-in-itself, therefore, leads Kant to that view of the self which finally gets expression in the quotations which were made in connection with Seth's second idea of the self. For it must be remembered that the introduction of the thing-in-itself into Kant's philosophy affects all the factors which enter into his account of knowledge—the nature of thought as well as the nature of sensation. It is not an excrescence which can be lopped off without reconstruction of the whole theory of knowledge. Do away with the thing-in-itself, and the conceptions, instead of being *merely* logical, are also real, for their whole existence and meaning will then be found in their synthetic relation to the sense manifold. And the transcendental self, instead of denoting a "logical exposition of thought in general," marks the synthetic union of the logical with the manifold of sense through regular principles of activity—marks, therefore, the objective character of the self. For if we reconstruct the Kantian theory of knowledge upon its own basis and method of analysis, doing away with the thing-in-itself, the result is to show that the *merely* logical, equally with the *merely* ontological, is an impossible abstraction. The *merely* logical is not at all; the logical *is* only as the thought factor in the entire determination of experience, requiring another factor in order to constitute the self. That Kant's position of the merely formal abstract character of the self is superior in consistency to that of some Neo-Kantians is, therefore, not so evident as is the inconsistency of the restatement of such a position by one who denies the whole notion of the thing-in-itself.

But even if we correct Kant's analysis by doing away with the thing-in-itself, retaining all features not inconsistent with it, can the result of the transcendental deduction stand without further interpretation? Admitting that the removal of the thing-in-itself would show the transcendental self not as a logical abstraction, but real as experience itself—more real, indeed, in the sense that the reality of experience is shown by analysis to involve the reality of this self, behind which we cannot go—would this removal give a self whose content was the same as the content of the known world? The answer must be in the negative. The known world is constituted by the manifold of sensation, as connected by the self through its principles of synthesis. The content of the world, as known, will not be equivalent to the whole significance of the self, therefore, unless sensation is capable of being connected by principles of synthesis which manifest the entire nature of the self. But the position of Kant (a position entirely independent of any notion of *Ding-an-sich*) is, that sensation is incapable of being so determined as to equal self-consciousness; or, if we put it from the other side, that self-consciousness, even as a real activity of synthesis, can never exhaust all its synthetic capacities upon a material of sense. Sense is, as it were, inadequate to the relations which constitute self-consciousness, and thus there must also remain a surplusage in the self, not entering into the make-up of the known world. The reason for this is that all the manifold of sense must be determined by certain forms of perception, space and time, before being determinable by the categories of thinking. Perhaps it would be more in accordance with the Kantian spirit to say that sensation, since it is in relation to space and time, must always present itself to the synthetic action of self as a manifold of mutually external particulars. The conceptions are thus not capable of determining sensation independently, but only as sensation is already subject to time- and space-*cadres*. Every category, therefore, must receive its value from its application to sensations already a manifold of external particulars, and the result can be only the system of objects in time and space. No category of experience can be found, accordingly, higher than that which determines most exhaustively the relations of objects and events in time and space, *viz.*, reciprocity. And, correspondingly, no object can be known which is not an object in space and time. Hence the impossibility of making the self an object, since it is the condition of all objects, through its synthetic action upon sense. Stated in more Kantian language, the result would be that self-consciousness is the unconditioned, while experience, owing to the necessary relation of the synthetic activity of self to a material already determined as externally limiting and limited, can never present an unconditioned.[1] There thus remains a distinction

[1] I do not mean to imply that I regard Kant as teaching that objects are first given as objects in space and time, and that the action of thought follows upon the presentation of such ready-made objects; or that there can be perception without conception. On the contrary, I think that Kant teaches very distinctly that space and time (and, of course, with them everything in space and time) do not exist as perceived objects without the action of thought. But he also holds that the manifold of sense which thought synthesizes has already a formal element which determines it to relations of externality. The

between self and experience, due not now to the shadow thrown on knowledge by the thing-in-itself, but by the incompatibility of sensation, as rendered a manifold of external particulars in space and time, to the unconditioned content of self-consciousness. Experience can never be complete enough to have a content equal to that of self-consciousness, for experience can never escape its limitation through space and time. Self-consciousness is real, and not merely logical; it is the ground of the reality of experience; it is wider than experience, and yet is unknown except so far as it is reflected through its own determinations in experience—this is the result of our analysis of Kant, the *Ding-an-sich* being eliminated but the Kantian method and all presuppositions not involved in the notion of the *Ding-an-sich* being retained. The resulting conception of the self is, evidently, not equivalent to either of Seth's two first definitions of the self. It is not a mere abstract and formal logical unity, for it involves the action of thought upon sense, and is thus synthetic and objective; and yet it is not one side of the world of experience. The world of experience is constituted by it, but the world of experience does not exhaust it.

We have next to consider the relation of this revised Kantian conception of self to the third notion of self stated in Seth's book—the idea of self-consciousness as the highest category of thought and of explanation. So far we have dealt only with the general idea of thinking as synthesis of sense according to principles. The different forms of synthesis, or the categories, we have not dealt with. Kant, as is well known, had twelve of them, which he derived without further examination from certain notions which he found to be involved in the formally logical theory of judgment. It was the work of Hegel, first, to give an *independent* derivation of them, as contrasted with Kant's taking them for granted; secondly, to

---

fact that thought never connects pure sensations as such, but only sensations partially determined by relations of perceptivity, would occupy much the same place now occupied by the notion of schematism in Kant's theory, if this theory were reconstructed merely on the basis of the elimination of the *Ding-an-sich*.

give an *organic* derivation of them, in placing them in relation to one another, as contrasted with the simple juxtaposition of them which is found in Kant; and, thirdly, to show the category of self-consciousness as their basis and system, instead of stopping short with reciprocity, and placing the categories in opposition to self-consciousness. Now, accepting Hegel's work so far as it thus relates to the categories, and accepting his criticisms upon the Kantian procedure in reference to them, let us again revise the Kantian results in view of Hegel's position. Will this give us the self as the supreme category of experience? The answer must be in the negative. In one way the Kantian conception will include more than the Hegelian; in another way, less. It includes more, because what Kant offers is not primarily the self as a category of explanation at all, but the self as the real ground (not, however, to be confused with cause) of experience.[2] It includes less, because, however ready Kant might be to admit the Hegelian criticism and derivation of the categories as superior to his own, he could not admit that self-consciousness may be used as a category of experience. Self-consciousness would still have the function of the Idea for Kant. It would be an ideal regulative of experience, not a category constitutive of it.

Considering first this latter point, we may say that, admitting Kant's derivation of the categories from the forms of syllogistic logic to be insufficient and artificial, granting that it is impossible to stop short with the category of reciprocity, it does not follow that the category of self-consciousness is a category of experience. The distinction between conceptions of *thought* and conceptions of *knowledge* still remains. The reason for this we have already seen. It is the peculiar relation of the categories to sense as qualified by the forms of space and time. While, therefore, we might have the thought of self-consciousness, and while as a thought it would not be empty but would be, in another sense from that in which Kant actually uses the term, the vehicle of all notions of thought—their organism, it would be impossible to use this

[2] It will be understood that we are now speaking of Kant as revised by the elimination of the *Ding-an-sich*.

category so as to determine sense by it. For it is impossible as long as we retain Kant's fundamental presupposition—the idea of the partial determination of sensation by relation to perception, apart from its relation to conception—to employ self-consciousness as a principle of explaining any fact of experience. Every fact of experience is capable of adequate explanation without any such category; or, conversely put, experience can never convey anything adequate to the notion of self. Self-consciousness would thus be an ideal category—that is to say, it would suggest the notion of a possible experience, unlike anything that *we* can possibly experience. It would be a notion which should regulate the successive organization of our present experience by pointing to a goal that yet we never could reach, and which should also point out the limitation of our present experience.[3]

The reconstruction of the Kantian theory of categories in the light of the Hegelian logic would give the following points. First, it would derive the conceptions from a common root and place them in some organic connection with one another. Secondly, it would place the Notion of the understanding and the Idea of reason in some connection with each other. The reason, with its Ideas, would not then appear, as it does now, an accidental afterthought of Kant, or an arbitrary derivation from the theory of the syllogism. The conception included under the Idea would follow by immanent development and criticism from what are now called Notions of the understanding, and would follow as their basis in thought. The distinction between them would be between conceptions that may be used to connect sensations subject to space- and time-forms and those that may not be so used. Thirdly, the ideas of organism and teleology, which also now appear to be unconnected with the rest of the Kantian philosophy, sprung upon us without intrinsic necessity, would form part of the content of the Idea as distinguished from the Notion. And,

---

[3] The distinction would thus be analogous to, perhaps identical with, the distinction Kant draws between our intelligence, in which the immediate and the mediate element never wholly coincide, and an intelligence which may be described either as Intuitive Reason or a Rational Intuition.

finally, the distinction Kant now makes between theoretical and practical reason, between the fact which is and the ideal which ought to be, would get an organic connection with the rest of the philosophy. This gives the outline of a reconstruction of his ethics; for it would appear that it is just the business of moral experience to overcome that distinction between experience and self-consciousness which theoretical knowledge cannot remove. All this we can get, if we read Kant with the eyes of Hegel; but self-consciousness as an actual category of our scientific experience we cannot get unless we simply substitute Hegel for Kant.

But it is time to turn to the other point: that the transcendental self of Kant is more than self-consciousness as a supreme category of explanation. It is more, because the self of Kant (the self as it would be with the *Ding-an-sich* eliminated) is more than any category: it is a real activity or being. And it cannot be said to be more than a category only because he has hypostatized a category—that if he had understood himself he would have seen that it was just a category. There is a fundamental distinction between the Kantian critique of pure reason and the Hegelian theory of categories which makes their results disparate. Kant's object is not the examination of *thought,* but the examination of *knowledge;* and his method is not a consideration of the significance, placing, relative adequacy and inadequacy of the conceptions or aspects of thought with a view to discovering the entire meaning of thought; his method is an analysis of the *actual* factors which actually constitute knowledge. One of these factors is thought, and, therefore, the complete carrying out of the method would undoubtedly involve an examination of thought as specified into its various conceptions. But because the Hegelian *Logic* is the development of one factor in Kant, it will hardly do to say that the purpose of the Kantian *Critique* is exhausted in the purpose of Hegel's *Logic.* At least, if we do say it, it should be with the distinct consciousness that we are not completing Kant, but are abandoning the characteristic feature of his undertaking and of his method. This is, I repeat, not an immanent "criticism of categories"

[175]

but an analysis of experience into its aspects and really constituent elements. And in the course of this analysis Kant comes upon a self which through various principles of synthesis puts together the manifold of sense and, thereby, constitutes experience. This, indeed, is not a theory of creation; it is not an attempt to tell how a self set to work, or by necessity would set to work, to make a universe. But because it is not a theory of creation, it does not follow that it is only a criticism of categories. The assumption that there is no middle ground between a theory of creation and a mere analysis of forms of objective thought is, to say the least, a curious one. Kant's method is the analysis of the known universe or of experience; and as a result it discovers a self acting through thought upon sensation. Thought as synthetic is action upon sense, and sense is through the synthetic action of thought. If we call them factors of experience it must be with the recognition of their intrinsic unity with each other. The self constitutes this unity; it is the activity which is the source of the correlative synthesis of thought and sense. That analysis of reality should give anything but reality would be a strange result. And the reality found by the Kantian method through analysis of reality is a self which through thought is synthetic of sense determined to be a manifold of limiting particulars by relation to space and time.

There are two strains in Kant: one is inquiry into the necessary thought or logical conditions of experience; the other is the inquiry into the actual nature of experience. The *Logic* of Hegel undoubtedly works out the former to its consistent results. The latter it does not come in contact with. The former inquiry asks what are the forms or principles by which we must think the world; or, from the other side, what the world must be, as thought. The answer is that to think the world in its completeness is to think it as self-consciousness. Now this proposition is, as I attempted to show in the earlier portion of this article, not convertible with the proposition that the world *is* self-consciousness, unless it is also shown that the world is only and just as it is for thought. But the result of Kant's inquiry into the *actual* nature of experience is to show (to his satisfaction, I mean, the *truth* of the results not being under examination) that it includes another element besides thought, namely, feeling, and that on account of this element—or at least on account of its peculiar relation to forms of perception—the world as experienced can never equal the world as thought. That is, while to *think* the world completely is to think it as self-consciousness, it is the very characteristic of experience or *knowledge* that it cannot be complete—and hence cannot give self-consciousness.

We have thus another conception of self-consciousness to put beside the three obtained from the analysis of Professor Seth. This is the conception which we reach in reconstructing Kant by means of the elimination of the *Ding-an-sich* and by that more complete working out of the logical side of his analysis of experience which was made by Hegel. This is the self as the activity of synthesis upon sense. Starting from this notion the other three notions may be at once placed with reference to it. The self as the *merely* logical or abstract unity of thought falls away entirely. Self-consciousness as a category of experience becomes changed into an ideal which serves at once to organize and to reveal the incompleteness of experience. Where (as in ethics) the ideal *is* the reality, self-consciousness is again a real category of experience—but of practical experience, not of theoretical. The self which could use the category of self as a category of both practical and theoretic experience would be a self whose content was the same as that of the world. "The self and the world are only two sides of the same reality" in this case. While from the standpoint of Hegel's *Logic* (I am not speaking of the rest of his philosophy) such a result could be reached only by substantiating a category, from the standpoint of Kant's *Critique* it would be reached as an analysis of the reality of experience —if it were reached at all. But it can be reached only as an ideal which serves by contrast to manifest the incompleteness of experience as it presents itself to us.

It is evident that we are now upon the verge of another difficulty. As long as sensation was regarded as given by a thing-in-itself, it was possible to form a conception of the self which did not identify it with the world. But when self is regarded as having meaning only because it is "there" as determined by thought, just as thought is "there" only as determining sense, it would seem either that the self is just their synthetic unity (thus equaling the world) or that it must be thrust back of experience, and become a thing-in-itself. The activity of the self can hardly be a third something distinct from thought and from sense, and it cannot be their synthetic union. What, then, is it? This is, I take it, the problem which finally emerges, when Kant is made self-consistent by the elimination of the thing-in-itself, and when the logical or thought factor of his philosophy is developed in the Hegelian manner. It is precisely, as it seems to me, the difficulty which comes to the front in Green's reconstruction of Kant. It is to meet this difficulty that he frames the idea of a completely realized self making an animal organism the vehicle of its own reproduction in time. The conditions of the problem are: a denial of the *Ding-an-sich;* the analysis of knowledge into thought, and feeling which is ἕτερον to thought; the recognition that this feeling, after all, exists only as determined by thought; and the belief that feeling enters into *our* knowledge only under conditions of space and time, although space and time, in themselves, are feeling determined by thought. No space remains to consider how far Green's conception of an eternal self communicating itself gradually through physical conditions, and thereby constituting a human self, meets the demands of the problem. But it is evident that, when the problem is conceived as just stated, the self cannot be thought of as equivalent, on the one hand, to the world, because this world, as knowable by us, is always subject to certain forms, namely, space and time, which condition sense; nor, on the other hand, as equivalent to the highest category of thought, because the self is more than thought, more than a category, namely, the activity of synthesis of sense through thought. It is, I think, this twofold character of time and space, as at once forms of knowledge conditioned by the self, and yet conditioning self as it works in us, that is the genesis of Green's notion. The truth of the conditions upon which it rests—that is, Kant read in the light of Hegel so far as is necessary to make Kant consistent—is not under examination here; but if we grant it, the theory of Green is a genuine attempt to meet a genuine problem, and not a mere hypostasis of an abstraction.

10

HOW DO CONCEPTS ARISE FROM PERCEPTS?

FAILURE to make some fundamental distinction may be the source of a confusion which makes all subsequent discussion mere blind thrashing in the air. The discussion of the nature of the concept has often suffered from failure to discriminate between a mental *state* and the *function* of that state. It is as if, in physiology, writers were to discuss the heart without having first decided whether they were writing of the *thing,* or of the *work* done by that thing and its *value* for the organism. Were such the case, it would not be surprising if one school of physiologists held the heart to be a definite, isolated thing, of a certain shape and size, composed of certain fibers, while another school held the heart to be a factor or member in an interconnected unity; not a thing but an activity; and its special structure a matter of indifference compared with the general purpose subserved by this structure.

Carrying out the needed discrimination in the case of the concept, it may be said that the concept is not a term denoting a mental state or existence, but an intellectual *function* or *value.* Every mental state is, as a bare existence (taken, that is, statically), an image. As such, it is a particular, numerically and qualitatively different from every other existence and enduring only for a limited time. The nominalist is, therefore, quite right when he asserts that there is no such thing as a general idea—provided he is speaking of mental existences. But so speaking, he does not touch the question at all. The concept is the *power* which a particular image has of standing for or conveying a certain meaning or intellectual value. Let

From *Public-School Journal,* November, 1891; 128-129.

me borrow an illustration from, I think, Mr. Bosanquet. It is a matter of indifference what kind of a flag be used as a danger signal on the railway. It may be eight inches square, or ten, or not square at all. It may be new or old, fresh or dirty, tattered or whole. *Prior* to its adoption as a signal, it may be of any color whatever. In other words, the main thing is not what the flag *is* as an existence. The main thing is what the flag *does*. So, when we are considering the structure of a particular mental image, we have not entered the domain of concepts, or universals, at all. The concept is something which the image does; some meaning which it conveys.

What meaning? The raising of this question brings us specifically to the question of the origin of the concept from the percept. My answer to the question is: the concept arises from the percept *through realizing the full meaning im*-plied, but not *ex*-plicit in the percept. For example, take the percept of a triangle. So far as this is a mere percept, it is regarded wholly as a particular thing. Knowledge of it from this point of view would be exhausted in getting its exact shape, size, length of sides, degree of angles, stuff made of, color, etc. The mind would nowhere be led beyond the consideration of the bare thing present. Even if it were found that the sum of its three interior angles was equal to two right angles, this would be a trait of the particular triangle, a bare item of information, of no more general value than that the length of one side was $1\frac{2}{17}$ inches. But suppose the mind advances beyond the particular triangle to the thought that there is a principle involved in the triangle; that the triangle, like everything in the world, is made upon a certain principle which is embodied in it; that this principle furnishes the plans and specifications according to which anything must exist in order to be a triangle at all; a principle which, if exceeded or come short of, there is no triangle at all. What shall we call this principle? Is it not evident that, since it is this principle which constitutes the particular thing a triangle, rather than a pumpkin or a stovepipe, it is this principle we really mean by triangle, and are attempting to know? Well, it is this principle which forms the concept, "triangle." The concept, "triangle," in other words, is the *way in which three lines are put together;* it is a *mode* or form of construction. Except as we know this mode of formation our idea of a triangle is exceedingly imperfect.

Hence, the characteristics of a concept. It is (1) "ideal" not sensuous. That is, as a mode or *way of mental action,* it cannot be felt or seen or heard. *It can be grasped only in and through the activity which constitutes it.* The only way to know the concept triangle is to make it—to go through the act of putting together the lines in the way called for. (I may remark, incidentally, that this reveals the impossibility of external or mechanical instruction. If a concept is the true meaning of a thing, and this true meaning is a mode of mental action, a process of intellectual construction, how possibly can true information be externally conveyed from one to another?) The concept is (2) general, not particular. Its generality lies in the very fact that it is a mode of action, a way of putting things or elements together. A cotton loom is particular in all its parts; every yard of cloth produced is particular, yet the way in which the parts go together and work together, the function of the loom is not particular.

So any given triangle, actual or as a mental existence, is particular. But the way of constructing triangles is not particular. It has no more to do with one triangle than with another. It is a principle in accordance with which any number of triangles may be brought into existence. *Anything* constituted in this way is a triangle.

It should be reasonably evident from what I have said that the concept of triangle contains not less but more than the percept. It is got, not by dropping traits, but by finding out what the real traits are.

It is true that certain features are excluded. But this dropping out of certain features is not what gives rise to the concept. On the contrary, *it is on the basis of the concept,* the principle of construction, *that certain features are omitted.* Nay, they are more than omitted. They are positively eliminated. They are declared to be irrelevant, to have nothing to do with the *real* triangle whatever.

[182]

The concept, in short, is knowledge of what the real object is—the object taken with reference to its principle of construction; while the percept, so called, is knowledge of the object in a more or less accidental or limited way. As to their intellectual value, concept means complete knowledge of an object—knowledge of it in its mode of genesis, and in its relations and bearings; while percept means incomplete [that is, "abstract," in the true sense of abstract] knowledge of an object—knowledge of the object in its qualitative, spatial, and temporal limitations.

It must, however, be added that the concept always returns into and enriches the percept, so that the distinction between them is not fixed but movable. Let me once get the concept triangle; let me, that is, once see into the process by which a triangle is made a triangle, and I carry the knowledge thus gained into every particular triangle I see. The concept becomes an enriching of the meaning of the percept.

In ideal, in completed development, the percept and concept would have the same content. It would exceed my limits here to show this to be the case; but let me suggest that complete knowledge of a particular object, say a given maple tree [the percept] would involve knowledge not merely of every detail of that tree, but of *how it came to be so*. On the other hand, complete knowledge of tree life [the concept] would involve not merely highly general ideas, but also knowledge of the particular circumstances and conditions under which tree life became deciduous or nondeciduous; of the conditions under which the deciduous differentiated into maple, oak, beech, etc.; of the still more particular circumstances under which maple life differentiated into this particular form of life, *this* maple tree.

Such a systematic knowledge, whether starting from an individual (when we call it percept) or starting from the principle (when we call it concept), is the ideal of every science. Our knowledge of the individual is limited until we have got at the principal involved in it. Our knowledge of the principle is imperfect (abstract) until we see how this principle acts under the multitude of different circumstances. As either is completed, it tends to approach the other.

[183]

11

THE SUPERSTITION OF NECESSITY

LEST my title give such offense as to prejudice unduly my
contention, I may say that I use the term in the way
indicated by its etymology: as a standing-still on the part of
thought; a clinging to old ideas after those ideas have lost
their use, and hence, like all superstitions, have become ob-
structions.[1] For I shall try to show that the doctrine of necessity is a survival; that it holds over from an earlier and unde-
veloped period of knowledge; that as a means of getting out
of and beyond that stage it had a certain value, but, having
done its work, loses its significance. Halting judgment may,
indeed, at one time have helped itself out of the slough of
uncertainty, vagueness, and inadequacy on to ground of more
solid and complete fact, by the use of necessity as a crutch;
once upon the ground, the crutch makes progress slower and,
preventing the full exercise of the natural means of locomotion, tends to paralyze science. The former support has become a burden, almost an intolerable one.

The beginning of wisdom in the matter of necessity is, I
conceive, in realizing that it is a term which has bearing or
relevancy only with reference to the development of judgment, not with reference to objective things or events. I do
not mean by this that necessity refers to the compelling force

From *The Monist*, April, 1893; 362-379.
[1] This article, as the title may indicate, was suggested by Mr. Peirce's article
upon "The Doctrine of Necessity Examined." As, however, my thought takes
finally a different turn, I have deemed it better to let it run its own course
from the start, and so have not referred, except, indirectly, to Mr. Peirce's
argument. I hope this will not be taken as a desire to slur over my indebted-
ness to him.

with which we are driven to make a given affirmation: I mean that it refers to the content of that affirmation, expressing the degree of coherence between its constituent factors. When we say something or other *must* be so and so, the "must" does not indicate anything in the nature of the fact itself, but a trait in our *judgment* of that fact; it indicates the degree with which we have succeeded in making a whole out of the various elements which have to be taken into account in forming the judgment. More specifically, it indicates a halfway stage. At one extreme we have two separate judgments which, so far as consciousness is concerned, have nothing to do with each other; and at the other extreme we have one judgment into which the contents of the two former judgments have been so thoroughly organized as to lose all semblance of separateness. Necessity, as the middle term, is the midwife which, from the dying isolation of judgments, delivers the unified judgment just coming into life—it being understood that the separateness of the original judgments is not as yet quite negated, nor the unity of the coming judgment quite attained. The judgment of necessity, in other words, is exactly and solely the transition in our knowledge from unconnected judgments to a more comprehensive synthesis. Its value is just the value of this transition; as negating the old partial and isolated judgments—in its backward look—necessity has meaning; in its forward look—with reference to the resulting completely organized subject matter—it is itself as false as the isolated judgments which it replaces. Its value is in what it rids judgment of. When it has succeeded, its value is nil. Like any go-between, its service consists in rendering itself uncalled for.

All science can ultimately do is to report or describe, to completely state, the reality. So far as we reach this standpoint regarding any fact or group of facts, we do not say that the fact *must* be such and such, but simply that it *is* such and such. There is no necessity attaching to the fact either as whole or as parts. *Qua* whole, the fact simply is what it is; while the parts, instead of being necessitated either by one another or by the whole, are the analyzed factors constituting, in their complete circuit, the whole. In stating the whole, we, as of course, state all that enters into it; if we speak of the various elements as *making* the whole, it is only in the sense of making it *up*, not of causing it. The fallacy of the necessitarian theory consists in transforming the determinate in the sense of the wholly defined, into the determined in the sense of something externally made to be what it is.

The whole, although first in the order of reality, is last in the order of knowledge. The complete statement of the whole is the goal, not the beginning of wisdom. We begin, therefore, with fragments, which are taken for wholes; and it is only by piecing together these fragments, and by the transformation of them involved in this combination, that we arrive at the real fact. There comes a stage at which the recognition of the unity begins to dawn upon us, and yet the tradition of the many distinct wholes survives; judgment has to combine these two contradictory conceptions; it does so by the theory that the dawning unity is an effect necessarily produced by the interaction of the former wholes. Only as the consciousness of the unity grows still more is it seen that instead of a group of independent facts, held together by "necessary" ties, there is one reality, of which we have been apprehending various fragments in succession and attributing to them a spurious wholeness and independence. We learn (but only at the end) that instead of discovering and then connecting together a number of separate realities, we have been engaged in the progressive definition of one fact.

There are certain points upon which there is now *practical* agreement among all schools. What one school has got at by a logical analysis of science, another school has arrived at by the road of a psychological analysis of experience. What one school calls the unity of thought and reality, another school calls the relativity of knowledge. The metaphysical interpretation further given to these respective statements may be quite different, but, so far as they go, they come to the same thing: that objects, *as known*, are not independent of the process of knowing, but are the content of our judgments. One school, indeed, may conceive of judgment as a mere associative or habitual grouping of sensations, the other as the correlative diversification and synthesis of the self; but the practical outcome, that the "object" (anyway as known) is a form of judgment, is the same. This point being held in common, both schools must agree that *the progress of judgment is equivalent to a change in the value of objects*—that objects as they are for us, as known, change with the development of our judgments. If this be so, truth, however it be metaphysically defined, must attach to late rather than to early judgments.

I am fortunate in being able to quote from authors who may be taken as typical of the two schools. Says Professor Caird in his article upon "Metaphysic" (lately reprinted, *Essays in Philosophy and Literature*):

> Our first consciousness of things is not an immovable foundation upon which science may build, but rather a hypothetical and self-contradictory starting-point of investigation, which becomes changed and transformed as we advance.

On the other hand, Mr. Venn writes (in the first chapter of his *Empirical Logic*):

> Select what object we please—the most apparently simple in itself, and the most definitely parted off from others that we can discover—yet we shall find ourselves constrained to admit that a considerable mental process has been passed through before that object could be recognized as being an object, that is, as possessing some degree of unity and as requiring to be distinguished from other such unities.

He goes on to illustrate by such an apparently fixed and given object as the sun, pointing out how its unity as a persistent thing involves a continued synthesis of elements very diverse in time and space, and an analysis, a selection, from other elements in very close physical juxtaposition. He goes on to raise the question whether a dog, for example, may be said to "see" a rainbow at all, because of the complex analysis and synthesis involved in such an object. The "mental whole" (to use Mr. Venn's words, the "ideal unity" as others might term it) is so extensive and intricate that

> One might almost as reasonably expect the dog to "see" the progress of democracy in the place where he lives, of which course of events the ultimate sensible constituents are accessible to his observation precisely as they are to ours.

As Mr. Venn is not discussing just the same point which I have raised, he does not refer to the partial and tentative character of our first judgments—our first objects. It is clear enough, however, that there will be all degrees between total failure to analyze and combine (as, say, in the case of the dog and rainbow) and fairly adequate grouping. The difference between the savage whose synthesis is so limited in scope that he sets up a new sun every day and the scientific man whose object is a unity comprehending differences through thousands of years of time and interactions going on through millions of miles of space is a case in point. The distinction between the respective objects is not simply a superimposition of new qualities upon an old object, that old object remaining the same; it is not getting new objects; it is a continual qualitative reconstruction of the object itself. This fact, which is the matter under consideration, is well stated by Mr. Venn, when he goes on to say:

> The act of predication, in its two-fold aspect of affirmation and denial, really is a process by which we are not only enabled to add to our information *about* objects, *but is also the process by the continued performance of which the objects had been originally acquired, or rather produced* [italics are mine].

This statement cannot be admitted at all without recognizing that the first judgments do not make the object once for all, but that the continued process of judging is a continued process of "producing" the object.

Of course the confused and hypothetical character of our

[188]

first objects does not force itself upon us when we are still engaged in constructing them. On the contrary, it is only when the original subject matter has been overloaded with various and opposing predicates that we think of doubting the correctness of our first judgments, of putting our first objects under suspicion. At the start, these objects assert themselves as the baldest and solidest of hard facts. The dogmatic and naïve quality of the original judgment is in exact proportion to its crudeness and inadequacy. The objects which are the content of these judgments thus come to be identified with reality *par excellence;* they are *facts*, however doubtful everything else. They hang on obstinately. New judgments, instead of being regarded as better definitions of the actual fact and hence as displacing the prior object, are tacked onto the old as best they may be. Unless the contradiction is too flagrant, the new predicates are set side by side with the old as simply additional information; they do not react into the former qualities. If the contradiction is too obvious to be overlooked the new predicate is used, if possible, to constitute another object, independent of the former. So the savage, having to deal with the apparently incompatible predicates of light and darkness, makes two objects; two suns, for two successive days. Once the Ptolemaic conception is well rooted, cycles and epicycles, almost without end, are superadded, rather than reconstruct the original object. Here, then, is our starting point: when qualities arise so incompatible with the object already formed that they cannot be referred to that object, it is easier to form a new object on their basis than it is to doubt the correctness of the old, involving as that does the surrender of the *object* (the fact, seemingly) and the formation of another object.

It is easier, I say, for there is no doubt that the reluctance of the mind to give up an object once made lies deep in its economies. I shall have occasion hereafter to point out the teleological character of the notions of necessity and chance, but I wish here to call attention to the fact that the forming of a number of distinct objects has its origin in practical needs of our nature. The analysis and synthesis which is first made

[189]

is that of most practical importance; what is abstracted from the complex network of reality is some net outcome, some result which is of value for life. As Venn says:

> What the savage mostly wants to do is to produce something or to avert something, not to account for a thing which has already happened. What interests him is to know how to kill somebody, not to know how somebody has been killed.

And again:

> What not only the savage, but also the practical man mostly wants, is a *general* result, say the death of his enemy. It does not matter whether the symptoms, *i.e.,* the qualifying circumstances, are those attendant on poison, or a blow from a club, or on incantation, provided the death is brought about. But they do desire *certainty* in respect of this general result.

Now it is this "general result," the net outcome for practical purposes, which is *the* fact, *the* object at first. Anything else is useless subtlety. That the man is dead—that is the fact; anything further is at most external circumstances which happen to accompany the fact. That the death is only a bare fraction of a fact; that the attendant "circumstances" are as much constituent factors of the real fact as the mere "death" itself (probably more so from the scientific point of view)— all this is foreign to conception. We pluck the fruit, and that fruit is the fact. Only when practical experience forces upon us the recognition that we cannot get the fruit without heeding certain other "conditions" do we consent to return upon our assumed object, put it under suspicion and question whether it is really what we took it to be. It is, we may presume, the savage who in order to get his living, has to regulate his conduct for long periods, through changes of seasons, in some continuous mode, who first makes the synthesis of one sun going through a recurring cycle of changes—the year.

As time goes on, the series of independent and isolated objects passes through a gradual change. Just as the recognition of incompatible qualities has led to setting up of separate things, so the growing recognition of similar qualities in these disparate objects begins to pull them together again. Some relation between the two objects is perceived; it is seen that neither object is just what it is in its isolation, but owes some of its meaning to the other objects. While in reality (as I hope later to point out), this "relationship" and mutual dependence means membership in a common whole, contribution to one and the same activity, a midway stage intervenes before this one fact, including as parts of itself the hitherto separate objects, comes to consciousness. The tradition of isolation is too strong to give way at the first suggestion of community. This passageway from isolation to unity, denying the former but not admitting the latter, is necessity or determinism. The wall of partition between the two separate "objects" cannot be broken at one attack; they have to be worn away by the attrition arising from their slow movement into one another. It is the "necessary" influence which one exerts upon the other that finally rubs away the separateness and leaves them revealed as elements of one unified whole. This done, the determining influence has gone too.

The process may be symbolized as follows: M is the object, the original synthesis of the elements seen to be of practical importance; a, b, c, etc., to h are predicates of constantly growing incompatibility. When the quality i is discovered, it is so manifestly incompatible with a that all attempt to refer it to the same subject M is resisted. Two alternatives are now logically open. The subject matter M, as the synthesis of the qualities a—h, may be taken up; it may be asked whether the object is really M with these qualities; whether it is not rather Σ, having instead of the predicates a, b, etc., the qualities $\rho\alpha$, $\rho\beta$, with which the new quality i is quite compatible. But this process goes against the practical grain of our knowledge; it means not only that we do not know what we thought we knew; it means that we did not *do* what we thought we did. Such unsettling of action is hardly to be borne. It is easier to erect a new object N, to which the more incompatible predicates are referred. Finally, it is discovered that both M and N have the same predicates r and s; that in virtue of this community of qualities there is a certain like element even in the qualities previously considered disparate. This mutual attraction continues until it becomes so marked a feature of the case that there is no alternative but to suppose that the r and s of one produces these qualities in the other, and thereby influences all the qualities of the other. This drawing together continues until we have the one reconstructed object Σ, with the traits $\rho\alpha$, $\rho\beta r$, etc. It is found that there is one somewhat comprehensive synthesis which includes within itself the several separate objects so far produced; and it is found that this inclusion in the larger whole reacts into the meaning of the several constituting parts—as parts of one whole, they lose traits which they seemed to possess in their isolation, and gain new traits, because of their membership in the same whole.

We have now to consider, more in detail, how the intermediate idea of necessity grows up and how it gives away upon the discovery of the one inclusive whole. Let us continue the illustration of the killing. The "general result," the death of the hated enemy, is at first the fact; all else is mere accidental circumstance. Indeed, the other circumstances at first are hardly that; they do not attract attention, having no importance. Not only the savage, but also the common-sense man of today, I conceive, would say that any attempt to extend the definition of the "fact" beyond the mere occurrence of the death is metaphysical refinement; that the *fact* is the killing, the death, and that that "fact" remains quite the same, however it is brought about. What has been done, in other words, is to abstract part of the real fact, part of *this* death, and set up the trait or universal thus abstracted as itself *fact*, and not only as fact, but as *the* fact, *par excellence*, with reference to which all the factors which constitute the reality, the concrete fact, of *this* death, are circumstantial and "accidental." [2]

[2] The reason of this abstraction is in practical nature, as already indicated. For all the savage *cares* about it, the death in general, *is* the real fact. It is all that interests him. It is hardly worth while to attempt to persuade the savage;

A fragment of the whole reality, of the actual fact individualized and specified with all kind of minute detail, having been thus hypostatized into an object, the idea of necessity is in fair way to arise. These deaths in general do not occur. Although the mere death of the man, his removal from the face of the earth, is the *fact,* none the less all *actual* deaths have a certain amount of detail in them. The savage has to hit his enemy with a club or spear, or perform a magic incantation, before he can attain that all-important end of getting rid of him. Moreover, a man with a coat of armor on will not die just the same way as the man who is defenseless. These circumstances have to be taken into account. Now, if the "fact" had not been so rigidly identified with the bare practical outcome, the removal of the hated one, a coherent interpretation of the need for these further incidents would be open. It could be admitted that the original death was a highly complex affair, involving a synthesis of a very large number of different factors; furthermore, the new cases of murder could be employed to reconstruct the original analysis-synthesis; to eliminate supposed factors which were not relevant, and to show the presence of factors at first not suspected. In other words, the real fact would be under constant process of definition, of "production." But the stiff-necked identification of the fragment which happened to have practical importance with the real object, effectually prevents any such reaction and reconstruction. What is to be done, however, with these conditions of spear, of stone, of armor, which so obviously have something *to do* with the real fact, al-

---

indeed, if he were not only a savage, but also a philosopher, he might boldly challenge the objector to present *any* definition of object which should not refer objectivity to man's practical activity; although he might, as a shrewd savage, admit that some one activity (or self) to which the object is referred has more content than another. In this case, I, for one, should not care about entering the lists against the savage. But when the common-sense philosopher, who resists all attempts to reconstruct the original object on the ground that a fact is a fact and all beyond that is metaphysics, is also a case-hardened nominalist (as he generally is), it is time to protest. It might be true that the real object is always relative to the value of some action; but to erect this pure universal into the object, and then pride one's self on enlightenment in rejecting the "scholastic figment" of the reality of universals is a little too much.

though, as it would seem, they are not the fact? They are considered as circumstances, *accidental*, so far as death in general is concerned; *necessary*, so far as *this* death is concerned. That is, wanting simply to get the net result of the removal of my enemy, so that he will no longer blight the fair face of nature, it is accidental how I do it; but having, after all, to kill a man of certain characteristics and surroundings in life, having to choose time and place, etc., it becomes necessary, *if* I am to succeed, that I kill him in a certain way, say, with poison, or a dynamite bomb. Thus we get our concrete, individual fact again.

Consider, then, that tortuous path from reality to reality, *via* a circuit of unreality, which calls the thought of necessity into existence. We first mutilate the actual fact by selecting some portion that appeals to our needs; we falsify, by erecting this fragment into the whole fact. Having the rest of the fact thus left on our hands for disposal, when we have no need of the concrete fact we consider it accidental, merely circumstantial; but we consider it necessary whenever we have occasion to descend from the outcome which we have abstracted back to the real fact, in all its individuality. Necessity is a device by which we both conceal from ourselves the unreal character of what we have called real, and also get rid of the practical evil consequences of hypostatizing a fragment into an independent whole.

If the purely teleological character of necessity is not yet evident, I think the following considerations will serve to bring it out. The practical value, the fruit from the tree, we pick out and set up for the entire fact so far as our past action is concerned. But so far as our *future* action is concerned, this value is a result *to be* reached; it is an end to be attained. Other factors, in reality all the time bound up in the one concrete fact or individual whole, have now to be brought in as means to get this end. Although after our desire has been met they have been eliminated as accidental, as irrelevant, yet when the experience is again desired their integral membership in the real fact has to be recognized. This is done under the guise of considering them as means which are necessary to bring about the end. Thus the idea of the circumstances as external to the "fact" is retained, while we get all the practical benefit of their being not external but elements of one and the same whole. Contingent and necessary are thus the correlative aspects of one and the same fact; conditions are accidental so far as we have abstracted a fragment and set it up as the whole; they are necessary the moment it is required to pass from this abstraction back to the concrete fact. Both are teleological in character—contingency referring to the separation of means from end, due to the fact that the end having been already reached the means have lost their value for us; necessity being the reference of means to an end *which has still to be got.* Necessary means *needed;* contingency means no longer required—because already enjoyed.

Note that the necessity of the means has reference to an end still to be attained, and in so far itself hypothetical or contingent, while the contingent circumstances are no longer needed precisely because they have resulted in a definite outcome (which, accordingly, is now a fact, and, in that sense, necessary), and we begin to see how completely necessity and chance are bound up with each other.

Their correlation may thus be stated: *If* we are to reach an end we *must* take certain means; while so far as we want an undefined end, an end in general, conditions which accompany it are mere accidents. Whichever way the relationship be stated, the underlying truth is that we are dealing with only partial phases of fact, which, having been unduly separated from each other through their erection into distinct wholes, have now to be brought back into their real unity.

In the first place, then, *if* I am to reach an end, certain means *must* be used. Here the end is obviously postulated; save as it is begged (presupposed), the necessity of the means has no sense. If, when starving, I am to live I must steal a dinner, but, having stolen, the logical but unsympathetic judge may question the relevancy (that is, the necessity) of my end, and thus cut the ground out from under the necessity of my means. My end requires *its* justification, the establishing of its validity, before the necessity of the means is anything more than hypothetical. The proximate end must be referred to a more ultimate and inclusive end to get any solid ground. Here we have our choice: we may deny the existence of any organic whole in life and keep chasing in a never-ending series, the *progressus ad infinitum,* after an end valid in itself. In this case we never get beyond a hypothetical necessity— something is necessary *if* we are to have something else, the necessity being relative to the implied doubt. Or, being convinced that life is a whole and not a series merely, we may say there is one comprehensive end which gives its own validity to the lesser ends in so far as they constitute it. While, on the other alternative, we reach only a hypothetical necessity, on this we reach none at all. The comprehensive end is no end at all in the sense of something by itself to be reached by means external to it. Any such end would be simply one in the infinite series and would be itself hypothetical. Whenever minor ends cease to be in turn means to further ends it is because they have become parts, constituent elements, of the higher end and thus ceased to be steps toward an end and beyond and outside of themselves. Given a final (*i.e.,* inclusive) end, eating and drinking, study and gossip, play and business, cease to be means *toward* an end and become its concrete definition, its analytic content. The minor activities state the supreme activity in its specific factors.

Our dilemma is the choice between an end which itself has no existence save upon presupposition of another end (is contingent), and an end which as an end in itself simply *is.*

The externality of means to end is merely a symptom of lack of specification or concreteness in the end itself. *If* I am going to invent some improvement in a typewriter, the necessity of going through certain preliminary steps is exactly proportionate to the indefiniteness of my conception of what the improvement is to be; when the end is realized, the operations which enter into the realization cease to be means necessary to an end and become the specific *content* of that end. The improvement is a *fact,* having such and such elements defining it. If I simply want, in general, to get my mail I *must* take this path (there being but one road); but if my end is not thus general, if it is individualized with concrete filling, the walk to the office may become a part of the end, a part of the actual fact. In so far, of course, it loses all aspect of necessitation. It simply *is*. And in general, so far as my end is vague, or abstract, so far as it is not specified as to its details, so far the filling up of its empty schema to give it particularity (and thus make it fact) appears as a means necessary to reach an end outside itself. The growth in concreteness of the end itself is transformed into ways of affecting an end already presupposed. Or, to state it in yet one other way, determination in the sense of definition in consciousness is hypostatized into determination in the sense of a physical making.

The point may come out more clearly if we consider it with the emphasis on chance instead of upon necessity. The usual statement that chance is relative to ignorance seems to me to convey the truth though not in the sense generally intended —*viz.*, that if we knew more about the occurrence we should see it necessitated by its conditions. Chance is relative to ignorance in the sense rather that it refers to an indefiniteness in our conception of what we are doing. In our consciousness of our end (our acts) we are always making impossible abstractions; we break off certain phases of the act which are of chief interest to us, without any regard to whether the concrete conditions of action—that is, the deed in its whole definition—permit any such division. Then, when in our actual doing, the circumstances to which we have not attended thrust themselves into consciousness—when, that is to say, the act appears in more of its own specific nature—we dispose of those events, foreign to our conscious purpose, as accidental; we did not want them or intend them—what more proof of their accidental character is needed? The falling of a stone upon a man's head as he walks under a window is "chance," for it has nothing to do with what the man proposed to do, it is no part of his conception of that walk. To an enemy who takes that means of killing him, it is anything but an accident, being involved in *his* conscious purpose. It is "Chance" when we throw a two and a six; for the concreteness of the act falls outside of the content of our intention.

We intended *a* throw, some throw, and in so far the result is not accidental, but this special result, being irrelevant to our conception of what we were to do, in so far is contingent. The vagueness or lack of determinateness in our end, the irrelevancy of actual end to conscious intent, chance, are all names for the same thing. And if I am asked whether a gambler who has a hundred dollars upon the outcome does not *intend* to throw double sixes, I reply that he has no such intention— unless the dice are loaded. He may *hope* to make that throw, but he cannot intend it save as he can define that act—tell how to do it, tell, that is, just *what* the act is. Or, once more, if I intend to get my mail and there are four paths open to me it is chance which I take, just in proportion to the abstractness of my end. If I have not defined it beyond the mere "general result" of getting mail, anything else is extraneous and in so far contingent. If the end is individualized to the extent, say, of getting the mail in the shortest possible time, or with the maximum of pleasant surroundings, or with the maximum of healthy exercise, the indifference of the "means," and with it their contingency, disappears. This or that path is no longer a mere means which *may* be taken to get a result foreign to its own value; the path is an intrinsic part of the end.

In so far as a man presents to himself an end in general, he sets up an abstraction so far lacking in detail as (taken *per se*) to exclude the possibility of realization. In order to exist as concrete or individual (and of course, nothing can exist except as individual or concrete) it must be defined or particularized. But so far as consciousness is concerned the original vague end is *the* reality; it is all that the man cares about and hence constitutes his act. The further particularization of the end, therefore, instead of appearing as what it really is, *viz.*, the discovery of the actual reality, presents itself as something outside that end. This externality to the end previously realized in consciousness is, taken as mere externality, contingency, or accident; taken as none the less so bound up with the desired end that it must be gone through before reaching that end, it is necessary. Chance, in other words, stands for the irrelevancy as the matter at first presents itself to consciousness; necessity is the required, but partial, negation of this irrelevancy. Let it be complete, instead of partial, and we have the one real activity defined throughout. With reference to this reality, conditions are neither accidental nor necessary, but simply constituting elements—they neither may be nor must be, but just are. What is irrelevant is now not simply indifferent; it is excluded, eliminated. What is relevant is no longer something required in order to get a result beyond itself; it is incorporated into the result, it is integral.

It now remains to connect the two parts of our discussion, the logical and the practical consideration of necessity, and show that, as suggested, logical necessity rests upon teleological—that, indeed, it is the teleological read backwards. The logical process of discovering and stating the reality of some event simply reverses the process which the mind goes through in setting up and realizing an end. Instead of the killing of an enemy as something to be accomplished, we have the fact of a murder to be accounted for. Just as on the practical side, the end, as it first arises in consciousness, is an end in general and thus contrasts with the concrete end which is individualized; so the fact, as at first realized in consciousness, is a *bare* fact, and thus contrasts with the actual event with its complete particularization. The actual fact, the murder as it really took place, is one thing; the fact as it stands in consciousness, the phases of the actual event which are picked out and put together, is another thing. The fact of knowledge, it is safe to say, is no *fact* at all; that is, if there had been in reality no more particularization, no more of detail, than there is consciousness, the murder would never have happened. But just as, practically, we take the end in general to be the real thing. (since it is the only thing of any direct interest), so in knowledge we take the bare fact as abstracted from the actual whole, as *the* fact. Just as the end of the savage is merely to kill his enemy, so the "fact" is merely the dead body with the weapon sticking in it. The fact, as it stands in consciousness, is indeterminate and partial, but, since it is in consciousness by itself, it is taken as a whole and as the certain thing. But as the abstractness of the "end in general" is confessed in the fact that means are required in order to make it real—to give it existence—so the unreal character of the "fact" is revealed in the statement that the causes which produced it are unknown and have to be discovered. The bare fact thus becomes a result to be accounted for: in this conception the two sides are combined; the "fact" is at once given a certain reality of its own while at the same time the lack of concreteness is recognized in the reference to external causes.

The gradual introduction of further factors, under the guise of causes accounting for the effect, defines the original vague "fact," until, at last, when it is accounted for, we have before us the one and only concrete reality. This done, we no longer have an effect to be accounted for, and causes which produce it, but one fact whose statement or description is such and such. But intermediate between the isolation and the integration is the stage when necessity appears. We have advanced, we will suppose, from the bare fact of the murder to the discovery of a large amount of "circumstantial" evidence regarding that fact. We hear of a man who had a quarrel with the deceased; he cannot account for himself at the time when the murder *must* have been committed; he is found to have had a weapon like that with which the murder *must* have been committed. Finally we conclude he *must* have been the murderer. What do these "musts" (the "must" of the time, weapon, and murderer) mean? Are they not obviously the gradual filling in of the previously empty judgment, through bringing things at first unconnected into relation with each other? The existence of the man M. N. is wholly isolated from the "fact" of the murder till it is learned that he had a grudge against the murdered man; this third fact, also distinct *per se,* brought into connection with the others (the "fact" of the murder and of the existence of M. N.) compels them to move together; the result is at first the possibility, later, as the points of connection get more and more marked and numerous, the "necessity," that M. N. is the murderer. Further, it is clear that this "must" marks not a greater certainty or actuality than a mere "is" would indicate, but rather a doubt, a surmise or guess gradually gaining in certainty. When the fact is really made out to our satisfaction, we drop the "must" and fall back on the simple *is*. Only so long as there is room for doubt, and thus for argument do we state that the time and weapon must have been such and such. So when we finally conclude that the murderer must have been M. N., it means that we have woven a large number of facts, previously discrete, into such a state of interrelationship that we do not see how to avoid denying their discreteness and incorporating them all into one concrete whole, or individual fact. That we still say "must" shows, however, that we have not quite succeeded in overcoming the partial and indefinite character of the original "fact." Had we succeeded in getting the whole fact before us the judgment would take this form: The murder *is* a fact of such and such definite nature, having as its content such and such precise elements. In this comprehensive whole all distinction, of effect to be accounted for and causes which produce, clean disappears. The idea of necessity, in a word, comes in only while we are still engaged in correcting our original error, but have not surrendered it root and branch; this error being that the fragment of reality which we grasp is concrete enough to warrant the appellation "fact."

A great deal of attention has been directed to the category of cause and effect. One striking feature of the ordinary consideration is that it takes for granted the matter most needing investigation and aims the inquiry at the dependent member of the firm. The effect seems to be so clearly *there,* while the cause is so obviously something to be searched for that the category of effect is assumed, and it is supposed that only the idea of causation is in need of examination. And yet this abstraction of certain phases of fact, the erection of the parts thus abstracted into distinct entities, which, though distinct, are still dependent in their mode of existence, is precisely the point needing examination. It is but another instance of the supreme importance of our practical interests. The effect is the end, the practical outcome, which interests us; the search for causes is but the search for the means which would produce the result. We call it "means and end" when we set up a result to be reached in the future and set ourselves upon finding the causes which put the desired end in our hands; we call it "cause and effect" when the "result" is given, and the search for means is a regressive one. In either case the separation of one side from the other, of cause from effect, of means from end, has the same origin: a partial and vague idea of the whole fact, together with the habit of taking this part (because of its superior practical importance) for a whole, for a fact.

I hope now to have made good my original thesis: that the idea of necessity marks a certain stage in the development of judgment; that it refers to a residuum, in our judgments and thus in our objects, of indeterminateness or vagueness, which it replaces without wholly negating; that it is thus relative to "chance" or contingency; that its value consists wholly in the impulse given judgment towards the *is,* or the concrete reality defined throughout. The analysis has been long; the reader may have found it not only tedious, but seemingly superfluous, since, as he may be saying to himself, no one nowadays regards necessity as anything but a name for fixed uniformities in nature, and of this view of the case nothing has been said. I hope, however, that when we come to a consideration of necessity as equivalent to uniformity, it will be found that the course of this discussion has not been irrelevant, but the sure basis for going further.

12

THE EGO AS CAUSE

PRETTY much all libertarians nowadays insist that their doctrine of freedom of will is quite distinct from the older theory of indifferent choice. They suggest that their opponents are quite out of date in devoting their attention to the latter doctrine, which, under present conditions, is wholly a man of straw; they profess themselves quite as devoted adherents of the doctrine of causation as are the determinists, holding that the sole difference is as to the nature of the cause involved in volition.[1] Now, in one sense, I believe this latter contention to be quite correct; only I should go a step further and say the idea of "causation" as implying a productive agency or determining force has no standing whatever in science—that it is a superstition, and accordingly the libertarian is the *only* believer in causation. Much of the opposition to determinism is due, I believe, to the fact that the determinist either is understood to, or actually does, carry over into his use of the term "cause" this sense of efficient agency, instead of using it in its sole justifiable scientific meaning—the analysis of a vague and unrelated fact into definite and cohering conditions.[2] For my own part, I wish by "causation" to mean nothing more nor less than the possibility of analyzing the vague undefined datum of a volition into a group of specific and concrete conditions, that is, factors.

Admitting then, for sake of argument, the libertarian's

From *The Philosophical Review,* May, 1894; 337-341.

[1] See, for example, the discussion by Dr. Gulliver in *The Philosophical Review,* January, 1894.

[2] With reference to this point I may be permitted to refer to [my] article "The Superstition of Necessity."

position that the ego is an efficient cause of volition, I wish
to make a confession of ignorance and a request for information. My confession is that I cannot frame to myself any conception of freedom of will (in the libertarian sense) which
does not come in the end to the old-fashioned doctrine of a
freedom of indifference. My request is that some libertarian
who sees the distinction clearly will point it out to me.

Let me indicate the special point where I need light. For
the sake of argument, it is conceded that the ego is the cause
of volition in general; that, then, is not the problem. The libertarian, however, puts great stress upon choice between alternatives; as I understand (or *if* I understand) him, the possibility of such choice is the essence of freedom. Now, in order
to avoid pure undeterminism (or the freedom of indifference), it becomes necessary to find a cause for this preference
of one alternative over the other. What is the cause of the
choice of one *rather* than the other? The ego simply as ego
in general *may* be (*ex hypothesi*) the cause of the volition;
but exactly the same ego cannot be the cause of two different
and even quite opposing effects; there must be some difference in the cause when it operates to bring about one effect
from that which would be operative in case the other is effected. I say, "cannot be" and "must be"; the reader will
please understand this not in a dogmatice sense, but as expressing my difficulty; I do not see how identically the same
cause, with no additional qualification whatever, can be regarded as a sufficient explanation of the choice of *a* rather
than of *b*, *except upon the basis of indifferentism*. A stroke
at billiards may be given so as to make a ball move either to
the right or the left; if the ball is so struck that it moves to the
left, it is because some further qualification has entered in
other than that involved in case it moves to the right. Is the
case the same or otherwise with the choice between alternatives? Does identically the same ego, without any further
modification or qualification, choose to steal a loaf of bread
that would also have chosen to go hungry? If yes, then how
does the Neo-libertarian differ from the old-fashioned indif-

ferentist? If no, how does he differ from a determinist—from a determinist that is, who sees that the introduction of this further modification is simply a further step in the concrete analysis of the act?

Be it remembered, it is not a cause for volition in general which is wanted; it is a cause for *this* volition rather than *that:* for choosing hunger rather than dishonesty. The old-fashioned indifferentist has an answer before which I stand rebuked. He, I imagine, would exclaim: "What, do you think to catch me in this easy way? When I tell you that the essence of freedom is the ability to choose either *a* or *b* without any further cause, am I supposed to be so simple as at once to contradict myself by attempting to assign a cause?" I should not know what the indifferentist means, but his meaning (if there be any meaning) would at least be self-consistent. But when I am told both that freedom consists in the ability of an independent ego to choose between alternatives, and that the reference to the *ego* meets the scientific demand with reference to the principle of causation, I feel as if I were being gratuitously fooled with. My libertarian informant must know as well as myself that the question is concerning motivation as to choice; if there is adequate statement for the choice of *a rather* than *b*, surely there is determinism; if there is not, surely there is freedom of indifference. The power of attention is now the favorite philosopher's resort. Putting the question in terms of attention: is there any reason in the conditions of the case, any specific or assignable reason, why attention gives its little boost to this side rather than to that? any assignable condition on the basis of which it gives a jog in this direction rather than in that? As I understand the matter, the whole question lies here: In considering the relation of attention to a given choice, can we (or if foiled in a given instance are we still to try to) carry back our analysis to scientific conditions, or must we stop at a given point because we have come upon a force of entirely a different order—an independent ego as entity in itself? If the action of the latter in swaying mental emphasis this way or that is one of the conditions, can we analyze *this* condition any further, or is it an ultimate fact? If the former, it seems to me an awkward determinism; if the latter, a frank indifferentism.[3]

The same point may be briefly repeated from the ethical side. When one man says to another, "You did that, and I shall hold you responsible for it," he means by his "you," not a metaphysical ego, but a definite individual—John Smith. Every step away from the concrete individual, John Smith, with his special aptitudes, habits, desires, ideas, and ignorances, every step toward an ego in general, means a weakening of the connection between the man and the act, and a release of the man from responsibility for the act. Determinism means that the individual and his act are one. What does libertarianism mean? Will not some libertarian explain to me the causal agency of the ego in volition in terms of some concrete self, instead of in terms of a metaphysical ego?

One point more. Why does the libertarian change his stand-

---

[3] It is somewhat aside from the point in discussion, but when Professor James says that views like the one quoted from Mr. John Fiske, on p. 577, Vol. II, of his *Psychology* are caricatures, arising from "not distinguishing between the possibles which really tempt a man and those which tempt him not at all," and that "free will, like psychology, deals with the former possibles exclusively," this seems partly only a mitigation of the scientific havoc wrought by the idea of free will; and partly to be entering on the deterministic path —and a mitigation *only* so far as the deterministic path is entered upon. From the anti-libertarian standpoint there is no break in the process; the fact of temptation and the fact of choice are related as the more undefined and the more definite establishing of relations within the self, or "between our Self and our own state of mind" (p. 568). Surely the determinist as well as the libertarian may recognize facts of uncertainty, of hesitation, of tentative action, of first trying on this and then that. And it is difficult to see why uncertainty will not do everything in giving zest and sting to life, that James thinks can be given only by sheer liberty (*Psychology*, Vol. I, p. 453). Our feeling that matters are "really being decided" looks to the future, not to the past; consequences *do* depend upon whether we act this way or that—*and this fact is one of the determining factors*. When Mr. James puts as the alternative to libertarianism "the rattling off of a chain that was forged innumerable ages ago," he must have in mind, not logical determinism, but theological *pre*determinism. And the theological view harks back to an independent entity or ego as Cause—to the "free-will" doctrine—not to the determinism of knowledge.

point so completely when considering the act *before* and *after* its performance? When considering the process of volition prior to the overt act, the presence in *consciousness* of two alternatives, the presence there of two attracting, yet incompatible ends, he treats as a fact in itself outside the freedom of will; it is capable of being accounted for on the ordinary principles of habit, association of ideas and desire. It is, he insists, an occasion for the exercise of freedom, but in itself lies outside of will proper. If he admitted the presence of the two alternatives to be an adequate basis for freedom, there would, of course, be no need whatever to call upon the outside entity, the ego. But if this consciousness of different ends, of competing interests, with the process of reflection upon them to ascertain their respective values, does not prove freedom, why use the *memory* of such consciousness—the conviction that we might have acted otherwise—to prove freedom? No determinist (that I know of) denies the facts of conflict of desire, denies that different ends with competing interests attaching to them come to consciousness, or denies the existence of deliberation or a tentative rehearsal of the different acts. He simply urges that choice, when it appears, is the normal psychological conclusion of this same process; that it no more requires the intervention of an outside faculty or entity as efficient cause, than the drawing of a conclusion from theoretical data requires more than recognition of the full meaning of the data.[4] In any case, we should have one interpretation or the other; not a mixture of two contradictory conceptions. Let us say, if we please, that our consciousness of ability to have acted otherwise does prove free-

[4] It is strange that Professor James, who recognizes so far as knowledge is concerned the entire uselessness of an ego outside and behind, who indeed has given that theory the hardest knocks it has yet received from the psychological side (Vol. I, pp. 360-370), should feel bound to set up its correlate when he comes to deal with will. If the stream of thought can run itself in one case, the stream of conduct may administer itself in the other. Why should he deny to the transcendentalist ego in knowing a power which he claims for attention in acting? Historically, I think the independent Ego in knowledge is a survival and transference from the action of an entity of Will in choice.

dom, because the presence in consciousness of alternative ends with the reflection which that calls out, *is* freedom; or, let us say that since this consciousness cannot prove freedom, no subsequent revival of it in memory can prove freedom. In either case, the role of ego as separate efficient agent in causation seems to be excluded.

13

THE PSYCHOLOGY OF INFANT LANGUAGE

I N his interesting and valuable article on *The Language of Childhood*,[1] Mr. Tracy undertakes, upon a basis of 5400 words used by at least twenty different children, to determine the relative frequency of the various parts of speech. Before making some remarks, I wish first to submit my own mite for the further use of students. A refers to a boy; B to a girl, 20 months younger.[2]

A at 19 months old

Parts of Speech		Per cent
Nouns	68	60
Verbs	24	21
Adjectives	13	11
Adverbs	4	3
Interjections	6	5
Total	115	100

Pronouns, prepositions, conjunctions, none.

From *The Psychological Review*, January, 1894; 63-66.

[1] *Am. Jour. Psychol.*, Vol. vi, No. 1, reprinted in *The Psychology of Childhood*, Boston, Heath & Co., 1893.

[2] The presence of other children in the family should always, I think, form part of the data with reference to a child's vocabulary. At least, it is one of the old wives' saws on this matter that the presence of other children both hastens and extends a vocabulary.

B[3] *at* 18 *months old*

Parts of Speech		Per cent
Nouns	76	53
Verbs	40	28
Adjectives	2	1
Adverbs	9	6
Interjections	7	5
Pronouns	8	6
Conjunctions	2	1
Total	144	100

Prepositions, none.

For purposes of comparison, I append the per cents reached by Mr. Tracy by averaging all his results:

Nouns	60
Verbs	20
Adjectives	9
Adverbs	5
Pronouns	2
Prepositions	2
Interjections	1.7
Conjunctions	0.3
	100.0

I wish to remark (1) concerning the relative frequency of verbs, and (2) concerning the different rates of distribution in different children:

1. Mr. Tracy notes that since the relative frequency of verbs in the language is but 11 per cent, the child, *comparatively* speaking, uses verbs with 1.81 the ease with which he uses nouns, and makes some judicious remarks concerning the prevalence of concepts of activity in the child mind. I think he could make his case much stronger. Mr. Tracy, I take it, has classified his words according to the sense which they have to an adult, and I have followed that principle in my own table.[4] In a sense, however, this is as artificial as Mr.

[3] A's vocabulaly was kept continuously; B's vocabulary was taken from words actually used within a period of five or six days; a number of words contained in her vocabulary four months previously do not appear at all.

[4] Phrases like "all light," "all dark," "all gone," "out" (for "go out"), etc., I have treated as verbs. It is obvious that they might be considered either as interjections or as adjectives. The relatively larger per cent of verbs in my table may be due to this classification.

Tracy notes that it is to put knife under *k* instead of under *n*, because *we spell* it with a *k*. The psychological classification is to class the word according to what it means to a child, not to an adult with his grammatical forms all differentiated.

Such a classification would in all probability increase immensely the percentage of verbs. It is true that such a method demands much more care in observation, and opens the way to the very variable error of interpretation; but the greater certainty of the method followed above is after all only seeming—it does not express the *child's* vocabulary, but our interpretation of it according to a fixed but highly conventional standard. It is out of the question to redistribute the language of A and B, given above; but I subjoin the vocabulary of a child in his twelfth month where contemporaneous observation makes me reasonably sure of what the child means:

See there; bye-bye; bottle; papa; mamma; grandma; Freddy; burn; fall; water; down; door; no, no; stop; thank you; boo (peek-a-boo); daw (used when he sees anything which he wants given to him)—17 in all.

Of the above, only the four proper nouns are, psychologically speaking, names of objects. Water is a verb as well as a noun; door is *always* accompanied by gestures of reaching, and an attempt to swing the door back and fro; "daw" is apparently a request, an expression of expectation of something good to eat and the name of a thing all together; bottle certainly has adjectival and verbal implications as well as nominal. At present I should regard it as a complex, "nominal-adjectival-verbal," the emphasis being on the noun, while six weeks previously it was, say, "verbal-adjectival-nominal." "Stop"; "no, no"; "burn"; "see there," etc., are equally interjections and verbs. "Thank you" is at times a request for something, and is almost invariably said when giving an article to anyone else. We have then a graded and continuous series, so far as *sense* is concerned, the proper names (23 per cent) at one end, and the interjectional forms "no, no," "peek-a-boo," at the other. These have a verbal coloring, however. Between these classes are a nominal-adjectival-verbal-interjectional complex, the verbal-interjectional meaning prevailing on the whole, the adjectival in all cases subordinate.[5] The tendency to apply the same term to a large number of objects ("ball" to ball, orange, moon, lamp globe, etc.) can be understood, I think, only if we keep in mind the extent to which the formal noun, "ball," has really an active sense. "Ball" is "to throw" just as much as it is the round thing. I do not believe that the child either confuses the moon with his ball, or abstracts the roundness of it; the roundness suggests to him something which he has thrown, so that the moon is something to throw —if he could only get hold of it.

What I would suggest, then, along the line of a study of the distribution of vocabulary into parts of speech is such observation and record as would note carefully the original sense to the child of his words, and the gradual *differentiation* of the original protoplasmic verbal-nominal-interjectional form (as it seems to me), until words assume their present rigidity.

2. No one can examine the statistics given without being struck by the great differences in different children. F, in Mr. Tracy's tables, has 15 per cent interjections; while K, with a vocabulary of 250 words, has none at all. F has 11 per cent adverbs; while K has but 2 per cent; in my own table, A has 4, while B has 9 per cent. So in my two, A has 11 per cent adjectives; B 1 per cent; while Mr. Tracy's vary from a maximum of 13 to a minimum of 3 per cent. I believe the tendency in all psychological investigation, at present, is to attempt to get a *uniform* mathematical statement, eliminating individual differences; for pedagogical and ethical purposes, at least, it is these differences which are, finally, most important. And on strictly psychological grounds the varying ratio of adverbs

[5] The fact that interjections fail so late, as a rule, in aphasia, taken with the highly immediate and emotional character of child life, indicates the defective character of a method of classification which reduces the percentage of interjections to 1.7. The philologist's objections to making interjections a primitive form of speech, however sound grammatically, seem to me to rest upon attaching a limited, technical sense to the concept *interjection*, which is without ground psychologically. In the infant mind (whether race or child) the emotional state and the tendency to react aroused by an object *must*, I should say, be fused, and both precede any clear recognition of the "object" as such, or of any objective quality.

and pronouns on one side and nouns and adjectives on the other must denote a very different psychological attitude— different methods of attaching interest and distributing attention. Observations of different mental traits as connected with these linguistic differences would not only add to the *terra incognita,* individual psychology (and it would seem that all psychology must be finally individual), but throw great light upon the psychology of language. How vague and formal at present our answers, for example, when we are asked to what psychological state and need an adverb corresponds!

14

THE THEORY OF EMOTION

I. EMOTIONAL ATTITUDES

IN this part of my examination of the theory of emotion I propose, assuming Darwin's principles as to the explanation of emotional attitudes, and the James-Lange theory of the nature of emotion, to bring these two into some organic connection with each other, indicating the modifications of statement demanded by such connection. This close dependence upon results already reached, together with the impossibility of an adequate discussion of all details in the given limits (to say nothing of the immediate availability of most of the details in every one's experience), must be my justification for the generic, and even schematic, quality of the discussion. This may be regarded either as a sketch map of a field previously surveyed, or as a possible outline for future filling in, not as a proved and finished account.

The necessity of bringing the two theories together may be seen from the fact that the very phrase "expression of emotion," as well as Darwin's method of stating the matter, begs the question of the relation of emotion to organic peripheral action, in that it assumes the former as prior and the latter as secondary.

1. Now this assumption, upon the basis of the discharge theory (as I shall call the James-Lange theory), is false. If one accept the latter theory, it is incumbent upon him to find the proper method of restating Darwin's principles, since there is no doubt of their substantial significance, however erroneous

From *The Psychological Review*, January, 1894; 553-569.

may be their underlying assumption as to the relation of emotion and peripheral disturbance.[1]

Professor James himself does not seem to me to have adequately realized the inconsistency of Darwin's principles, as the latter states them, with his own theory; or the needed restatement would already have been performed by a much more competent hand than my own. At least he quotes, with apparent approval, explanations from Darwin which assume the priority of an emotion of distress to the contraction of the brows; and even suggests that Darwin does not go far enough in recognizing the principle of reacting similarly to analogous feeling stimuli.[2] Surely if James's conception of the origin of emotion is true, the statement that we react similarly to stimuli which feel alike must be translated into the statement that activities which involve, in like fashion, the same peripheral structures feel alike.[3]

2. One does not, however, need to be committed to James's

[1] While Darwin's language is that of the dependence of "expression" upon emotion, it is interesting to note that so careful an observer has, in one place, anticipated and definitely stated the discharge theory, *Expression of Emoions*, p. 239. (My references are to the American edition.) "Most of our emotions are so closely connected with their expression that they hardly exist if the body remains passive—the nature of the expression depending in chief part on the nature of the actions which have been habitually performed under this particular state of mind." (Note in this latter phrase the assumption of the priority of emotion; but the coutinuation is unambiguous in the other sense.) "A man, for instance, may know that his life is in extremest peril, and may strongly desire to save it; yet as Louis XVI said when surrounded by a fierce mob, 'Am I afraid? Feel my pulse.' So a man may intensely hate another, *but until his bodily frame is affected* he cannot be said to be enraged." (Italics mine.)

[2] *Psychology*, Vol. II, pp. 480-81. The exactness of the latter statement may be doubted, as Darwin recognizes the facts, but includes them under the principle of serviceable associated habits (*Expression*, 256), as he certainly has a right to; for Mr. James himself recognizes (p. 481, footnote) that the "analogous feeling" principle goes back to the teleology of the movements concerned.

[3] The *facts* conveyed in this principle seem to me of themselves a strong argument for the discharge theory. Left as Darwin and Wundt state it, all mediating machinery, physiological and psychological, is absent, and we cannot even start a hypothesis as to *how* a feeling (recognizing that it feels *like* another feeling!) sets out along the same afferent paths. Upon the discharge theory the mystery vanishes and we have the practical tautology: like affections of like structures give like feeling, the interest lying in the gentic tracing of the details.

theory to feel the need of a different way of stating the particular undoubted facts discovered by Darwin. Physiologists agree that there are no muscles intended primarily for purposes of expression. A psychological translation of this would be that there is no such thing (from the standpoint of the one having the experience) as expression. We call it expression when looking at it from the standpoint of an observer—whether a spectator or the person himself as scientifically reflecting upon his movements, or aesthetically enjoying them. The very word "expression" names the facts not as they are, but in their second intention.[4] To an onlooker my angry movements are expressions—signs, indications; but surely not to me. To rate such movements as primarily expressive is to fall into the psychologist's fallacy: it is to confuse the standpoint of the observer and explainer with that of the fact observed. Movements *are*, as matter of fact, expressive, but they are also a great many other things. In themselves they are movements, acts, and must be treated as such if psychology is to take hold of them right end up.

3. I shall attempt to show, hereafter, that this standpoint of expression of pre-existent emotion complicates and aborts the explanation of the relevant facts in the cases of "antithesis" and "direct nervous discharge." At this stage I wish to point out that in the case of "serviceable associated habits," the principle of explanation *actually* used, whatever the form of words employed, is that of survival, in the form of attitudes, of acts originally useful not *qua* expressing emotion, but *qua* acts—as serving life. In the discussion of movements in animals the reference to emotion is not even nominal. It is a matter of "satisfaction of desire" and "relieving disagreeable sensations"—practical ends. The expressions of grief and of anxiety (Chs. VI and VII) are explained, in their detail, whatever the general phraseology employed, by reference to acts

---

[4] This, of course, is in no way inconsistent with the development of certain movements to serve as expressive. On the contrary, since movements take place in a social medium, and their recognition and interpretation by others is a fact of positive import in the struggle for existence, we might expect the development of gesture and signs through selection.

useful in themselves. It would take up too much space to follow all cases in particular, but the book is open and the reader may easily discover whether in every case the idea of expression of emotion does not enter in only to confuse. *The reference to emotion in explaining the attitude is wholly irrelevant; the attitude of emotion is explained positively by reference to useful movements.*

An examination of one apparent exception may serve to clear up the principle. Of laughter, Mr. Darwin says, "We can see in a vague manner how the utterance of sounds of some sort would naturally become associated with a pleasurable state of mind." But Darwin does not use this idea, even in a "vague" way. With his inevitable candor he goes on, "But why the sounds which man utters when he is pleased have the peculiar reiterated character of laughter we do not know."

Now I am not so rash as to attempt to deal in detail with laughter and its concomitant features, but I think something at least a little less vague than Mr. Darwin's account may be given. I cannot see, even in the vaguest way, why pleasure *qua* feeling (emotion?) should express itself in uttering sounds. As matter of fact it does not, nor even in smiles;[5] it is pleasure of a certain qualitative excitement or vivacity which breaks out in laughter, and what we can see, in a "vague way," is why excitement affecting the entire organism should discharge in the vocal apparatus. The problem is the discovery of that special form of excited action which differentiates the laugh from other excitations. Observe a crowd of amateurs just from a game. Note how, irrespective of what they say, you can judge whether they have won or lost. In one case postures are erect, lungs frequently expanded, movements quick, abrupt, and determined; there is much gesturing, talking, and laughing in high keys—a scene which, looking at it "ejectively," we term one of liveliness, exhilaration, etc. In the other case there is little speaking, and that subdued; all move-

[5] The "pleasures" of eating have their characteristic attitude—smacking lips, rolling tongue; the pleasures of sex theirs, etc. Many pleasures are accompanied by holding the breath to maintain the excitation at its maximum, not at all by the expiration found in laughter.

ments tend to be slow, or, if rapid, indicate a desire to escape or expel something; meditative postures are frequently observed, etc.—a scene of depression. It is the contrast between spontaneous overflow and lowering of overt activity.

What is the difference? In either case the energy, muscular, nervous and visceral, aroused in the game persists to some extent. What determines the antithetical lines of discharge of this surplus energy (that antithesis of "dejection" and "elation" running through all our terms)? In one case, I answer, there are frictionless lines of action, harmonized activity; or, in more psychological language, all existing kinesthetic images reinforce and expand one another; in the other case there are two more or less opposed lines of activity going on—the images of the present situation and those of the past game cannot be co-ordinated. The energy is largely directed "inward"; that is, it is used up in rethinking the game, in making hypothetical changes, in recalling blunders (that is, images which one wants to expel), etc. The movements appropriate to the present activity cannot be identified with the nervous and motor energies which image the game. In the case of exhilaration, etc., there is identification of the thoughts (the nerve and muscular activities relative to the past game) and the present motor discharges.

The connection between *il penseroso* and melancholy more or less mild, and between *l'allegro* and joy, is thus organic and literal, not one of chance or analogy—as if analogy were somehow a force! When one can put up with his defeat, it ceases to bother him, he does not consider it longer. That is, the "downcast" emotion and the intellectual reflection vanish together—the moment there is identification of images. The essential identity of the attitudes of thought and of regret is because of the condition of divided activity; there is still a struggle. Means and end are apart. The identity of attitudes of joy and of activity, of life (alert, wide awake, brisk, animated, vivacious, cheerful, gay—showy, lively, sprightly), is because of the unification of activity. Meditation and regret are both activities of arrest, of conflict; joy and "lively" movement, of stimulation—expansion. No wonder, then, they have the same signs.

Thinking, to be sure, in certain professions, though not for the ordinary man, is an end in itself. In so far as thinking is an end in itself, the activity is unified and has its own joys. It ceases to be occupied with merely instrumental, and (therefore) more or less burdensome, movements. Yet the pangs, the travail of thought, the arduousness of reflection, the loneliness of meditation, the heaviness of deliberation, are all proverbial. Only in rare cases is the whole system involved or unified, and the joy voluminous. Its ordinary form is the "thrill" of identification or the satisfaction of "good taste" in a clear, neat discrimination. When a long and comprehensive process is concluding and approaching its final successful or unified discharge, then, indeed, the hand of a Newton may tremble and joy become intoxicating. But I cannot admit, even in a half-hearted way, the idea that the sense of abundance and ease in thought may be purely cerebral.[6] It appears to me that it is in a literal sense that the object "sets trains going"—these are revivals of motor discharge and organic reinforcement. Upon such occasions thinking becomes really wholehearted; it takes possession of us altogether, and passes over into the aesthetic.

This, however, is only preparatory to the question of the specific "sign" of joy, the laugh. How is that to be brought under this principle of being an actual portion of a useful activity? Why should the excitation, admitting that it affects the vocal organs, manifest itself in this form? While I feel pretty sure of the following explanation, I cannot hope that it will convince many. Though the result of considerable observation, it can be briefly summed up. The laugh is by no means to be viewed from the standpoint of humor; its connection with humor is secondary. It marks the ending (that is, the attainment of a unity) of a period of suspense, or expectation,

---

[6] Such distinctions as James makes here—in reality purely verbally—between spiritual and physiological, instead of between cerebral and visceromotor, are what give the opponent the sole reason for labeling the theory materialistic —as if the bowels were really more material than the brain!

an ending which is sharp and sudden. Rhythmical activities, as peek-a-boo, call out a laugh at every culmination of the transition, in an infant. A child of from one and a half to two years uses the laugh as a sign of assent; it is his emphatic "I do" or "yes" to any suggested idea to which he agrees or which suddenly meets his expectations.

A very moderate degree of observation of adults will convince one that a large amount of laughter is wholly irrelevant to any joke or witticism whatever. It is a constant and repeated "sign" of attaining suddenly to a point. Now all expectancy, waiting, suspended effort, etc., is accompanied, for obvious teleological reasons, with taking in and holding a full breath, and the maintenance of the whole muscular system in a state of considerable tension. It is a divided activity, part of the kinesthetic images being fixed upon the immediately present conditions, part upon the expected end. Now let the end suddenly "break," "dawn," let one see the "point" and this energy discharges—the getting the point is the unity, the discharge. This sudden relaxation of strain, so far as occurring through the medium of the breathing and vocal apparatus, is laughter. Its rhythmical character seems to be simply a phase of the general teleological principle that all well-arranged or economical action is rhythmical.[7] The laugh is thus a phenomenon of the same general kind as the sigh of relief. The difference is that the latter occurs when the interest is in the *process,* and when the idea of labor, slow and continuous, is at its height; while the laugh occurs when the interest is all in the outcome, the result—the sudden, abrupt appearance of the "point." In one case the effort is continued until it accomplishes something; in the other case the effort is arrested, and then the energy accumulated is set free from a seemingly outside source. The connection of humor with the laugh, and the ideas of relative superiority–triviality, and of incongruity, involved in humor, etc., seem to be simply more complex, and more intellectually loaded, differentiations of this general principle.

[7] Acute crying, etc., is non-rhythmical; when it does take the form of rhythmical sobbing, one experiences a sensation of relief—grief has "moderated."

Not only are joy and grief practically in a peculiar qualitative antithesis, seeming to imply a common principle of which they are the extremes, but the "signs" of joy and grief, especially when these become violent, are identical. This fact, otherwise so meaningless, becomes natural if we adopt the above explanation. Both crying and laughing fall under the same principle of action—the termination of a period of effort. If we fix our attention upon the conventional and literary conceptions of grief, this will seem farfetched; if we take children and simple cases, it seems to stare us in the eyes. Crying is either a part of an effort to expel an intruder,[8] an effort so general as to engage spasmodically the lungs and vocal organs (a sort of general gripe); or, as we see so often in children, an explosion of energy, accumulated in preparation for some act, suddenly discharged *in vacuo* upon the missing of the essential part, the finishing factor of the act.[9]

Beginning with the simpler case, the phenomena of matured grief become easily explainable. They are phenomena of *loss*. Reactions surge forth to some stimulus, or phase of a situation; the object appropriate to most of these, the factor necessary to co-ordinate all the rising discharges, is gone; and hence they interfere with one another—the expectation, or kinesthetic image, is thrown back upon itself.

4. In dealing with grief we have unconsciously entered upon a new field. The point of our third head is that the principle which Darwin calls that of "movements useful in expressing an emotion" explains the relevant facts only when changed to read "useful as parts of an act which is useful as

[8] While Darwin's explanation of shutting the eyes—to protect blood vessels from gorging on account of the violent screaming—undoubtedly accounts for the selection of this attitude, it can hardly account for its origin. I think originally it had the same end as screaming—to shut out or off some threatening object, as the ostrich, etc., or as one shuts his eyes on firing a gun the first time.

[9] I suppose everyone has seen a young child go into a rage of screams and violent movements upon being handed, say, a broken cooky. The thing explains itself on the above principle. The concluding factor in a co-ordination of energy does not appear, and the child goes literally to pieces. I should like to see any explanation upon the anti-James theory, save that offered by Saint Augustine for similar phenomena of his infancy—total depravity.

movement." In dealing with grief we have passed over into the phenomena of the breakdown of a given teleological co-ordination, and the performance of acts which, therefore, objectively viewed, are not only useless but may be harmful. My proposition at this point is that the phenomena referred to the principle of direct nervous discharge (the response to an idiopathic stimulus) are cases of the failure of habitual teleological machinery, through some disturbance in one or more of the adjusted members of the habit.

In order to avoid misconception, let me point out a great ambiguity in the use of the term idiopathic. In one sense even the "associated useful" movements are idiopathic, provided, that is, they originally were useful in reaching an end, and not simply in expressing an emotion. They are the reactions to their appropriate stimuli, and the sole difference between them and the liver changes, nausea, palpitation of heart, etc., usually classed as idiopathic, is that in them stimuli and reaction are more definitely limited to certain particular channels than in the latter cases; there is a defined, as against a vague and diffuse, direct nervous discharge. The fact that this defined discharge happens to be useful may state the kind of idiopathic response we have, but cannot make it other than a response. Furthermore, upon evolutionary principles, the limited, adjusted, and useful discharge must be a differentiation, selected and perpetuated because of its utility in the struggle for life, out of an original more diffuse and irradiating wave of discharge.

Admitting, then, that all emotional attitudes whatever are idiopathic in the broad sense, the sole difference being in the definiteness or limitation of the stimulus and its response, what are we to do with the cases now disposed of as "idiopathic" in the narrower sense?—such phenomena as Mr. James briefly but excellently sums up. My proposition, I repeat, is that all such idiopathic discharges, possessing emotional quality, are in reality disturbances, defects, or alienations of the *adjusted* movements. While not immediately teleological in the sense that they themselves are useful, they are teleologically conditioned. They are cases of the disintegration of associations (co-ordinations) which are serviceable, or are the use of means under circumstances in which they are totally inappropriate.

Idiopathic discharges which are not themselves adjusted movements or the disturbances of such adjusted movements do not appear to me to have any *emotional* quality at all. The trembling with cold or sheer fatigue is certainly qualitatively different from the tremble of rage or fear. The sensations of weakness in the bowels and of nausea, which are idiopathic to their appropriate stimuli, can be called emotional only by such a stretch of the term as renders all sensations and impulses emotions. Professor James seems to me wholly successful in dealing with the charge brought that, upon his theory, all laughing ought to give the mirthful emotion, all vomiting that of disgust, etc.[10] The diffusive wave in one case is incomplete; but is there no reason or meaning in this difference? There is no doubt, in my own mind, that, *under existing conditions,* the supplying of the missing organic excitations will change the laugh and the nausea into mirth and disgust as emotions—this without any change in the "object." But whence and why these "existing conditions"? The change from mere cachinnation to mirthful emotion is a distinct change in psychical quality, and this change of quality does not seem to be adequately *accounted* for by mere addition of more discharges—though, I repeat, simply adding on more discharges will undoubtedly *make* this difference. If these supplementary factors report the meaning or value of past co-ordinations, this change of quality is reasonable and inevitable; if not, if they are simply some more accidental discharges, the peculiar qualitative "feel" is miraculous—it admits of no explanation.

This is but to say, from the psychological side, that all normal emotion of terror has an *object,* and involves an attitude *toward* that object; this attitude, under the given circumstances, perhaps not being useful, nay, being harmful, but yet the reproduction of an attitude or, rather, a mixture of attitudes which have been useful in the past. The useless-

[10] *Psychological Review,* September, 1894; 522.

ness of the attitude is due to the fact that some feature in the stimulus (the situation or object) awakens its appropriate reactions, but these do not co-ordinate with the reactions aroused by other features of the situation. The pathological emotion is, as Mr. James calls it, the *objectless* emotion, but its content is controlled by the active attitudes previously assumed toward objects, and, *from its own standpoint,* it is not objectless; it goes on at once to supply itself with an object, with a rational excuse for being.[11] This immediate correlation of the emotion with an "object," and its immediate tendency to assume the "object" when it is not there, seem to me mere tautology for saying that the emotional attitude is normally rational in content (*i.e.,* adjusted to some end), and, even in pathological cases, sufficiently teleological in form to subsume an object for itself.

In any case, upon James's theory, the admission of any idiopathic cases which cannot be reduced to abnormal use of teleological adjustments is more or less intolerable. Their permanent resistance to such reduction would be a strong objection to the theory. Hope, fear, delight, sorrow, terror, love, are too important and too relevant in our lives to be in the main[12] the "feel" of bodily attitudes which have themselves no meaning. If the attitude is wholly accidental, then the emotion itself is brute and insignificant, upon a theory which holds that the emotion is the "feel" of such an attitude.

One more word of general explanation. The antithesis here is between the merely accidental and the adjusted excitation—not between the mechanical and the teleological. I add this because of the following sentence in James: "It seems as if even the changes of blood-pressure and heart-beat during emotional excitement might, instead of being teleologically determined, prove to be purely mechanical or physiological out-

[11] The pathological emotion is to the normal as hallucination is to perception. An unusual stimulus takes advantage of and controls the lines of coordination and discharge which have been built up with reference to the usual or normal stimulus. Psychologically the process is quite regular; it is only in its teleology that it is "off."

[12] In the main, I say; for doubtless it is pedantry to hold that every slight feature of the attitude is conditioned by an activity directed toward an object.

pourings through the easiest drainage-channels." Certainly, if these are the alternatives, I should go a step further and say that even the clenching of the fist and the retraction of the lips in anger are simply mechanical outpourings through the easiest available channel. But these are not the alternatives. The real question is simply how this particular channel came to be the easiest possible, whether purely accidentally or because of the performance of movements having some value for life preservation. The ground taken here is that the easiest path is determined by habits which, upon the whole, were evolved as useful.[13]

Coming a little more to details, it is obvious that the teleological principle carries within itself a certain limitation. Normal and usual are identical; the habit is based upon the customary features of the situation. The very meaning of habit is limitation to a certain average range of fluctuation. Now if an entirely strange (forgive the contradiction in terms) stimulus occurs, there will be no disturbance of function, though the organism may be destroyed by the impact of the foreign force. But let some of the features of a situation habitually associated in the past with other features be present while these others fail, or let the ordinary proportion or relative strength of stimuli be changed, or let their mode of connection be reversed, and there is bound to be a disturbance and a resulting activity which, *objectively viewed,* is non-teleological. We thus get an *a priori* canon, as it were, for determining when, in a given emotion, we shall get symptoms falling under the "serviceable associated habit" principle and when under the idiopathic. Whenever the various factors of the act, muscular movement, nutritive, respiratory, and circulatory changes, are co-ordinated and reinforce each other,

[13] It is admitted, of course, as Mr. James puts it, that there are "reactions incidental to others evolved for utility's sake, but which would never have been evolved independently." Indeed, in one sense of the term "incidental" this is a necessary part of my proposition. The only qustion is whether "incidental" means purposeless, or means having their purpose not in themselves, but as relative to, as facilitating or reinforcing, some other useful act. The fact, once more, that upon Darwin's method of statement no such relative or incidental movements can be admitted is an undoubted objection to Darwin's mode of statement of the principle of useful habit.

it is the former; whenever they interfere (the "idiopathic"), the "feel" of this interference *is* (applying the general principle of James) the pathological rage, or terror, or expectation.

Once more, we work in a wrong, a hopeless direction when we start from the emotion and attempt to derive the movements as its expression; while the situation clears itself up when we start from the character of the movement, as a completed or disturbed co-ordination, and then derive the corresponding types of normal and pathological emotion. We can understand why the so-called idiopathic principle comes into play in all cases of extreme emotion, the maximum limit seeming to be the passage into spasm when it assumes a rigid type, of hysteria when it involves complete breakdown of co-ordination.

The attitude of normal fear may be accounted for upon direct teleological principles; the holding of breath marks the effort; the opening of mouth, the act arrested halfway; the opening of eyes, the strained attention; the shiver, of retraction; the crouching down, the beginning of escape; the rapid beating of heart, the working up of energy for escape, etc. Now if these activities go on to complete themselves, if, that is, they suggest the further reaction which will co-ordinate into a definite response, we get judicious fear—that is, caution. Now if these do not suggest a further movement which completes the act, some or all of these factors begin to assert themselves in consciousness, isolatedly or in alternation—there is confusion. Moreover, each particular phase of the act which is normal in co-ordination, as the more rapid beating of the heart, being now uncontrolled by lack of its relevant motor associates, is exaggerated and becomes more and more violent. The response to the normal demand for more nutrition finds no regular outlet in supplying the motor energy for the useful act, and the disturbances of viscera and associated organs propagate themselves. The trembling marks, so far as I can see, simply this same disco-ordination on the side of the muscular system. It is the extreme of vacillating indecision; we start to do this, that, and the other thing, but each act falls athwart its predecessor.

Speaking roughly, there is exaggeration of the entire vegetative functions of the activity, and defect of the motor side—
the unstriped muscles being included, on a functional basis,
with the vegetative system. Now this is just what we might
expect when there is a great stirring up of energy preparatory
to activity, but no defined channel of discharge. Thus the
agent becomes entirely taken up with its own state and is unable to attend to the object.

The pathological emotion is, then, simply a case of morbid
self-consciousness. Those factors of the organism which relate
most immediately to the welfare of the organism, the vegetative functions, absorb consciousness, instead of being, as they
normally are, subsidiary to the direction of muscular activity
with reference to the "object." This is equally true in extreme
terror, and in being "beside one's self" with anger. The cases
in which sanguine excitement and apprehension affect the
bladder will be found, I believe, to be almost uniformly cases
where it is not possible to do anything at once with the
aroused activities; they cannot be controlled by being directed
toward the putting forth of effort upon the "object," that
being too remote or uncertain.

Certainly, the principle for attitudes commonly called those
of morbid self-consciousness is precisely the one just laid
down. In these cases muscular (not vegetative) functions normally useful in the attainment of an end are first aroused in
response to stimuli, and then, not being completely co-
ordinated into action, are *not* used with reference to the end,
and so stand out in consciousness on their own account. I
shall not attempt any detailed statement here, but leave it
to the reader to answer if the above does not give a precise
generic description of the sensations of awkwardness, of bash-
fulness, of being ridiculous (as when one starts an appropriate
movement, but is made conscious of it in itself apart from its
end) on one side, and of affected grace, mincing ease, pom-
posity and conceit on the other.

All these facts taken cumulatively seem to me to render it
fairly certain that the "idiopathic" cases, as a rule, are to be
conceived of as the starting of activities formerly useful for

a given end, but which now, for some reason, fail to function, and therefore stand out in consciousness apart from the needed end.

5. I come now to the principle of antithesis. According to Mr. Darwin, when certain movements have been habitually of service in connection with certain emotions, there is a tendency, when a directly opposite state of mind is induced, to the performance of movements of a directly opposite nature, *"though these have never been of any use"* (italics mine). Here we have a crucial case; if the antithesis of the emotion determines the antithesis of expression, James's theory is, in so far, overthrown; if, on the other hand, the antithesis of "expression" goes back to activities having their own ends, the ground is at least cleared for the discharge theory.

Beginning with animals, Mr. Darwin illustrates his principle of antithesis from the cat and dog. No one can read his account or examine the pictures without being convinced that the movements *are* antithetical. But there is something intolerable to the psychologist in the supposition that an opposite emotion can somehow select for itself channels of discharge not already used for some specific end, and those channels such as give rise to directly opposed movements. Antithesis is made a causal force. Such an idea is not conceivable without some presiding genius who opens valves and pulls strings. The absence of mediating machinery, of interlinking phenomena, is even more striking in this case than in that of "analogous feeling."

If, again, the matter be treated as a case of the connection of movements with reference to certain acts, the mystery vanishes. Mr. Darwin's cases are taken from domestic animals. Now wild animals have, speaking roughly, just two fundamental characteristic attitudes—those connected with getting food, including attack upon enemies, and those of defense, including flight, etc. A domestic animal, by the very fact that it is domestic, has another characteristic attitude, that of reception—the attitude of complete adaptation to something outside itself. This attitude is constituted, of course, by a certain co-ordination of movements; and these are antithetical

THE THEORY OF EMOTION

to those movements involved in the contrary attitude, that of resistance or opposition. A study of dogs will show that the attitude of opposition is naturally self-centered and braced, the best position from which to fall, on one side, into an attitude of overt attack, and, upon the other side, into that of resistance to attack. The attitude of "humility" and "affection" consists, as Mr. Darwin well says, in continuous, flexuous movements. These movements are precisely those of response and adaptation. The center of gravity is, as it were, in the master, and the lithe and sinuous movement is the solution of the problem of maintaining balance with respect to every change in this external center of gravity. It is the attitude of receiving favor and food from another. The dependence is actual, not symbolic. Unless Mr. Darwin were prepared to equip the animal with a full-fledged moral consciousness, the "humble" attitude of the dog can hardly be other than the habitual attitude of reception, or the "affectionate" attitude other than the recurrence of movements associated with the food getting. The same general principle will apply to the antithetical cat expressions, save that the dependence in the case of the cat assumes more the form of passive contact and less that of active adjustment. The reminiscence of sexual attitude is possibly also more marked.[14]

The other cases of antithesis given by Mr. Darwin are the shrug of impotence, and the raising of the hands in great astonishment. I feel certain that the rational hypothesis is to suppose that these are survivals of certain acts, and not symbolic indications of certain emotions. As a contribution to such a working hypothesis, I suggest the possibility that the throwing up of the arms in attention is partly the survival of a movement of warding off the approaching hostile object,

[14] Being unable to do anything with these cases, I called them to the notice of my friend and colleague, Mr. G. H. Mead. The explanation given, which seems to me indubitable, is his. The relation between the vegetative and the motor functions, given above in discussion of pathological emotion and to be used again below, I also owe to him. While I have employed the point only incidentally, Mr. Mead rightly makes it essential to the explanation of emotion and its attitudes, as distinct from the identification and description which alone I have attempted. I hope, therefore, that his whole theory may soon appear in print.

and partly a reinforcement of the holding of the chest full of air characteristic of expectancy and of astonishment—a movement whose analogue is found in the raising and drawing back of the arms in yawning.[15] The shrug of impotence seems to be complex; the union of survivals of three or four distinct acts. The raising of the brows is the act of retrospect, of surveying the ground to see if anything else could have been done; the pursing of the lips, the element of tentative rejection (doubt); the raising of the shoulders, the act of throwing a burden off (cf. "he shouldered it off on someone else"); the holding out of the hand, palm up, the attitude of asking or taking. To my introspection the *quale* of the emotion agrees entirely; it is a feeling of "I don't see how I could possibly have done anything else, so far as I am concerned, but I'm willing to hear what you have to offer"—of "I don't know; you tell." It thus has the distinctly expressive or social element in it, and marks the passing over of emotional attitude into gesture.

Summing up, we may say that all so-called expressions of emotions are, in reality, the reduction of movements and stimulations originally useful into attitudes. But we note a difference in the form and nature of the reduction, and in the resulting attitudes, which explain the apparent diversity of the four principles of "serviceable associated habits," of "analogous stimuli," of "antithesis," and of "direct nervous discharge." A given movement or set of movements may be useful either as preparatory to, as leading up to, another set of acts, or in themselves as accomplished ends. Movements of effort, of bracing, of reaching, etc., evidently come under the former head. Here we have the case of useful associated movements in its strict sense. The culmination of all these preparatory adjustments is the attainment of food or of the sexual embrace. In so far as we have attitudes which reflect these acts, satisfying in themselves, we get cases of so-called analogous stimuli. The antithetical attitudes of joy and grief, and

---

[15] Since writing the text, I have repeatedly noticed this attitude of the arms, without the rigidity, assumed by a child of two years while watching the preparation of his food.

all that is differentiated from them, mark the further development of actual attainment of an end (or failure to get it) occurring when the activity specially appropriate to the particular end reached (or missed) is reinforced and expanded by a wide range of contributory muscular and visceral changes. The cases of failure bring us to the breakdown of co-ordinations habitually useful, to their alienation, or to reciprocal disturbance of their various factors, and thus to the facts usually subsumed under the idiopathic principle. In this progression we have a continually changing ratio of the vegetative to the motor functions. In the preparatory adjustments the latter has the highest exponent, and the strictly emotional *quale* of feeling is at its minimum. In joy and grief, as in less degree with "sweetness," disgust, etc., the organic resonance is at its height, but strictly subservient to the motor performances. In the idiopathic these vegetative functions break loose and run away, and thus, instead of reinforcing the efficiency of behavior, interefere by their absorption of consciousness.

II. THE SIGNIFICANCE OF EMOTIONS[16]

[In the foregoing] I endeavored to show that all the so-called expressions of emotion are to be accounted for not by reference to emotion, but by reference to movements having some use, either as direct survivals or as disturbances of teleological co-ordinations. I tried to show that, upon this basis, the various principles for explaining emotional attitudes may be reduced to certain obvious and typical *differentiae* within the teleological movements. [Now] I wish to reconsider the James-Lange, or discharge, theory of the nature of emotion from the standpoint thus gained; for if all emotions (considered as "emotional seizures," *Affect* or "feel," as I may term it) are constituted by the reflexion of the teleological attitude, the motor and organic discharges, into consciousness, the same principle which explains the attitude must serve to analyze the emotion.

[16] From *The Psychological Review,* January, 1895; 13-32.

The fact, if it be a fact, that all "emotional expression" is a phase of movements teleologically determined, and not a result of pre-existent emotion, is itself a strong argument for the discharge theory. I had occasion to point out [above] that the facts brought under the head of "antithesis" and "analogous stimuli" are absolutely unaccountable upon the central theory, and are matters of course upon the James theory. But this statement may be further generalized. If every emotional attitude is referred to useful acts, and if the emotion is *not* the reflex of such act, where does it come in, and what is its relation to the attitude? The first half of the hypothesis prevents its being the antecedent of the attitude; the latter half of the hypothesis precludes its being the consequent. If it is said that the emotion is a mere side issue of that central excitation (corresponding to the purpose) which issues in the muscular and organic changes, then we are entitled to ask, *a priori*, for some explanation of its unique appearance at this point, some sort of mechanical or teleological *causa essendi;* and, *a posteriori*, to point out that, as matter of fact, everyone now supposes that his emotion, say of anger, does have *some* kind of direct relation to his movements—in fact, common usage compels us to speak of them as movements of anger. I think, then, that logic fairly demands either the surrender of the "central" theory of emotion or else a refutation of [my analysis of emotional attitudes] and a proof that emotional attitudes are to be explained by reference to emotion, and not by reference to acts.

More positively, this reference to serviceable movement in explanation of emotional attitudes, taken in connection with the hypothesis that the emotional "feel" is always due to the return wave of this attitude, supplies a positive tool for the analysis of emotion in general and of particular emotions in especial. As indicating the need of a further consideration, it may be pointed out that Mr. James himself lays the main emphasis of his theory upon its ability to account for the *origin* of emotions, and as supplying emotion with a "physical basis," not upon the psychological analysis which it might yield of the nature of emotional experience. Indeed, James definitely relegates to the background the question of classification,[17] saying that the question of genesis becomes all-important. But every theory of genesis must become a method of analysis and classification. The discharge theory does, indeed, give the *coup de grâce* to the fixed pigeonhole method of classification, but it opens the door for the genetic classification. In other words, it does for the emotions precisely what the theory of evolution does in biology; it destroys the arbitrary and subjective schemes, based on mere possession of likenesses and differences, and points to an objective and dynamic classification based on descent from a given functional activity, gradually differentiated according to the demands of the situation. The general conclusion indicated regarding the nature of emotion is that:

Emotion in its entirety is a mode of behavior which is purposive, or has an intellectual content, and which also reflects itself into feeling or Affects, as the subjective valuation of that which is objectively expressed in the idea or purpose.[18]

This formula, however, is no more than a putting together of James's theory with the revision of Darwin's principles [I] attempted. If an attitude (of emotion) is the recurrence, in modified form, of some teleological movement, and if the specific differentia of emotional consciousness is the resonance of such attitude, then emotional excitation is the felt process of realization of ideas. The chief interest lies in making this formula more specific.

In the first place, this mode of getting at it relieves Mr. James's statement of the admittedly paradoxical air which has surrounded it. I can but think that Mr. James's critics

---

[17] *Psychology*, Vol. II, p. 454 and p. 485.

[18] In my *Psychology*, e.g., p. 19 and pp. 246-249, it is laid down, quite schematically, that feeling is the internalizing of activity or will. There is nothing novel in the doctrine; in a way it goes back to Plato and Aristotle. But what first fixed my especial attention, I believe, upon James's doctrine of emotion was that it furnishes this old idealistic conception of feeling, hitherto blank and unmediated, with a medium of translation into the terms of concrete phenomena. I mention this bit of personal history simply as an offset to those writers who have found Mr. James's conception so tainted with materialism. On the historical side, it may be worth noting that a crude anticipation of James's theory is found in Hegel's *Philosophie des Geistes*, § 401.

have largely made their own difficulties, even on the basis of his "slap-dash" statement that "we feel sorry because we cry, angry because we strike, afraid because we tremble." The very statement brings out the idea of *feeling* sorry, not of *being* sorry. He expressly refers to his task as "subtracting certain *elements of feeling* from an emotional state supposed to exist *in its fulness*" (italics mine). And in his article,[19] he definitely states that he is speaking of an *Affect*, or emotional seizure. By this I understand him to mean that he is not dealing with emotion as a concrete whole of experience, but with an abstraction from the actual emotion of that element which gives it its differentia—its feeling *quale*, its "feel." As I understand it, he did not conceive himself as dealing with that state which we term "being angry," but rather with the peculiar "feel" which anyone has when he is angry, an element which may be intellectually abstracted, but certainly has no existence by itself, or as full-fledged emotion-experience.

What misled Mr. James's critics, I think, was not so much his language, as it was the absence of all attempts on his part to connect the emotional seizure with the other phases of the concrete emotion-experience. What the whole condition of *being* angry, or hopeful or sorry may be, Mr. James nowhere says, nor does he indicate why or how the "feel" of anger is related to them. Hence the inference either that he is considering the whole emotion-experience in an inadequate way, or else—as Mr. Irons took it—that he is denying the very existence of emotion, reducing it to mere consciousness of bodily change as such. Certainly, even when we have admitted that the emotional differentia, or "feel," is the reverberation of organic changes following upon the motor response to stimulus, we have still to *place* this "feel" with reference to the other phases of the concrete emotion-experience. "Common sense" and psychological sense revolt at the supposed implication that the emotional "feel" which constitutes so much of the meaning of our lives is a chance arrival, or a chance superimposition from certain organic changes

[19] *The Psychological Review,* September, 1894.

which happen to be going on. It is this apparently arbitrary isolation which offends.

If, preparatory to attempting such a placing, we put before us the whole concrete emotional experience, we find, I think, that it has two phases beside that of *Affect*, or seizure. (1) It is a disposition, a mode of conduct, a way of behaving. Indeed, it is this practical aspect of emotion which common speech mainly means to refer to in its emotional terms. When we say that John Smith is very resentful at the treatment he has received, or is hopeful of success in business, or regrets that he accepted a nomination for office, we do not simply, or even chiefly, mean that he has a certain "feel" occupying his consciousness. We mean he is in a certain practical attitude, has assumed a readiness to act in certain ways. I should not fear a man who has simply the "feel" of anger, nor should I sympathize with one having simply the "feel" of grief.[20] Grief means *unwillingness* to resume the normal occupation, practical discouragement, breaking up of the normal reactions, etc., etc. Just as anger means a tendency to explode in a sudden attack, not a mere state of feeling. We certainly do not deny nor overlook the "feel" phase, but in ordinary speech the behavior side of emotion is, I think, always uppermost in consciousness. The connotation of emotion is primarily ethical, only secondarily psychical. Hence our insulted feeling when told (as we hastily read it—our interpretation is "slapdash" rather than the sentence itself) that we are not angry until we strike, for the sudden readiness to injure another is precisely what we mean by anger. Let the statement read that we do not have the emotional seizure, the "feel" of anger, till we strike, or clench our fist, or have our blood boil, etc., and the statement not only loses its insultingly paradox-

[20] I take it that this separation of "feel" from practical attitude is precisely what makes the difference between an emotional and a sentimental experience. The fact that the "feel" may be largely, though never wholly, simulated, by arousing certain organic excitations apart from the normal practical readiness to behave in a certain way, has played a sufficiently large part in our "evangelical" religions. The depth, in a way, and the hollowness, in another way, of the subjectively induced religious sentiments seems to me, in itself, a most admirable illustration of the truth of James's main contention.

ical quality, but (unless my introspection meets a different scene from that of others) is verified by every passing emotion. (2) But the full emotional experience also always has its "object" or intellectual content. The emotion is always "about" or "toward" something; it is "at" or "on account of" something, and this prepositional reference is an integral phase of the single pulse of emotion; for emotion, as well as the idea, comes as a whole carrying its distinctions of value within it. The child who ceases to be angry *at* something—were it only the floor at last—but who keeps up his kicking and screaming, has passed over into sheer spasm. It is then no more an emotion of anger than it is one of aesthetic appreciation. Disgust, terror, gratitude, sulkiness, curiosity—take all the emotions seriatim and see what they would be without the intrinsic reference to idea or object. Even the pathological or objectless emotion is so only to the rational spectator. To the experiencer (if I may venture the term) it subsumes at once its own object as source or aim. This feeling of depression must have its reason; the world is dark and gloomy; no one understands me; I have a dread disease; I have committed the unpardonable sin. This feeling of buoyancy must have its ideal reference; I am a delightful person, or one of the elect or have had a million dollars left me.[21]

It is perhaps at this point that the need of some reconstruction which will enable us to place the phases of an entire emotional experience becomes most urgent. In Mr. James's statement the experience is apparently (apparently, I say; I do not know how much is due to the exigency of discussion which necessitates a seeming isolation) split up into three separate parts: First comes the object or idea which operates only as stimulus; secondly, the mode of behavior taken as discharge of this stimulus; third, the *Affect,* or emotional excitation, as the repercussion of this discharge. No such seriality or separation attaches to the emotion as an experience. Nor does reflective analysis seem to establish this order as the best expression of the emotion as an object of psychological ab-

[21] I do not mean, of course, that every "pathological" emotion creates an intellectual delusion; but it does carry with it a changed intellectual coloring, a different direction of attention.

straction. We might almost infer from the way Mr. James leaves it that he is here a believer in that atomic or mosaic composition of consciousness which he has so effectively dealt with in the case of intellectual consciousness. However this may be, Mr. James certainly supplies us, in the underlying *motif* of this "chapter" on emotion, with an adequate instrument of reconstruction. This is the thought that the organic discharge is an *instinctive* reaction, not a response to an idea as such.

Following the lead of this idea, we are easily brought to the conclusion that *the mode of behavior is the primary thing, and that the idea and the emotional excitation are constituted at one and the same time; that, indeed, they represent the tension of stimulus and response within the co-ordination which makes up the mode of behavior.*

It is sheer reflective interpretation to say that the activity in anger is set up by the object, if we by object mean something consciously apprehended as object. This interpretation, if we force it beyond a mere way of speaking into the facts themselves, becomes a case of the psychological fallacy. If my bodily changes of beating heart, trembling and running legs, sinking in stomach, looseness of bowels, etc., follow from and grow out of the conscious recognition, *qua conscious recognition,* of a bear, then I see no way for it but that the bear is already a bear of which we are afraid—our idea must be of the bear as a fearful object. But if (as Mr. James's fundamental idea would imply, however his language may read at times) this reaction is not to the bear as *object,* nor to the *idea* of bear, but simply expresses an instinctive co-ordination of two organic tendencies, then the case is quite different. It is not the idea of the bear, or the bear as object, but a certain *act of seeing,* which by habit, whether inherited or acquired, sets up other acts. It is the kind of *co-ordination of acts* which, brought to sensational consciousness, constitutes the bear a fearful or a laughable or an indifferent object. The following sentence, for example, from James[22] seems to involve a mixture of his own theory with the one which he is

[22] *The Psychological Review,* September, 1894; 518 [italics Dewey's].

engaged in combatting: "Whatever be our reaction on the situation, in the last resort it is an *instinctive reaction* on that one of its elements which strikes us for the time being *as most vitally important.*" The conception of an instinctive reaction is the relevant idea; that of reaction upon an element "which strikes us as important" the incongruous idea. Does it strike us, *prior* to the reaction, as important? Then, most certainly, it already has emotional worth; the situation is already delightful and to be perpetuated, or terrible and to be fled, or whatever. What does recognition of importance mean aside from the ascription of worth, value—that is, aside from the projection of emotional experience? [23] But I do not think James's expression in this and other similar passages is to be taken literally. The reaction is not made on the basis of the apprehension of some quality in the object; it is made on the basis of an organized habit, of an organized co-ordination of activities, one of which instinctively stimulates the other. The outcome of this co-ordination of activities constitutes, for the first time, the object with such and such an import—terrible, delightful, etc.—or constitutes an emotion referring to such and such an object. For, we must insist once more, the frightful object and the emotion of fear are two names for the same experience.

Here, then, is our point of departure in placing the "feel," the "idea," and the "mode of behavior" in relation to one another. The idea or object which precedes and stimulates the bodily discharge is in no sense the idea or object (the intellectual content, the "at" or "on account of") of the emotion itself. The particular idea, the specific quality or object to which the seizure attaches, is just as much due to the discharge as is the seizure itself. More accurately and definitely, the idea or the object is an abstraction from the activity just

[23] It seems to me that the application of James's theory of emotion to his theory of attention would give some very interesting results. As it now stands, the theory "in attention" of preferential selection on the *basis* of interest seems to contradict the theory of emotional value as the *outcome* of preferential selection (that is, specific reaction). But the contradiction is most flagrant in the case of effort, considered, first, as emotion and then as an operation of will.

as much as is the "feel" or seizure. We have certain organic activities initiated, say in the eye, stimulating, through organized paths of association in the brain, certain activities of hands, legs, etc., and (through the co-ordination of these motor activities with the vegetative functions necessary to maintain them) of lungs, heart, vasomotor system, digestive organs, etc. The "bear" is, psychologically, just as much a discrimination of certain values, within this total pulse or co-ordination of action, as is the feeling of "fear." The "bear" is constituted by the excitations of eye and co-ordinated touch centers, just as the "terror" is by the disturbances of muscular and glandular systems. The reality, the co-ordination of these partial activities, is that whole activity which may be described equally well as "that terrible bear," or "Oh, how frightened I am." It is precisely and identically the same actual concrete experience; and the "bear," considered as one experience, and the "fright," considered as another, are distinctions introduced in reflection upon this experience, not separate experience. It is the psychological fallacy again if the differences which result from the reflection are carried over into the experience itself. If the fright comes, then the bear is not the bear of that particular experience, is not the object to which the feeling attaches, *except* as the fright comes. Any other supposition is to confuse the abstract bear of science with the concrete (*just this*) bear of experience.

The point may be further illustrated by the objection which Mr. Irons has brought against the James theory. "How can one perceptive process of itself suffuse with emotional warmth the cold intellectuality of another?" Note here the assumption of two distinct "processes," apparently recognizing themselves as distinct, or anyhow somehow marked out as different in themselves. The continued point of Mr. Irons's objection is that Mr. James makes intellectual and emotional "states" (values), the knowledge of an object and the emotion referred to it, both due to currents from the periphery, and the same kind of current cannot be supposed to induce such radically different things as an intellectual and an emotional process. The objection entirely overlooks the fact that we have but the one organic pulse, the frightful bear, the frightened man, whose reality is the whole concrete co-ordination of eye—leg—heart, etc., activity, and that the distinction of cold intellectuality and warm emotionality is simply a *functional* distinction within this one whole of action. We take a certain phase which *serves a certain end,* namely, giving us information, and call that intellectual; we take another phase, having another end or value, that of excitement, and call that emotional. But does anyone suppose that, *apart from our interpretation of values,* there is one process in itself intellectual, and another process in itself emotional? I cannot even frame an idea of what is meant. I can see that the eye-touch process gives us information mainly, and so we call that intellectual; and that the heart-bowels process gives us the valuation of this information in terms of our own inner welfare—but aside from this distinction of *values* within a concrete whole, through reflection upon it, I can see nothing.

If, then, I may paraphrase Mr. James's phraseology, the statement would read as follows: Our customary analysis, reading over into the experience itself what we find by interpreting it,[24] says we have an idea of the bear as something to be escaped, and so run away. The hypothesis here propounded is that the factors of a co-ordination (whether due to inherited instinct or to individually acquired habit) begin to operate and we run away; running away, we get the idea of "running-away-from-bear," or of "bear-as-thing-to-be-run-from." I suppose everyone would admit that the complete, mature idea came only in and through the act of running, but might hold that an embryonic suggestion of running came before the running. I cannot disprove this position, but everything seems to point the other way. It is more natural to suppose that as the full idea of running away comes in from the full execu-

[24] This is simply circumlocution for "common sense." Common sense is practical, and when we are practical it is the value of our experience, what we can get out of it or think we can, that appeals to us. The last thing that concerns us is the actual process of experiencing, *qua* process. It might almost be said that the sole difficulty in psychology, upon the introspective side, is to avoid this substitution of a practical interpretation of an experience for the experience itself.

tion, so the vague suggestion comes through the vague start-ing-up-of the system, mediated by discharge from the centers.

The idea of running away must certainly involve, as part of its content, an excitation of the "motor centers" actually concerned in running; it would seem as if this excitation must involve some, however slight, innervation of the peripheral apparatus involved in the act.[25] What ground is there for sup-posing that the idea comes to consciousness save through the sensorial return of this peripheral excitation? Is there any conceivable statement, either in terms of introspection or of nervous structure, of an idea of movement coming to con-sciousness absolutely unmediated peripherally? Sensorial con-sciousness, mediated by the incoming current, is an un-doubted fact; it is *vera causa*. Putting the two hypotheses side by side simply as hypotheses, surely the logical advantage of economy and of appeal to *vera causa* is on the side of the theory which conceives the idea of movement in terms of a return of discharge wave, and against that which would make it a purely central affair.[26]

But this is far from being all. I suppose one is fairly en-titled now to start from the assumption of a sensory contin-uum, the "big, buzzing, blooming confusion," out of which particular sensory quales are differentiated. Discrimination, not integration, is the real problem. In a general way we all admit that it is through attention that the distinctions arise, through selective emphasis. Now we may not only rely upon the growing feeling that attention is somehow bound up with

[25] I do not mean that this innervation comes to consciousness as such; on the contrary.

[26] There are further logical grounds for expecting acquiescence from those who accept the general standpoint of Mr. James. To say nothing of the in-sistence upon consciousness as essentially reactive or motor, "idea" and emo-tional seizure hang together. Fear-of-bear, bear-as-fearful-object cannot be separated. Besides, when I introspect for my "fringe" in the stream of thought I always find its particular sensorial basis in shiftings of directions and quan-tity of breath, and other slight adjustments, just as certainly as I always can pick out the sensorial basis for my emotional seizures. *A priori*, it is difficult to see what the "fringe" can be save the feeling of the running accompani-ment of aborted acts, having their value now only as signs or cues, but orig-inally complete in themselves.

motor adjustment and reaction, but we can point to the specific facts of sensorial discrimination which show that, as a matter of fact, the range and fineness of discrimination run parallel to the apparatus for motor adjustments. We can also show that, in the only case in which there has, as yet, been a serious attempt to work out the details of discrimination, namely, space distinctions, all hands agree that they come through motor adjustments—the question whether "muscular" or joint surface sensations are primary, having here no importance. Such being the case, how can the particular stimulus which excites the discharge be defined as *this* or *that* object apart from our reaction to it? I do not care to go into the metaphysics of objective qualities, but dealing simply with the psychological recognition of such qualities, what basis or standard for qualitative definiteness can we have, save the consciousness of differences in our own organic response? The bear may be a thousand times an individual entity or distinct object metaphysically, if you please; you may even suppose, if you will, that the particular wave lengths which deflect from the bear, somehow sort themselves out from the wave lengths coming from all the rest of the environment, and come to the brain as a distinct bundle or package by themselves—but the recognition of just *this* object out of the multitude of possible objects, of just this bundle of vibrations out of all the other bundles, still remains to be accounted for. The predominating motor response supplies the conditions for its objectification, or selection. There is no competing hypothesis of any other machinery even in the field.

We return, then, confirmed, to our belief that the mode of behavior, or co-ordination of activities, constitutes the ideal content of emotion just as much as it does the *Affect* or "feel," and that the distinction of these two is not given in the experience itself, but simply in reflection upon the experience. The mode of action constituted by the organic co-ordination of certain sensorimotor (or ideomotor) activities, on one side; and of certain vegetative-motor activities on the other, is the reality, and this reality has a value, which, when interpreted, we call intellectual, and a value which, when interpreted we call Affect, or "feel." In the terms of our illustration, the mode of behavior carried with it the concept of the bear as a thing to be acted toward in a certain way, and of the "feel" of our reaction. It is brown and chained—a "beautiful" object to be looked at. It is soft and fluffy—an "aesthetic" object to be felt of. It is tame and clumsy—an "amusing" object to while away time with. It is hungry and angry—and is a "ferocious" object to be fled. The consciousness of our mode of behavior as affording data for other possible actions constitutes the bear an objective or ideal content. The consciousness of the mode of behavior as something in itself—the looking, petting, running, etc.—constitutes the emotional seizure. In all concrete experience of emotion these two phases are organically united in a single pulse of consciousness.

It follows from this that all emotion, as excitation, involves inhibition. This is not absolute inhibition; it is not suppression or displacement. It is incidental to the co-ordination. The two factors of the co-ordination, the "exciting stimulus" and the excited response, have to be adjusted, and the period of adjustment required to affect the co-ordination, marks the inhibition of each required to effect its reconstruction as an integral part of the whole act. Or, since we have recognized that the exciting stimulus does not exist as fact, or object, until constituted such by the coordination in the final act, let us say that the activities needing adjustment, and so partial inhibition, are the kinesthetic (sensorimotor or ideomotor) activities which translate themselves into the "object," and the vegetative-motor activities which constitute the "reaction" or "response" to the "object."

But here, again, in order to avoid getting on the wrong track it must be noted that this distinction of "object" and "response" is one of interpretation, or value, and not a plain matter of course difference in the experiencing. I have already tried to show that the "object" itself is an organic excitation on the sensorimotor, or, mediately, ideomotor side, and that it is not *the* peculiar object *of* the emotion until the mode of behavior sets in, and the diffusive wave repercussates in consciousness. But it is equally necessary to recognize that the very distinction between exciting or stimulating sensorimotor activity and excited or responding vegetative-motor activity is teleological and not merely factual. It is because these two activities have to be coordinated in a single act, to accomplish a single end, and have therefore to be so adjusted as to cooperate with each other, that they present themselves as stimulus and response. When we consider one activity, say the sensori-ideo-motor activity, which constructs or constitutes the bear as an "object," not in itself, but from the standpoint of the final act into which it merges—the stopping to look at the bear and study it scientifically, or enjoy its clumsy movements—that activity takes the form of stimulus. So the vegetative-motor activity, which is, in itself as direct experience, simply the intrinsic organic continuation of the sensorimotor activity, being interpreted again as a reduced factor of, or contribution to, the final outcome, assumes the form of response. But, I repeat, this distinction of stimulus and response is one of interpretation, and of interpretation from the standpoint of the value of some act considered as an accomplished end.

The positive truth is that the prior and the succeeding parts of an activity are in operation together; that the prior activity besides passing over into the succeeding also persists by itself, and yet that the necessary act cannot be performed until these two activities reinforce each other, or become contributing factors to a unified deed. The period of maximum emotional seizure corresponds to this period of adjustment. If we look at the deflection or reconstruction which either side undergoes during this adjustment, we shall call it inhibition —it is arrest of discharge which the activity would perform, if existing by itself. If we look at the final outcome, the completed adjustment, we have co-ordination.

I think it must be obvious that this account in no way runs athwart Mr. James's denial of inhibition as a necessary phase of the *Affect (Psychology,* Vol. II., p. 476, note). He there speaks of inhibition as if it could mean only complete suppression—which is no inhibition at all, psychologically, since with suppression or displacement, all tension vanishes. It is, indeed, a question of primary impulsive tendencies, but of these tendencies as conflicting with one another and therefore mutually checking, at least temporarily, one another. Acts, which in past times, have been *complete* activities, now present themselves as contemporaneous phases of one activity. In so far as they were once each complete in itself, there is struggle of each to absorb or negate the other. This must either occur or else there is a readjustment and a new whole, or co-ordination, appears, they now being contributory factors. The inhibition once worked out, whether by displacement of one or by reconstruction of both contending factors, the *Affect* dies out.

This sort of inhibition the James theory not only permits, but demands—otherwise the whole relation between the exciting stimulus and the instinctive response, which is the nerve of the theory, disappears. If the exciting stimulus does not persist over into the excited response, we get simply a case of habit. The familiar fact that emotion as excitement disappears with definiteness of habit simply means that in so far as one activity serves *simply* as means, or cue, to another and gives way at once to it, there is no basis for conflict and for inhibition. But if the stimulating and the induced activities need to be co-ordinated together, if they are both means contributing to one and the same end, then the conditions for mere habit are denied, and some struggle, with incidental inhibitory deflection of the immediate activity, sets in. In psychological terms, this tension is always between the activity which constitutes, when interpreted, the object as an intellectual content, and that which constitutes the response or mode of dealing with it. There is the one phase of organic activity which constitutes the bear as object; there is the other which would attack it, or run away from it, or stand one's ground before it. If these two co-ordinate *without friction,* or if one immediately displaces the other, there is no emotional seizure. If they coexist, both pulling apart as complete in themselves and pulling together as parts of a new whole, there is great emotional excitement.[27] It is this tension which makes it impossible to describe any emotion whatever without using dual terms—one for the *Affect* itself, the other for the object "at," "toward," or "on account of," which it is.

We may now connect this analysis with the result of the consideration of the emotional attitudes. The attitude is precisely that which was a complete activity once, but is no longer so. The activity of seizing prey or attacking an enemy, a movement having its meaning in itself, is now reduced or aborted; it is an attitude simply. As an instinctive reaction it is thoroughly ingrained in the system; it represents the actual co-ordinations of thousands and thousands of ancestors; it tends to start into action, therefore, whenever its associated stimulus occurs. But the very fact that it is now reduced to an attitude or tendency, the very fact that it is now *relatively* easy to learn to control the instinctive blind reaction when we are stimulated in a certain way, shows that the primary activity is inhibited; it no longer exists as a whole by itself, but simply as a co-ordinated phase, or a contributory means, in a larger activity. There is no reason to suppose that the original activity of attack or seizure was emotional, or had any *quale* attached to it such as we now term "anger." The animal or our ancestor so far as it was given up without restraint to the full activity undoubtedly had a feeling of activity; but just because the activity was undivided, it was not "emotion"; it was not "at," or "toward" an object held in tension against itself. This division could come in only when there was a need of co-ordinating the activity which corresponded to the

[27] See James, II, 496-497. But more particularly I should apply to the difference between relatively indifferent and emotionally excited consciousness precisely what James says of the difference between habitual and reasoned thinking. (II, p. 366.) "In the former, an entire system of cells vibrating at any one moment discharges in its totality into another system, the order of the discharges tends to be a constant one in time; whilst in the latter a part of the prior system still keeps vibrating in the midst of the subsequent system, and the order . . . has little tendency to fixedness in time." Add to this that it is necessary to perform a unified act—or reconstitute a single, comprehensive system, and the reality (though strictly incidental character) of inhibition appears.

perception and that which corresponded to the fighting, as means to an activity which was neither perceiving nor fighting. The animal growling and lashing its tail as it *waits* to fight may have an emotional consciousness, but even here, there may be, for all we know, simply a unified consciousness, a complete concentration on the act of maintaining that posture, the act of waiting being the *adequate* response to the given stimulus. Certainly,[28] so far as I can trust my own introspection, whenever my anger or any strong emotion has gained complete possession of me, the peculiar *Affect quale* has disappeared. I remember well a youthful fight, with the emotions of irritation and anger before, and of partial fear and partial pride afterwards, but as to the intervening period of the fight nothing but a strangely vivid perception of the other boy's face as the hypnotizing focus of all my muscular activities. On the other side, my most intense and vengeful feelings of anger are associated with cases where my whole body was so sat on as to prevent the normal reaction. Everyone knows how the smart and burn of the feeling of injustice increases with the feeling of impotency; it is, for example, when strikes are beginning to fail that violence from anger or revenge, as distinct from sheer criminality, sets in. It is a commonplace that the busy philanthropist has no occasion to feel the extreme emotion of pathos which the spectator or

[28] I have no intention here of constructing, *a priori*, the animal consciousness. I use this merely as hypothetical illustration; *if* unification of activity, then no emotion; *if* emotion, then tenson of intellectual recognition on one side and consideration of how to behave toward object recognized on the other. I must add, however, that such interpretations as Darwin's umbrella case (in his *Descent of Man*), as illustrating a rude sense of the supernatural, seem to me most unwarrantably anthropomorphic. Surely, the only straightforward interpretation is, there was interruption of a reaction which had started to discharge, and that such a change in stimulus suddenly set up another discharge totally at cross-purposes with the first, thus disintegrating the animal's co-ordinations for a moment. Unless the animal recognizes or objectifies the familiar reaction, and recognizes also the unexpected reaction in such a way that there tension arises between the two, there can be no *emotion* in the animal, but simply a shock of interrupted activity—the sort of fit which James speaks of, Vol. II, 420. It may well be that the feeling of the supernatural in man, however, *is* precisely the feeling of such tension—instead of there being an idea of the supernatural, and then an associated feeling of terror toward it.

[247]

reader of literature feels. Cases might be multiplied *ad libitum.*

It is then in the reduction of activities once performed for their own sake, to attitudes now useful simply as supplying a contributory, a reinforcing or checking factor, in some more comprehensive activity, that we have all the conditions for high emotional disturbance. The tendency to large diffusive waves of discharge is present, and the inhibition of this outgoing activity through some perception or idea is also present. The need of somehow reaching an adjustment of these two sides is urgent. The attitude stands for a recapitulation of thousands of acts formerly done, ends formerly reached; the perception or idea stands for multitudes of acts which may be done, ends which may be acted upon. But the immediate and present need is to get this attitude of anger which reflects the former act of seizing into some connection with the act of getting even or of moral control, or whatever the idea may be. The conflict and competition, with incidental inhibition and deflection, is the disturbance of the emotional seizure.

Upon this basis, the apparent strangeness or absurdity in the fact that a mere organic repercussation should have such tremendous values in consciousness disappears. This organic return of the discharge wave stands for the entire effort of the organism to adjust its formed habits or co-ordinations of the past to present necessities as made known in perception or idea. The emotion is, *psychologically, the adjustment or tension of habit and ideal,* and the organic changes in the body are the literal working out, in concrete terms, of the struggle of adjustment. We may recall once more the three main phases presented in this adjustment as now giving us the basis of the classification of the emotions. There may be a failure to adjust the vegetative-motor function, the habit, to the sensori- (or ideo-) motor; there may be the effort, or there may be the success. The effort, moreover, also has a double form according as the attempt is in the main so to use the formed reactions as to avoid or exclude the idea or object, setting up another in its place, or to incorporate and assimilate it—*e.g.,* terror and anger, dread and hope, regret and complacency, etc.[29]

I shall not carry out this classification; but further suggest that, in my judgment, we now have the means for discriminating emotion as *Gefühlston,* as emotional disturbance, or *Affect* (with which we have been dealing so far) and as interest.

Interest is the feeling which arises with the completed coordination. Let the tension solve itself by successive displacements in time, *i.e.,* means assuming a purely serial form in which one stimulates the next, and we get the indifference of routine. But let the various means succeed in organizing themselves into a simultaneous comprehensive whole of action, and we have interest. All interest, *qua* interest, it would follow from this, is qualitatively alike, being differentiated simply by the idea to which it attaches. And experience seems to verify this inference. Interest is undisturbed action, absorbing action, unified action, and all interests, *as interests,* are equally interesting. The collection of postage stamps is as absorbing, if it *is* absorbing or an interest, as the discovery of double stars; and the figuring of indefinite columns of statistics as the discovery of the nature of sympathy. Nor is this a pathological principle, as it might seem to be were we to instance merely fads or hobbies. The multiplicity of deeds which demand doing in this world is too great to be numbered; that principle which secures that if only full or organic activity go into each end, each act shall equally satisfy in its

[29] Because of the tension, however, these cannot be set over against each other absolutely. All terror, till it passes into pathological fright, involves anger, and anger some fear, etc. All moral experience is only too full of the subtle and deceiving ways in which regret (condemnation) and complacency (self-approbation) run into each other. There is the Pharisee who can maintain his sense of his own goodness only by tension with his thought of evil; or who can make his depth of remorse material for self-gratulation. And there is the sentimental selfish character which disguises its own disgrace from itself by emotional recognitions of the beauty of goodness, and of its own misfortunes in not being able, in the past, to satisfy this ideal. I have never known other such touching tributes to goodness as can proceed from the sentimental egoist, when he gets into "trouble," as he euphemistically terms it.

time and place, is the highest ethical principle; it is the statement of the only religious emotional experience which really
seems worth while—the sense of the validity of all necessary
doing. I cannot dwell upon this matter of interest, but I suggest the case of purely scientific interest as crucial. On one
side, it seems wholly unemotional, so free from all disturbance or excitation may it become; on the other, it represents
a culmination of absorption, of concentrated attention. How
this apparent paradox is to be dealt with save on the supposition that emotion (as *Affect*) is the feeling of tension in action, while interest is the feeling of a complex of relevant
activity unified in a single channel of discharge, I do not see.

As for the *Gefühlston,* I shall only state the conclusion
that would seem to follow from a thoroughgoing application
of the principle already laid down. I do not know that this
complete application is advisable, much less necessary, but I
share somewhat in the feeling of Mr. Baldwin[30] that there is
a presumption that a unitary principle holds all the way
through.[31] At all events, those who have followed me so far
may like to see how the hypothesis already propounded might
conceivably apply to the case of, say, delight in certain tones,
colors or tastes, while those who do not accept the hypothesis
will hardly be shocked at one absurdity the more.

The suggestion, then, is that the *Gefühlston* represents the
complete consolidation of a large number of achieved ends
into the organic habit or co-ordination. It is interest read
backwards. That represents the complete identification of the
habits with a certain end or aim. The tone of sense-feeling
represents the reaction, the incorporate identification, of the
successful ends into the working habit. It is not, as I have
hitherto indicated, habit as habit which becomes feelingless;
it is only the habit which serves as mere means, or serial stim-

[30] *The Psychological Review,* November, 1894; 617.

[31] It hardly seems fair, though, to charge Mr. James with inconsistency because he declines to force his theory beyond the limits of the facts upon which
he feels himself to have a sure hold. Surely we may admire this reserve, even
if we cannot imitate it, instead of virtually accusing him of giving away his
whole case by admitting, hypothetically, the existence of facts whose explanation would require an opposite principle.

ulus. That a given co-ordination should assume into itself the value of all associated co-ordinations is a fact of everyday experience. Our eye-consciousness takes up into itself the value of countless motor and touch experiences; our ear takes up the value of motor and visual experiences, etc. There is no apparent reason why this vicarious assumption should not become so organically registered—*pace* Weismann—as to become hereditary; and become more and more functionally incorporated into structure.

To sum up: Certain movements, formerly useful in themselves, become reduced to tendencies to action, to attitudes. As such they serve, when instinctively aroused into action, as means for realizing ends. But so far as there is difficulty in adjusting the organic activity represented by the attitude with that which stands for the idea or end, there is temporary struggle and partial inhibition. This is reported as *Affect,* or emotional seizure. Let the co-ordination be effected in one act, instead of in a successive series of mutually exclusive stimuli, and we have interest. Let such co-ordinations become thoroughly habitual and hereditary, and we have *Gefühlston.*

15

THE REFLEX ARC CONCEPT
IN PSYCHOLOGY

THAT the greater demand for a unifying principle and controlling working hypothesis in psychology should come at just the time when all generalizations and classifications are most questioned and questionable is natural enough. It is the very cumulation of discrete facts creating the demand for unification that also breaks down previous lines of classification. The material is too great in mass and too varied in style to fit into existing pigeonholes, and the cabinets of science break of their own dead weight. The idea of the reflex arc has upon the whole come nearer to meeting this demand for a general working hypothesis than any other single concept. It being admitted that the sensorimotor apparatus represents both the unit of nerve structure and the type of nerve function, the image of this relationship passed over into psychology, and became an organizing principle to hold together the multiplicity of fact.

In criticizing this conception it is not intended to make a plea for the principles of explanation and classification which the reflex arc idea has replaced; but, on the contrary, to urge that they are not sufficiently displaced, and that in the idea of the sensiorimotor circuit, conceptions of the nature of sensation and of action derived from the nominally displaced psychology are still in control.

The older dualism between sensation and idea is repeated in the current dualism of peripheral and central structures

From *The Psychological Review*, July, 1896; 357-370.

and functions; the older dualism of body and soul finds a distinct echo in the current dualism of stimulus and response. Instead of interpreting the character of sensation, idea and action from their place and function in the sensorimotor circuit, we still incline to interpret the latter from our preconceived and preformulated ideas of rigid distinctions between sensations, thoughts and acts. The sensory stimulus is one thing, the central activity, standing for the idea, is another thing, and the motor discharge, standing for the act proper, is a third. As a result, the reflex arc is not a comprehensive, or organic, unity, but a patchwork of disjointed parts, a mechanical conjunction of unallied processes. What is needed is that the principle underlying the idea of the reflex arc as the fundamental psychical unity shall react into and determine the values of its constitutive factors. More specifically, what is wanted is that sensory stimulus, central connections and motor responses shall be viewed, not as separate and complete entities in themselves, but as divisions of labor, functioning factors, within the single concrete whole, now designated the reflex arc.

What is the reality so designated? What shall we term that which is not sensation-followed-by-idea-followed-by-movement, but which is primary; which is, as it were, the psychical organism of which sensation, idea and movement are the chief organs? Stated on the physiological side, this reality may most conveniently be termed co-ordination. This is the essence of the facts held together by and subsumed under the reflex arc concept. Let us take, for our example, the familiar child-candle instance. The ordinary interpretation would say the sensation of light is a stimulus to the grasping as a response, the burn resulting is a stimulus to withdrawing the hand as response and so on. There is, of course, no doubt that is a rough practical way of representing the process. But when we ask for its psychological adequacy, the case is quite different. Upon analysis, we find that we begin not with a sensory stimulus, but with a sensorimotor co-ordination, the optical-ocular, and that in a certain sense it is the movement which is primary, and the sensation which is secondary, the movement of body, head and eye muscles determining the quality of what is experienced. In other words, the real beginning is with the act of seeing; it is looking, and not a sensation of light. The sensory quale gives the value of the act, just as the movement furnishes its mechanism and control, but both sensation and movement lie inside, not outside, the act.

Now if this act, the seeing, stimulates another act, the reaching, it is because both of these acts fall within a larger co-ordination; because seeing and grasping have been so often bound together to reinforce each other, to help each other out, that each may be considered practically a subordinate member of a bigger co-ordination. More specifically, the ability of the hand to do its work will depend, either directly or indirectly, upon its control, as well as its stimulation, by the act of vision. If the sight did not inhibit as well as excite the reaching, the latter would be purely indeterminate, it would be for anything or nothing, not for the particular object seen. The reaching, in turn, must both stimulate and control the seeing. The eye must be kept upon the candle if the arm is to do its work; let it wander and the arm takes up another task. In other words, we now have an enlarged and transformed co-ordination; the act is seeing no less than before, but it is now seeing-for-reaching purposes. There is still a sensorimotor circuit, one with more content or value, not a substitution of a motor response for a sensory stimulus.

Now take the affairs at its next stage, that in which the child gets burned. It is hardly necessary to point out again that this is also a sensorimotor co-ordination and not a mere sensation. It is worth while, however, to note especially the fact that it is simply the completion, or fulfilment, of the previous eye-arm-hand co-ordination and not an entirely new occurrence. Only because the heat-pain quale enters into the same circuit of experience with the optical-ocular and muscular quales, does the child learn from the experience and get the ability to avoid the experience in the future.

More technically stated, the so-called response is not merely *to* the stimulus; it is *into* it. The burn is the original seeing, the original optical-ocular experience enlarged and transformed in its value. It is no longer mere seeing; it is seeing-of-a-light-that-means-pain-when-contact-occurs. The ordinary reflex arc theory proceeds upon the more or less tacit assumption that the outcome of the response is a totally new experience; that it is, say, the substitution of a burn sensation for a light sensation through the intervention of motion. The fact is that the sole meaning of the intervening movement is to maintain, reinforce or transform (as the case may be) the original quale; that we do not have the replacing of one sort of experience by another, but the development or (as it seems convenient to term it) the mediation of an experience. The seeing, in a word, remains to control the reaching, and is, in turn, interpreted by the burning.[1]

The discussion up to this point may be summarized by saying that the reflex arc idea, as commonly employed, is defective in that it assumes sensory stimulus and motor response as distinct psychical existences, while in reality they are always inside a co-ordination and have their significance purely from the part played in maintaining or reconstituting the co-ordination; and (secondly) in assuming that the quale of experience which precedes the "motor" phase and that which succeeds it are two different states, instead of the last being always the first reconstituted, the motor phase coming in only for the sake of such mediation. The result is that the reflex arc idea leaves us with a disjointed psychology, whether viewed from the standpoint of development in the individual or in the race, or from that of the analysis of the mature consciousness. As to the former, in its failure to see that the arc of which it talks is virtually a circuit, a continual reconstitution, it breaks continuity and leaves us nothing but a series of jerks, the origin of each jerk to be sought outside the process of experience itself, in either an external pressure of "environment," or else in an unaccountable spontaneous variation from within the "soul" or the "organism." [2] As to the latter,

[1] See, for a further statement of mediation, my *Syllabus of Ethics*, p. 15.
[2] It is not too much to say that the whole controversy in biology regarding the source of variation, represented by Weismann and Spencer respectively,

failing to see the unity of activity, no matter how much it may prate of unity, it still leaves us with sensation or peripheral stimulus; idea, or central process (the equivalent of attention); and motor response, or act, as three disconnected existences, having to be somehow adjusted to each other, whether through the intervention of an extra-experimental soul, or by mechanical push and pull.

Before proceeding to a consideration of the general meaning for psychology of the summary, it way be well to give another descriptive analysis, as the value of the statement depends entirely upon the universality of its range of application. For such an instance we may conveniently take Baldwin's analysis of the reactive consciousness. In this there are, he says, "three elements corresponding to the three elements of the nervous arc. First, the receiving consciousness, the stimulus—say a loud, unexpected sound; second, the attention involuntarily drawn, the registering element; and, third, the muscular reaction following upon the sound—say flight from fancied danger." Now, in the first place, such an analysis is incomplete; it ignores the status prior to hearing the sound. Of course, if this status is irrelevant to what happens afterwards, such ignoring is quite legitimate. But is it irrelevant either to the quantity or the quality of the stimulus?

If one is reading a book, if one is hunting, if one is watching in a dark place on a lonely night, if one is performing a chemical experiment; in each case, the noise has a very different psychical value; it is a different experience. In any case, what proceeds the "stimulus" is a whole act, a sensorimotor co-ordination. What is more to the point, the "stimulus" emerges out of this co-ordination; it is born from it as its matrix; it represents as it were an escape from it. I might here fall back upon authority, and refer to the widely accepted sensation continuum theory, according to which the sound

---

arises from beginning with stimulus or response instead of with the co-ordination with reference to which stimulus and response are functional divisions of labor. The same may be said, on the psychological side, of the controversy between the Wundtian "apperceptionists" and their opponents. Each has a *disjectum membrum* of the same organic whole, whichever is selected being an arbitrary matter of personal taste.

cannot be absolutely *ex abrupto* from the outside, but is simply a shifting of focus of emphasis, a redistribution of tensions within the former act; and declare that unless the sound activity had been present to some extent in the prior co-ordination, it would be impossible for it now to come to prominence in consciousness. And such a reference would be only an amplification of what has already been said concerning the way in which the prior activity influences the value of the sound sensation. Or, we might point to cases of hypnotism, mono-ideism and absent-mindedness, like that of Archimedes, as evidences that if the previous co-ordination is such as rigidly to lock the door, the auditory disturbance will knock in vain for admission to consciousness. Or, to speak more truly in the metaphor, the auditory activity must already have one foot over the threshold, if it is ever to gain admittance.

But it will be more satisfactory, probably, to refer to the biological side of the case, and point out that as the ear activity has been evolved on account of the advantage gained by the whole organism, it must stand in the strictest histological and physiological connection with the eye, or hand, or leg, or whatever other organ has been the overt center of action. It is absolutely impossible to think of the eye center as monopolizing consciousness and the ear apparatus as wholly quiescent. What happens is a certain relative prominence and subsidence as between the various organs which maintain the organic equilibrium.

Furthermore, the sound is not a mere stimulus, or mere sensation; it again is an act, that of hearing. The muscular response is involved in this as well as sensory stimulus; that is, there is a certain definite set of the motor apparatus involved in hearing just as much as there is in subsequent running away. The movement and posture of the head, the tension of the ear muscles, are required for the "reception" of the sound. It is just as true to say that the sensation of sound arises from a motor response as that the running away is a response to the sound. This may be brought out by reference to the fact that Professor Baldwin, in the passage quoted, has inverted the real order as between his first and second elements. We do not have first a sound and then activity of attention, unless sound is taken as mere nervous shock or physical event, not as conscious value. The conscious sensation of sound depends upon the motor response having already taken place; or, in terms of the previous statement (if stimulus is used as a conscious fact, and not as a mere physical event) it is the motor response or attention which constitutes that which finally becomes the stimulus to another act. Once more, the final "element," the running away, is not merely motor, but is sensorimotor, having its sensory value and its muscular mechanism. It is also a co-ordination. And, finally, this sensorimotor co-ordination is not a new act, supervening upon what preceded. Just as the "response" is necessary to constitute the stimulus, to determine it as sound and as this kind of sound, of wild beast or robber, so the sound experience must persist as a value in the running, to keep it up, to control it. The motor reaction involved in the running is, once more, into, not merely to, the sound. It occurs to change the sound, to get rid of it. The resulting quale, whatever it may be, has its meaning wholly determined by reference to the hearing of the sound. It is that experience mediated[3] What we have is a circuit; not an arc or broken segment of a circle. This circuit is more truly termed organic than reflex, because the motor response determines the stimulus, just as truly as sensory stimulus determines movement. Indeed, the movement is only for the sake of determining the stimulus, of fixing what kind of a stimulus it is, of interpreting it.

I hope it will not appear that I am introducing needless refinements and distinctions into what, it may be urged, is

[3] In other words, every reaction is of the same type as that which Professor Baldwin ascribes to imitation alone, viz., circular. Imitation is simply that particular form of the circuit in which the "response" lends itself to comparatively unchanged maintenance of the prior experience. I say comparatively unchanged, for as far as this maintenance means additional control over the experience, it is being psychically changed, becoming more distinct. It is safe to suppose, moreover, that the "repetition" is kept up only so long as this growth or mediation goes on. There is the new-in-the-old, if it is only the new sense of power.

after all an undoubted fact, that movement as response follows sensation as stimulus. It is not a question of making the account of the process more complicated, though it is always wise to beware of that false simplicity which is reached by leaving out of account a large part of the problem. It is a question of finding out what stimulus or sensation, what movement and response mean; a question of seeing that they mean distinctions of flexible function only, not of fixed existence; that one and the same occurrence plays either or both parts, according to the shift of interest; and that because of this functional distinction and relationship, the supposed problem of the adjustment of one to the other, whether by superior force in the stimulus or an agency *ad hoc* in the center or the soul, is a purely self-created problem.

We may see the disjointed character of the present theory, by calling to mind that it is impossible to apply the phrase "sensorimotor" to the occurrence as a simple phrase of description; it has validity only as a term of interpretation, only, that is, as defining various functions exercised. In terms of description, the whole process may be sensory or it may be motor, but it cannot be sensorimotor. The "stimulus," the excitation of the nerve ending and of the sensory nerve, the central change, are just as much, or just as little, motion as the events taking place in the motor nerve and the muscles. It is one uninterrupted, continuous redistribution of mass in motion. And there is nothing in the process, from the standpoint of description, which entitles us to call this reflex. It is redistribution pure and simple; as much so as the burning of a log, or the falling of a house or the movement of the wind. In the physical process, as physical, there is nothing which can be set off as stimulus, nothing which reacts, nothing which is response. There is just a change in the system of tensions.

The same sort of thing is true when we describe the process purely from the psychical side. It is now all sensation, all sensory quale; the motion, as psychically described, is just as much sensation as is sound or light or burn. Take the withdrawing of the hand from the candle flame as example. What we have is a certain visual-heat-pain-muscular-quale, transformed into another visual-touch-muscular-quale—the flame now being visible only at a distance, or not at all, the touch sensation being altered, etc. If we symbolize the original visual quale by v, the temperature by h, the accompanying muscular sensation by m, the whole experience may be stated as vhm-vh$m$-vhm'; m being the quale of withdrawing, m' the sense of the status after the withdrawal. The motion is not a certain kind of existence; it is a sort of sensory experience interpreted, just as is candle flame, or burn from candle flame. All are on a par.

But, in spite of all this, it will be urged, there is a distinction between stimulus and response, between sensation and motion. Precisely; but we ought now to be in a condition to ask of what nature is the distinction, instead of taking it for granted as a distinction somehow lying in the existence of the facts themselves. We ought to be able to see that the ordinary conception of the reflex arc theory, instead of being a case of plain science, is a survival of the metaphysical dualism, first formulated by Plato, according to which the sensation is an ambiguous dweller on the borderland of soul and body, the idea (or central process) is purely psychical, and the act (or movement) purely physical. Thus the reflex arc formulation is neither physical (or physiological) nor psychological; it is a mixed materialistic-spiritualistic assumption.

If the previous descriptive analysis has made obvious the need of a reconsideration of the reflex arc idea, of the nest of difficulties and assumptions in the apparently simple statement, it is now time to undertake an explanatory analysis. The fact is that stimulus and response are not distinctions of existence, but teleological distinctions, that is, distinctions of function, or part played, with reference to reaching or maintaining an end. With respect to this teleological process, two stages should be discriminated, as their confusion is one cause of the confusion attending the whole matter. In one case, the relation represents an organization of means with reference to a comprehensive end. It represents an accomplished adaptation. Such is the case in all well developed instincts, as when we say that the contact of eggs is a stimulus to the hen to set;

or the sight of corn a stimulus to pick; such also is the case with all thoroughly formed habits, as when the contact with the floor stimulates walking. In these instances there is no question of consciousness of stimulus *as* stimulus, of response *as* response. There is simply a continuously ordered sequence of acts, all adapted in themselves and in the order of their sequence, to reach a certain objective end, the reproduction of the species, the preservation of life, locomotion to a certain place. The end has got thoroughly organized into the means. In calling one stimulus, another response, we mean nothing more than that such an orderly sequence of acts is taking place. The same sort of statement might be made equally well with reference to the succession of changes in a plant, so far as these are considered with reference to their adaptation to, say, producing seed. It is equally applicable to the series of events in the circulation of the blood, or the sequence of acts occurring in a self-binding reaper.[4]

Regarding such cases of organization viewed as already attained, we may say, positively, that it is only the assumed common reference to an inclusive end which marks each member off as stimulus and response, that apart from such reference we have only antecedent and consequent;[5] in other words, the distinction is one of interpretation. Negatively, it must be pointed out that it is not legitimate to carry over, without change, exactly the same order of considerations to cases where it is a question of *conscious* stimulation and response. We may, in the above case, regard, if we please, stimulus and response each as an entire act, having an individuality of its own, subject even here to the qualification that individuality means not an entirely independent whole, but a division of labor as regards maintaining or reaching an end.

[4] To avoid misapprehension, I would say that I am not raising the question as to how far this teleology is real in any one of these cases; real or unreal, my point holds equally well. It is only when we regard the sequence of acts *as if* they were adapted to reach some end that it occurs to us to speak of one as stimulus and the other as response. Otherwise, we look at them as a *mere* series.

[5] Whether, even in such a determination, there is still not a reference of a more latent kind to an end is, of course, left open.

But in any case, it is an act, a sensorimotor co-ordination, which stimulates the response, itself in turn sensorimotor, not a sensation which stimulates a movement. Hence the illegitimacy of identifying, as is so often done, such cases of organized instincts or habits with the so-called reflex arc, or of transferring, without modification, considerations valid of this serial co-ordination of acts to the sensation-movement case.

The fallacy that arises when this is done is virtually the psychological or historical fallacy. A set of considerations which hold good only because of a completed process, is read into the content of the process which conditions this completed result. A state of things characterizing an outcome is regarded as a true description of the events which led up to this outcome; when, as a matter of fact, if this outcome had already been in existence, there would have been no necessity for the process. Or, to make the application to the case in hand, considerations valid of an attained organization or co-ordination, the orderly sequence of minor acts in a comprehensive co-ordination, are used to describe a process, *viz.*, the distinction of mere sensation as stimulus and of mere movement as response, which takes place only because such an attained organization is no longer at hand, but is in process of constitution. Neither mere sensation, nor mere movement, can ever be either stimulus or response; only an act can be that; the *sensation* as stimulus means the lack of and search for such an objective stimulus, or orderly placing of an act; just as mere movement as response means the lack of and search for the right act to complete a given co-ordination.

A recurrence to our example will make these formulae clearer. As long as the seeing is an unbroken act, which is as experienced no more mere sensation than it is mere motion (though the onlooker or psychological observer can interpret it into sensation and movement), it is in no sense the sensation which stimulates the reaching; we have, as already sufficiently indicated, only the serial steps in a co-ordination of *acts*. But now take a child who, upon reaching for bright light (that is, exercising the seeing-reaching co-ordination), has sometimes had a delightful exercise, sometimes found something good to eat and sometimes burned himself. *Now the response is not only uncertain, but the stimulus is equally uncertain; one is uncertain only in so far as the other is.* The real problem may be equally well stated as either to discover the right stimulus, to constitute the stimulus, or to discover, to constitute, the response. The question of whether to reach or to abstain from reaching is the question what sort of a bright light have we here? Is it the one which means playing with one's hands, eating milk, or burning one's fingers? The stimulus must be constituted for the response to occur. Now it is at precisely this juncture and because of it that the distinction of sensation as stimulus and motion as response arises.

The sensation or conscious stimulus is not a thing or existence by itself; it is that phase of a co-ordination requiring attention because, by reason of the conflict within the co-ordination, it is uncertain how to complete it. It is to doubt as to the next act, whether to reach or no, which gives the motive to examining the act. The end to follow is, in this sense, the stimulus. It furnishes the motivation to attend to what has just taken place; to define it more carefully. From this point of view the discovery of the stimulus is the "response" to possible movement as "stimulus." We must have an anticipatory sensation, an image, of the movements that may occur, together with their respective values, before attention will go to the seeing to break it up as a sensation of light, and of light of this particular kind. It is the initiated activities of reaching, which, inhibited by the conflict in the co-ordination, turn round, as it were, upon the seeing, and hold it from passing over into further act until its quality is determined. Just here the act as objective stimulus becomes transformed into sensation as possible, as conscious, stimulus. Just here also, motion as conscious response emerges.

In other words, sensation as stimulus does not mean any particular psychical *existence*. It means simply a function, and will have its value shift according to the special work requiring to be done. At one moment the various activities of reaching and withdrawing will be the sensation, because they are that phase of activity which sets the problem, or creates the demand for, the next act. At the next moment the previous act of seeing will furnish the sensation, being, in turn, that phase of activity which sets the pace upon which depends further action. Generalized, sensation as stimulus is always that phase of activity requiring to be defined in order that a co-ordination may be completed. What the sensation will be in particular at a given time, therefore, will depend entirely upon the way in which an activity is being used. It has no fixed quality of its own. The search for the stimulus is the search for exact conditions of action; that is, for the state of things which decides how a beginning co-ordination should be completed.

Similarly, motion, as response, has only a functional value. It is whatever will serve to complete the disintegrating co-ordination. Just as the discovery of the sensation marks the establishing of the problem, so the constitution of the response marks the solution of this problem. At one time, fixing attention, holding the eye fixed, upon the seeing and thus bringing out a certain quale of light is the response, because that is the particular act called for just then; at another time, the movement of the arm away from the light is the response. There is nothing in itself which may be labeled response. That one certain set of sensory quales should be marked off by themselves as "motion" and put in antithesis to such sensory quales as those of color, sound and contact, as legitimate claimants to the title of sensation, is wholly inexplicable unless we keep the difference of function in view. It is the eye and ear sensations which fix for us the problem; which report to us the conditions which have to be met if the co-ordination is to be successfully completed; and just the moment we need to know about our movements to get an adequate report, just that moment, motion miraculously (from the ordinary standpoint) ceases to be motion and become "muscular sensation." On the other hand, take the change in values of experience, the transformation of sensory quales. Whether this change will or will not be interpreted as movement, whether or not any consciousness of movement will arise, will depend upon whether this change is satisfactory, whether or not it is regarded as a harmonious development of a co-ordination, or whether the change is regarded as simply a means in solving a problem, an instrument in reaching a more satisfactory co-ordination. So long as our experience runs smoothly we are no more conscious of motion as motion than we are of this or that color or sound by itself.

To sum up: the distinction of sensation and movement as stimulus and response respectively is not a distinction which can be regarded as descriptive of anything which holds of psychical events or existences as such. The only events to which the terms stimulus and response can be descriptively applied are to minor acts serving by their respective positions to the maintenance of some organized co-ordination. The conscious stimulus or sensation, and the conscious response or motion, have a special genesis or motivation, and a special end or function. The reflex arc theory, by neglecting, by abstracting from, this genesis and this function gives us one disjointed part of a process as if it were the whole. It gives us literally an arc, instead of the circuit; and not giving us the circuit of which it is an arc, does not enable us to place, to center, the arc. This arc, again, falls apart into two separate existences having to be either mechanically or externally adjusted to each other.

The circle is a co-ordination, some of whose members have come into conflict with each other. It is the temporary disintegration and need of reconstitution which occasions, which affords the genesis of, the conscious distinction into sensory stimulus on one side and motor response on the other. The stimulus is that phase of the forming co-ordination which represents the conditions which have to be met in bringing it to a successful issue; the response is that phase of one and the same forming co-ordination which gives the key to meeting these conditions, which serves as instrument in effecting the successful co-ordination. They are therefore strictly correlative and contemporaneous. The stimulus is something to be discovered; to be made out; if the activity affords its own adequate stimulation, there is no stimulus save in the objective sense already referred to. As soon as it is adequately determined, then and then only is the response also complete. To attain either, means that the co-ordination has completed itself. Moreover, it is the motor response which assists in discovering and constituting the stimulus. It is the holding of the movement at a certain stage which creates the sensation, which throws it into relief.

It is the co-ordination which unifies that which the reflex arc concept gives us only in disjointed fragments. It is the circuit within which fall distinctions of stimulus and response as functional phases of its own mediation or completion. The point of this story is in its application; but the application of it to the question of the nature of psychical evolution, to the distinction between sensational and rational consciousness, and the nature of judgment must be deferred to a more favorable opportunity.

16

THE PSYCHOLOGY OF EFFORT

THERE are three distinguishable views regarding the psychical quales experienced in cases of effort. One is the conception that effort, as such, is strictly "spiritual" or "intellectual," unmediated by any sensational element whatever; it being admitted, of course, that the expression or putting forth of effort, in so far as it occurs through the muscular system, has sensational correlates. This view shades into the next in so far as its upholders separate "physical" from "moral" effort, and admit that in the former the consciousness of effort is more or less sensational in character, while in the latter remaining wholly non-sensuous in quality. The third view declines to accept the distinction made between moral and physical effort as a distinction of genesis, and holds that all sense of effort is sensationally (peripherally) determined. For example, the first theory, in its extreme or typical form, would say that when we put forth effort, whether to lift a stone, to solve a refractory problem, or to resist temptation, the sense of effort is the consciousness of pure psychical activity, to be carefully distinguished from any sense of the muscular and organic changes occurring from the actual putting forth of effort, the latter being a return wave of resulting sensations. The second view would discriminate between the cases alluded to, drawing a line between effort in lifting the stone, which is considered as itself due to sense of strain and tension arising from the actual putting forth of energy (and hence sensuously conditioned), and the two other cases. Various writers would, however, apparently draw

From *The Philosophical Review,* January, 1897; 43-56.

the line at different places, some conceding the sense of effort in intellectual attention to be sensational, mediated through feeling the contraction of muscles of forehead, fixation of eyes, changes in breathing, etc. Others would make the attention, as such, purely spiritual (*i.e.,* in this use, non-sensational), independently of whether the outcome is intellectual or moral in value. But the third view declares unambiguously that the sense of effort is, in any case, due to the organic reverberations of the act itself, the "muscular," visceral, and breathing sensations.[1]

In the following paper I purpose, for the most part, to approach this question indirectly rather than directly, my underlying conviction being that the difference between the "sensational" and "spiritual" schools is due to the fact that one is thinking of a distinctly psychological fact, the way in which the sense or *consciousness* of effort is mediated, while the other is, in reality, discussing a logical or moral problem —the interpretation of the category of effort, the value which it has as a part of experience. To the point that the distinction between "physical" and "spiritual" effort is one of interpretation, of function, rather than of kind of existence, I shall return in the sequel. Meantime, I wish to present a certain amount of introspective evidence for the position that the sense of effort (as distinguished from the fact or the category) is sensationally mediated; and then to point out that if this is admitted, the real problem of the psychology of effort is only stated, not solved; this problem being to find the sensational *differentia* between the cases in which there is, and those in which there is not, a sense of effort.

The following material was gathered, it may be said, not

[1] Professor James, to whom, along with Ferrier, we owe, for the most part the express recognition of the sensational quales concerned in effort, appears to accept the second of these three types of views. I do not know that the question has been raised as to how this distinction is reconcilable with his general theory of emotion; nor yet how his ground for making it—the superiority of the spiritual over the physical—is to be adjusted to his assertion (*Psychology*, II, p. 453) that the sensational theory of emotions does not detract from their spiritual significance.

with reference to the conscious examination of the case in hand, but in the course of a study of the facts of choice; this indirect origin makes it, I believe, all the more valuable. The cases not quoted are identical in kind with those quoted, there being no reports of a contrary sense. "In deciding a question that had to be settled in five minutes, I found myself turned in the chair, till I was sitting on its edge, with the left arm on the back of the chair, hand clenched so tightly that the marks on the nails were left in the palm, breathing so rapid that it was oppressive, winking rapid, jaws clenched, leaning far forward and supporting my head by the right hand. The question was whether I should go to the city that day. When I decided to go I felt more like resting than starting."

The next instance relates to an attempt to recall lines of poetry formerly memorized. "There is a feeling of strain. This I found to be immediately dependent upon a hard knitting of the brows and forehead—especially upon a fixing and converging of the eyes. At the same time there is a general contraction of the system as a whole. The breathing is quiet, slow, and regular, save where emotional accompaniments break it up. The meter is usually kept by a slight movement of the toes in the shoes or by a finger of the hand. As the recollection proceeds, there is a sensation of peering, of viewing the whole scene. The fixation exhausts the eyes much more than hard reading."

The succeeding instance relates to the effort involved in understanding an author. "First, I am conscious of drawing myself together, my forehead contracts, my eyes and ears seem to draw themselves in and shut themselves off. There is tension of the muscles of limbs. Secondly, a feeling of movement or plunge forward occurs. My particular sensations differ in different cases, but all have this in common: First, a feeling of tension, and then movement forward. Sometimes the forward movement is accompanied by a muscular feeling in the arms as if throwing things to right and left, in clearing a road to a desired object. Sometimes it is a feeling of climbing, and planting my foot firmly as on a height attained." [2]

Now of course I am far from thinking that these cases, or any number of such cases, prove the sensational character of the consciousness of effort. Logically, the statements are all open to the interpretation that we are concerned here with products or incidental *sequelae* of effort, rather than with its essence. But I have yet to find a student who, with growing power of introspection, did not report that to him such sensations seemed to constitute the "feel" of effort. Moreover, the cumulative force of such statements is very great, if not logically conclusive. Many state that if they relax their muscles entirely it is impossible to keep up the effort. Sensations frequently mentioned are those connected with breathing— stopping the respiration, breathing more rapidly, contracted chest and throat; others are contraction of brow, holding head fixed, or twisting it, compression of lips, clenching of fist, contraction of jaws, sensations in pit of stomach, goneness in legs, shoulders higher, head lower than usual, fogginess or mistiness in visual field, trying to see something which eludes vision, etc.

But upon the whole I intend rather to assume that the sense of effort is, in all its forms, sensationally conditioned. We have in this fact (if it be a fact) no adequate psychology of effort, but only the preliminary of such theory. The conception up to this point has, for theoretical purposes, negative value only; it is useful in overthrowing other theories of effort, but throws no positive light upon its nature. The problem of interest, as soon as the rival theories are dismissed, comes to be this: Granted the sensational character of the consciousness of effort, what is its specific *differentia?* What we wish now to know is what set of sensory values marks off experiences of effort from those closely resembling, but not felt as cases of effort. So far as I know this question has not been raised.

How then does, say, a case of perception with effort differ

---

[2] A number of cases, on further questioning, reported a similar rhythm of contraction and movement accompanying mental effort. This topic would stand special inquiry.

from a case of "easy" or effortless perception? The difference, I repeat, shall be wholly in sensory quale; but in *what* sensory quale?

At this point a reversion to a different point of view, and the introduction of a different order of ideas is likely to occur. We may be told, as an explanation of the difference, that in one case we have a feeling of activity, a feeling of the putting forth of energy. I found that persons who in special cases have become thoroughly convinced of the sensational quality of all consciousness of effort, will make this answer. The explanation is, I think, that the point of view unconsciously shifts from effort as a psychical fact, as fact of direct consciousness, to effort as an objective or teleological fact. We stop thinking of the sense of effort, and think of the reference or import of the experience. Effort, as putting forth of energy, is involved equally in all psychical occurrences. It exists with a sense of ease just as much as with a sense of strain. There may be more of it in cases of extreme absorption and interest, where no effort is felt, than in cases of extreme sense of effort. Compare, for example, the psychophysical energy put forth in listening to a symphony, or in viewing a picture gallery, with that exercised in trying to fix a small moving speck on the wall; compare the energy, that is, as objectively measured. In the former case, the whole being may be intensely active, and yet there may be, at the time, absolutely no consciousness of effort or strain. The latter may be, objectively, a very trivial activity, and yet the consciousness of strain may be the chief thing in the conscious experience. In some cases it seems almost as if the relation between effort as an objective fact, and effort as a psychical fact, were an inverse one. If a monotonous physical movement be indefinitely repeated, it will generally be found that as long as "activity" is put forth, and accomplishes something objectively (as measured in some dynometric register), there is little sense of effort. Let the energy be temporarily exhausted and action practically cease, then the sense of effort will be at its maximum. Let a wave of energy recur, and there is at once a sense of lightness, of ease. And in all cases, the sense of effort and ease follows, never precedes, the change in activity as objectively measured.

We are not concerned, accordingly, with any question of the existence or non-existence of spiritual activity, or even of psychophysical activity. The reference to this, as furnishing the *differentia* of cases of consciousness of effort from those of ease, is not so much false as irrelevant.

Where, then, shall we locate the discriminative factor? Take the simplest possible case: I try to make out the exact form, or the nature, of a faint marking on a piece of paper a few feet off, at about the limit of distinct vision. What is the special sensation carrier of the sense of effort here? Introspectively I believe the answer is very simple. In the case of felt effort, certain sensory quales, usually fused, fall apart in consciousness, and there is an alternation, an oscillation, between them, accompanied by a disagreeable tone when they are apart, and an agreeable tone when they become fused again. Moreover, the separation in consciousness during the period when the quales are apart is not complete, but the image of the fused quale is at least dimly present. Specifically, in ordinary or normal vision, there is no distinction within consciousness of the ocular-motor sensation which corresponds to fixation, from the optical sensations of light and color. The two are so intimately fused that there is but one quale in consciousness. In these cases, there is feeling of ease, or at least absence of sense of effort. In other cases, the sensations corresponding to frowning, to holding the head steady, the breathing fixed—the whole adjustment of motor apparatus—come into consciousness of themselves on their own account. Now we are not accustomed to find satisfaction in the experience of motor adjustment; the relevant sensations have value and interest, not in themselves, but in the specific quales of sound, color, touch, or whatever they customarily introduce. In at least ninety-nine one-hundreths of our experience, the "muscular" sensations are felt simply as passing over into some other experience which is either aimed at, or which, when experienced, affords satisfaction. A habit of expectation, of looking forward to some other experience, thus comes to be the normal associate of motor experience. It is felt as fringe, as "tendency," not as psychical resting place. Whenever it persists as motor, whenever the expectation of other sensory quales of positive value is not met, there is at least a transitory feeling of futility, of thwartedness, or of irritation at a failure. Hence the disagreeable tone referred to. But in the type of cases taken as our illustration, more is true than a failure of an expected consequent through mere inertia of habit. The image of the end aimed at persists, and, through its contrast with the partial motor quale, emphasizes and reinforces the sense of incompleteness. That is to say, one is continually imaging the speck as having some particular form—an oval or an angular form; as having a certain nature —an inkspot, a flyspeck. Then this image is as continually interfered with by the sensations of motor adjustment coming to consciousness by themselves. Each experience breaks into, and breaks up, the other before it has attained fullness. Let the image of a five-sided inkspot be acquiesced in apart from the motor adjustment (in other words, let one pass into the state of reverie), or let the "muscular" sensations be given complete sway by themselves (as when one begins to study them in his capacity as psychologist), and all sense of effort disappears. It is the rivalry, with the accompanying disagreeable tone due to failure of habit, that constitutes the sense of effort.

It will be useful to apply the terms of this analysis to some attendant phenomena of effort. First, it enables us to account for the growing sense of effort with fatigue, without having to resort to a set of conceptions lying outside the previously used ideas. The sense of fatigue increases effort, just because it marks the emergence into consciousness of a distinct new set of sensations which resist absorption into, or fusion with, the dominant images of the current habit or purpose. Upon the basis of other theories of effort, fatigue increases sense of effort because of sheer exhaustion; upon this theory, because of the elements introduced which distract attention. Other theories, in other words, have to fall back upon an extra-psychical factor, and something which is heterogeneous with

[273]

the other factors concerned. Moreover, they fail to account for the fact that if the feeling of fatigue is surrendered to, it ceases to be disagreeable, and may become a delicious languor.

In a similar way certain facts connected with sense of effort, as related to the mastery of novel acts, may be explained. Take the alternation of ridiculous excess of effort, with total collapse of effort in learning to ride a bicycle. Before one mounts one has perhaps a pretty definite visual image of himself in balance and in motion. This image persists as a desirability. On the other hand, there comes into play at once the consciousness of the familiar motor adjustments— for the most part, related to walking. The two sets of sensations refuse to coincide, and the result is an amount of stress and strain relevant to the most serious problems of the universe. Or, again, the conflict becomes so unregulated that the image of the balance disappears, and one finds himself with only a lot of "muscular" sensations at hand; the effort entirely vanishes. I have taken an extreme case, but surely everyone is familiar, in dealing with unfamiliar occupations, of precisely this alternation of effort, out of all proportion to the objective significance of the end, with the complete mind-wandering and failure of endeavor. If the sense of effort is the sense of incompatibility between two sets of sensory images, one of which stands for an end to be reached, or a fulfillment of a habit, while the other represents the experiences which intervene in reaching the end, these phenomena are only what are to be expected. But if we start from a "spiritual" theory of effort, I know of no explanation which is anything more than an hypostatized repetition of the facts to be explained.

It probably has already occurred to the reader, that when the theory of the sensational character of the consciousness of effort is analyzed, instead of being merely thrown out at large, the feeling that it deals common sense a blow in the face disappears. If we state the foregoing analysis in objective, instead of in psychical, terms, it just says that effort is the feeling of opposition existing between end and means. The kinesthetic image of qualitative nature (*i.e.,* of color, sound, contact) stands for the end, whether consciously desired, or as furnishing the culmination of habit. The "muscular" sensations[3] represent the means, the experiences to which value is not attached on their own account, but as intermediaries to an intrinsically valuable consciousness.

Practically stated, this means that effort is nothing more, and also nothing less, than tension between means and ends in action, and that the sense of effort is the awareness of this conflict. The sensational character of this experience, which has been such a stumbling to some, means that this tension of adjustment is not merely ideal, but is actual (*i.e.,* practical); it is one which goes on in a struggle for existence. Being a struggle for realization in the world of concrete quales and values, it makes itself felt in the only media possible—specific sensations, on the one hand, and muscular sensations, on the other. Instead of denying, or slurring over, effort, such an account brings it into prominence. Surely what common sense values in effort is not some transcendental act, occurring before any change in the actual world of qualities, but precisely this readjustment within the concrete region. And if one is somewhat scandalized at being told that the awareness of effort is a sense of changes of breathing, of muscular tensions, etc., it is not, I conceive, because of what is said, but rather because of what is left unsaid—that these sensations report the state of things as regards effective realization.

It is difficult to see, upon a more analytic consideration than common sense is called upon to make, what is gained for the "spiritual" nature of effort by relegating it to a purely extrasensational region. That "spiritual" is to be so interpreted as to mean existence in a sphere transcending space and time determinations is, at best, a piece of metaphysics, and not a piece of psychology; and as a piece of metaphysics, it cannot escape competition with the theory which finds the meaning of the spiritual in the whole process of realizing the concrete values of life. I do not find that any of the upholders

[3] Perhaps it would be well to state that sensations of tendons, joints, internal contacts, etc., are what is meant by this term—the whole report of the motor adjustment.

of the non-sensational quality of effort has ever made a very specific analysis of the experience. Professor Baldwin's account, however, being perhaps the most thoroughgoing statement of effort as preceding sensation, in "physical" as well as "spiritual" effort, is, perhaps, as explicit as any. In one passage, effort is "distinct consciousness of opposition between what we call self and muscular resistance." Now a consciousness of muscular resistance, whatever else it may or may not be, would seem to involve sensations, and the consciousness of effort to be, so far forth, sensationally mediated—which is contrary to the hypothesis. Moreover, it is extremely difficult to see how there can be any consciousness of opposition between the self in general, and the muscles in general. Until the "self" actually starts to do something (and then, of course, there are sensations), how can the muscles offer any opposition to it? And even when it does begin to do something, how can the muscles, as muscles, offer opposition? If because the act is unfamiliar, then certainly what we get is simply a case of difficulty in the having of a unified consciousness—the kinesthetic image of the habitual movement will not unify with the proposed sensory image, and there is rivalry. But this is not a case of muscles resisting the self; it is a case of divided activity of the self. It means that the activity already going on (and, therefore, reporting itself sensationally) resists displacement, or transformation, by or into another activity which is beginning, and thus making its sensational report.

But Professor Baldwin gives another statement which is apparently different. "In all voluntary movement, therefore, there is an earlier fiat than the will to move, *i.e.,* the fiat of attention to the particular idea of movement." And it is repeatedly intimated that the real difficulty in effort is, not in the muscular execution, but in holding a given idea in consciousness. (In fact, it is distinctly stated that, even in muscular effort, the real effort is found in "attending" to the idea.) Now, this statement is certainly preferable to the other, in that it avoids the appearance of making the muscles offer resistance to the self. But now, what has become of the resistance, and, hence, of the effort? Is there anything left to offer opposition *to* the self? Can an idea, *qua* pure idea, offer resistance and demand effort? And is it the self, as barely self, to which resistance is made? Such questions may, perhaps, serve to indicate the abstractness of the account, and suggest the fact that effort is never felt, save when a *change of existing activity is proposed*. In this case, the effort may be centered in the introduction of the new idea as against the persistence of the present doing, or it may be to maintain the existing habit against the suggested change. In the former, the new activity will probably be categorized as duty; in the latter case, as temptation or distraction. But in either alternative, effort is felt with reference to the adjustment of factors in an action. Neither of these is exclusively self, neither the old nor the new factor; and the one which happens to be especially selected as self varies with the state of action. At one period, the end or aim is regarded as self, and the existing habit, or mode of action, as the obstruction to the realization of the desired self; at the next stage, the end having been pretty well defined, the habit, or existing line of action, since the only means or instrument for attaining this end, is conceived as self, and the ideal as "beyond," and at once as resisting and as soliciting the self.

I do not suppose anyone will question this account, so far as relates to the fact that the sense of effort arises only with reference to a proposed change in the existing activity, and that at least the existing activity has its sensational counterpart. Doubt is more likely to arise as regards the proposed end, or the intruding distraction. This, it may be said, is pure idea, not activity, and, hence, has no sensational report. But whoever takes this position must be able to explain the *differentia* between instances of logical manipulation of an idea, aesthetic contemplation, and cases of sense of effort. I may take the idea of something I ought to do, but which is repulsive to me; may say that I ought to do it, and may then hold the idea as an idea or object in consciousness, may revolve it in all lights, may turn it over and over, may chew it as a sweet or a bitter cud, and yet have absolutely no sense of effort. It is only, so far as I can trust my own observation,

[277]

when this idea passes into at least nascent or partial action, and thus comes head up against some other line of action, that the sense of effort arises.

In other words, the sense of effort arises, not because there is an activity struggling against resistance, or a self which is endeavoring to overcome obstacles outside of it; but it arises within activity, marking the attempt to co-ordinate separate factors within a single whole. Activity is here taken not as formal, but as actual and specific. It means an act, definitely doing something definite. An act, as something which occupies time, necessarily means conflict of acts. The demand for time is simply the result of a lack of unity. The intervening process of execution, the use of means, is the process of disintegrating acts hitherto separate and independent, and putting together the result, or fragments, into a single piece of conduct. Were it not for the division of acts and results in conflict, the deed, or co-ordination, would be accomplished at once.

One of the conflicting acts stands for the end or aim. This, at first, is the sensory image which gives the cue and motive to the reaction or response. In the case previously cited, it is the image of the colored speck, as determining the movements of the head and eye muscles.[4] That we are inclined to view only the motor response as act, and regard the image, either as alone psychical, or as pure idea, is because the image is already in existence, and, therefore, its active side may be safely neglected. Being already in possession of the field, it does not require any conscious activity to keep it in existence. The movement of the muscles, being the means by which the desired end may be reached, becomes the all-important thing, or *the* act; in accordance with the general principle that attention always goes to the weakest part of a co-ordination in process of formation, meaning by weakest, that part least under the immediate control of habit. This being conceived alone as act, everything lying outside of it is conceived as

---

[4] It must not be forgotten that both sensory stimulus and motor response are both in reality sensorimotor, and, therefore, each is itself an act or psychical whole. On this point, see my "The Reflex Arc Concept."

resistance; thus recognition is avoided of the fact, that the real state of things is, that there are two acts mutually opposing each other, during their transformation over into a third new and inclusive act.

We have here, I think, an adequate explanation of all that can be said about the tremendous importance of effort, of all that Professor James has so conclusively said. This importance is not due to the fact that effort is the one sole evidence of a free spiritual activity struggling against outward and material resistance. It is due to the fact that effort is the critical point of progress in action, arising whenever old habits are in process of reconstruction, or of adaptation to new conditions; unless they are so readapted, life is given over to the rule of conservatism, routine, and over-inertia. To make a new co-ordination the old co-ordination must, to some extent, be broken up, and the only way of breaking it up is for it to come into conflict with some other co-ordination; that is, a conflict of two acts, each representing a habit, or end, is the necessary condition of reaching a new act which shall have a more comprehensive end. That sensations of the bodily state report to us this conflict and readjustment, merely indicates that the reconstruction going on is one of acts, and not mere ideas. The whole prejudice which supposes that the spiritual sense of effort is lost when it is given sensational quality, is simply a survival of the notion that an idea is somehow more spiritual than an act.

Up to this time I have purposely avoided any reference to the attempt to explain effort by attention. My experience has been that this mode of explanation does not explain, but simply shifts the difficulty, at the same time making it more obscure by claiming to solve it. There is some danger that attention may become a psychological pool of Bethesda. If we have escaped the clutch of associationalism, only to fall into attentionalism, we have hardly bettered our condition in psychology. But the preceding account would apply to any concrete analyses of effort in terms of attention. The psychological fallacy besets us here. We confuse attention as an objective fact, attention for the observer, with attention as consciously experienced. During complete absorption an onlooker may remark how attentive such a person is, or after such an absorption one may look back and say how attentive one was; but taking the absorption when it occurs, it means that only the subject matter is present in consciousness, not attention itself. We are conscious of being attentive only when our attention is divided, only when there are two centers of attention competing with each other, only when there is an oscillation from one group of ideas to another, together with a tendency to a third group of ideas, in which the two previous groups are included. The sense of strain in attention, instead of being coincident with the activity of attention, is proof that attention itself is not yet complete.

To establish the identity of attention with the formation of a new act, through the mutual adaptation of two existing habits, would take us too far away from our present purpose; but there need be no hesitation, I believe, in admitting that the sense of attention arises only under the conditions of conflict already stated.

17

INTERPRETATION OF THE SAVAGE MIND

THE psychical attitudes and traits of the savage are more than stages through which mind has passed, leaving them behind. They are outgrowths which have entered decisively into further evolution, and as such form an integral part of the framework of present mental organization. Such positive significance is commonly attributed, in theory at least, to animal mind; but the mental structure of the savage, which presumably has an even greater relevancy for genetic psychology, is strangely neglected.

The cause of this neglect I believe lies in the scant results so far secured, because of the abuse of the comparative method—which abuse in turn is due to the lack of a proper method of interpretation. Comparison as currently employed is defective—even perverse—in at least three respects. In the first place, it is used indiscriminately and arbitrarily. Facts are torn loose from their context in social and natural environment and heaped miscellaneously together, because they have impressed the observer as alike in some respect. Upon a single page of Spencer[1] which I chanced to open in looking for an illustration of this point, appear Kamschadales, Kirghiz, Bedouins, East Africans, Bechuanas, Damaras, Hottentots, Malays, Papuans, Fijians, Andamanese—all cited in reference to establishing a certain common property of primitive minds. What would we think of a biologist who appealed successively to some external characteristic of, say, snake, butterfly, elephant, oyster and robin in support of a

From *The Psychological Review*, May, 1902; 217-230.
[1] *Sociology*, I, p. 57.

statement? And yet the peoples mentioned present widely remote cultural resources, varied environments and distinctive institutions. What is the scientific value of a proposition thus arrived at?

In the second place, this haphazard, uncontrollable selection yields only static facts—facts which lack the dynamic quality necessary to a genetic consideration. The following is a summary of Mr. Spencer's characterizations of primitive man, emotional and intellectual:

He is explosive and chaotic in feeling, improvident, childishly mirthful, intolerant of restraint, with but small flow of altruistic feeling attentive to meaningless detail and incapable of selecting the facts from which conclusions may be drawn, with feeble grasp of thought, incapable of rational surprise, incurious, lacking in ingenuity and constructive imagination. Even the one quality which is stated positively, namely, keenness of perception, is interpreted in a purely negative way, as a character antagonistic to reflective development. "In proportion as the mental energies go out in restless perception, they cannot go out in deliberate thought." And this from a sensationalist in psychology!

Such descriptions as these also bear out my first point. Mr. Spencer himself admits frequent and marked discrepancies, and it would not be difficult to bring together a considerable mass of proof-texts to support the exact opposite of each of his assertions. But my point here is that present civilized mind is virtually taken as a standard, and savage mind is measured off on this fixed scale.

It is no wonder that the outcome is negative; that primitive mind is described in terms of "lack," "absence": its traits are incapacities. Qualities defined in such fashion are surely useless in suggesting, to say nothing of determining, progress, and are correspondingly infertile for genetic psychology, which is interested in becoming, growth, development.

The third remark is that the results thus reached, even passing them as correct, yield only loose aggregates of unrelated traits—not a coherent scheme of mind. We do not escape from an inorganic conglomerate conception of mind by just abusing the "faculty" psychology. Our standpoint must be more positive. We must recognize that mind has a pattern, a scheme of arrangement in its constituent elements, and that it is the business of a serious comparative psychology to exhibit these patterns, forms or types in detail. By such terms, I do not mean anything metaphysical; I mean to indicate the necessity of a conception such as is a commonplace with the zoologist. Terms like articulate or vertebrate, carnivor or herbivor, are "pattern" terms of the sort intended. They imply that an animal is something more than a random composite of isolated parts, made by taking an eye here, an ear there, a set of teeth somewhere else. They signify that the constituent elements are arranged in a certain way; that in being co-adapted to the dominant functions of the organism they are of necessity co-related with one another. Genetic psychology of mind will advance only as it discovers and specifies generic forms or patterns of this sort in psychic morphology.

It is a method for the determination of such types that I wish to suggest in this paper. The biological point of view commits us to the conviction that mind, whatever else it may be, is at least an organ of service for the control of environment in relation to the ends of the life process.

If we search in any social group for the special functions to which mind is thus relative, occupations at once suggest themselves.[2] Occupations determine the fundamental modes of activity, and hence control the formation and use of habits. These habits, in turn, are something more than practical and overt. "Apperceptive masses" and associational tracts of necessity conform to the dominant activities. The occupations determine the chief modes of satisfaction, the standards of success and failure. Hence they furnish the working classifi-

[2] We might almost say, in the converse direction, that biological genera are "occupational" classifications. They connote different ways of getting a living with the different instrumentalities (organs) appropriate to them, and the different associative relations set up by them.

cations and definitions of value; they control the desire processes. Moreover, they decide the sets of objects and relations that are important, and thereby provide the content or material of attention, and the qualities that are interestingly significant. The directions given to mental life thereby extend to emotional and intellectual characteristics. So fundamental and pervasive is the group of occupational activities that it affords the scheme or pattern of the structural organization of mental traits. Occupations integrate special elements into a functioning whole.

Because the hunting life differs from, say, the agricultural, in the sort of satisfactions and ends it furnishes, in the objects to which it requires attention, in the problems it sets for reflection and deliberation, as well as in the psychophysic coordinations it stimulates and selects, we may well speak, and without metaphor, of the hunting psychosis or mental type. And so of the pastoral, the military, the trading, the manually productive (or manufacturing) occupations and so on. As a specific illustration of the standpoint and method, I shall take the hunting vocation, and that as carried on by the Australian aborigines. I shall try first to describe its chief distinguishing marks; and then to show how the mental pattern developed is carried over into various activities, customs and products, which on their face have nothing to do with the hunting life. If a controlling influence of this sort can be made out—if it can be shown that art, war, marriage, etc., tend to be psychologically assimilated to the pattern developed in the hunting vocation, we shall thereby get an important method for the interpretation of social institutions and cultural resources —a psychological method for sociology.

The Australian lives in an environment upon the whole benign, without intense or violent unfavorable exhibition of natural forces (save in alternations of drought and flood in some portions), not made dangerous by beasts of prey, and with a sufficient supply of food to maintain small groups in a good state of nutrition though not abundant enough to do this without continual change of abode. The tribes had no cultivated plants, no domesticated animals (save the dingo dog), hence no beasts of burden, and no knowledge or use of metals.[3]

Now as to the psychic pattern formed under such circumstances. How are the sensory-motor co-ordinations common to all men organized, how stimulated and inhibited into relatively permanent psychic habits, through the activities appropriate to such a situation?

By the nature of the case, food and sex stimuli are the most exigent of all excitants to psychophysic activity, and the interests connected with them are the most intense and persistent. But with civilized man, all sorts of intermediate terms come in between the stimulus and the overt act, and between the overt act and the final satisfaction. Man no longer defines his end to be the satisfaction of hunger as such. It is so complicated and loaded with all kinds of technical activities, associations, deliberations and social divisions of labor, that conscious attention and interest are in the process and its content. Even in the crudest agriculture, means are developed to the point where they demand attention on their own account, and control the formation and use of habits to such an extent that they are the central interests, while the food process and enjoyment as such is incidental and occasional.

The gathering and saving of seed, preparing the ground, sowing, tending, weeding, care of cattle, making of improvements, continued observation of times and seasons, engage thought and direct action. In a word, in all post-hunting situations the end is mentally apprehended and appreciated not as food satisfaction, but as a continuously ordered series of activities and of objective contents pertaining to them. And hence the direct and personal display of energy, personal put-

[3] All these points are important, for the general hunting psychosis exhibits marked differentiations when developed in relation to ferocious beasts; in relation to a very sparse or very abundant food supply; in relation to violently hostile natural forces; and when hunting is pursued in connection with various degrees of agriculture or domesticated herds or flocks. For economy of space, I have omitted reference to the few portions of Australia where the food supply (generally fish in such circumstances) is sufficiently abundant to permit quasi-permanent abodes, though the psychological variations thus induced are interesting.

ting forth of effort, personal acquisition and use of skill are not conceived or felt as immediate parts of the food process. But the exact contrary is the case in hunting. There are no intermediate appliances, no adjustment of means to remote ends, no postponements of satisfaction, no transfer of interest and attention over to a complex system of acts and objects. Want, effort, skill and satisfaction stand in the closest relations to one another. The ultimate aim and the urgent concern of the moment are identical; memory of the past and hope for the future meet and are lost in the stress of the present problem; tools, implements, weapons, are not mechanical and objective means, but are part of the present activity, organic parts of personal skill and effort. The land is not a means to a result but an intimate and fused portion of life— a matter not of objective inspection and analysis, but of affectionate and sympathetic regard. The making of weapons is felt as a part of the exciting use of them. Plants and animals are not "things," but are factors in the display of energy and form the contents of most intense satisfactions. The "animism" of primitive mind is a necessary expression of the immediacy of relation existing between want, overt activity, that which affords satisfaction and the attained satisfaction itself. Only when things are treated simply as *means*, are marked off and held off against remote ends, do they become "objects."

Such immediacy of interest, attention and deed is the essential trait of the nomad hunter. He has no cultivated plants, no system of appliances and tending and regulating plants and animals; he does not even anticipate the future by drying meat. When food is abundant, he gorges himself, but does not save. His habitation is a temporary improvised hut. In the interior, he does not even save skins for clothes in the cold of winter, but cooks them with the rest of the carcass. Generally even by the water he has no permanent boats, but makes one of bark when and as he needs it. He has no tools or equipment except those actually in use at the moment of getting or using food—weapons of the chase and war. Even set traps and nets which work for the savage are practically unknown. He catches beast, bird and fish with his own hands when he does not use club or spear; and if he uses nets he is himself personally concerned in their use.

Now such facts as these are usually given a purely negative interpretation. They are used as proofs of the incapacities of the savage. But in fact they are parts of a very positive psychosis which, taken in itself and not merely measured against something else, requires and exhibits highly specialized skill and affords intense satisfactions—psychical and social satisfactions, not merely sensuous indulgences. The savage's repugnance to what we term a higher plane of life is not due to stupidity or dullness or apathy—or to any other merely negative qualities—such traits are a later development and fit the individual only too readily for exploitation as a tool by "superior races." His aversion is due to the fact that in the new occupations he does not have so clear or so intense a sphere for the display of intellectual and practical skill, or such opportunity for a dramatic play of emotion. Consciousness, even if superficial, is maintained at a higher intensity.[4]

The hunting life is of necessity one of great emotional interest, and of adequate demand for acquiring and using highly specialized skills of sense, movement, ingenuity, strategy and combat. It is hardly necessary to argue the first point. Game and sport are still words which mean the most intense immediate play of the emotions, running their entire gamut. And these terms still are applied most liberally and most appropriately to hunting. The transferred application of the hunting language to pursuit of truth, plot interest, business adventure and speculation, to all intense and active forms of amusement, to gambling and the "sporting life," evidences how deeply imbedded in later consciousness is the hunting pattern or schema.[5]

[4] For good statements by competent authorities of the Australian's aversion to agriculture, etc., see Hodginkson, *Australia, from Port Macquarie to Moreton Bay*, p. 243; and Grey, *Two Expeditions*, etc., II, p. 279.

[5] See Thomas's "The Gaming Instinct," *American Journal of Sociology*, Vol. VI, p. 750. I am indebted to Dr. Thomas (through personal conversation as well as from his articles) for not only specific suggestions, but for the point of view here presented to such an extent that this article is virtually a joint contribution.

The interest of the game, the alternate suspense and movement, the strained and alert attention to stimuli always changing, always demanding graceful, prompt, strategic and forceful response; the play of emotions along the scale of want, effort, success or failure—this is the very type, psychically speaking, of the drama. The breathless interest with which we hang upon the movement of play or novel are reflexes of the mental attitudes evolved in the hunting vocation.

The savage loses nothing in enjoyment of the drama because it means life or death to him.[6] The emotional interest in the game itself is moreover immensely reinforced and deepened by its social accompaniments. Skill and success mean applause and admiration; it means the possibility of lavish generosity—the quality that wins all. Rivalry and emulation and vanity all quicken and feed it. It means sexual admiration and conquests—more wives or more elopements. It means, if persistent, the ultimate selection of the individual for all tribal positions of dignity and authority.

But perhaps the most conclusive evidence of the emotional satisfactions involved is the fact that the men reserve the hunting occupation to themselves, and give to the women everything that has to do with the vegetable side of existence (where the passive subject matter does not arouse the dramatic play), and all activity of every sort that involves the more remote adaptation of means to ends—and hence, drudgery.[7]

The same sort of evidence is found in the fact that, with change to agricultural life, other than hunting types of action are (if women do not suffice) handed over to slaves, and the energy and skill acquired go into the game of war. This also explains the apparent contradiction in the psychic retrogression of the mass with some advances in civilization. The gain is found in the freed activities of the few, and in the cumulation of the objective instrumentalities of social life, and in

[6] Though some writers even say that the savage's interest in the game of hunting is so great that he hunts for the excitement rather than for food. See Lumholtz, *Among Cannibals*, p. 161 and p. 191.

[7] This collateral development of a different mental pattern in women is a matter of the greatest significance, in itself, in its relation to subsequent developments and in relation to present mental interests.

the final development, under the discipline of subjection, of new modes of interest having to do with remoter ends—considerations, however, which are psychologically realized by the mass only at much later periods.

As to the high degree of skill, practical and intellectual, stimulated and created by the hunting occupation, the case is equally clear—provided, that is, we bear in mind the types of skill appropriate to the immediate adjustments required, and do not look for qualities irrelevant because useless in such a situation.

No one has ever called a purely hunting race dull, apathetic or stupid. Much has been written regarding the aversion of savages to higher resources of civilization—their refusal to adopt iron tools or weapons, for example, and their sodden absorption in routine habits. None of this applies to the Australian or any other *pure* hunting type. Their attention is mobile and fluid as is their life; they are eager to the point of greed for anything which will fit into their dramatic situations so as to intensify skill and increase emotion. Here again the apparent discrepancies strengthen the case. It is when the native is forced into an alien use of the new resources, instead of adapting them to his own ends, that his workmanship, skill and artistic taste uniformly degenerate.

Competent testimony is unanimous as to the quickness and accuracy of apprehension evinced by the natives in coming in contact even for the first time with complicated constructive devices of civilized man, provided only these appliances have a direct or immediate action-index. One of the commonest remarks of travelers, hardly prepossessed in favor of the savage, is their superiority in keenness, alertness and a sort of intelligent good humor to the average English rustic. The accuracy, quickness and minuteness of perception of eye, ear and smell are no barren accumulation of meaningless sense detail as Spencer would have it; they are the cultivation to the highest point of skill and emotional availability of the instrumentalities and modes of a dramatic life. The same applies to the native's interest in hard and sustained labor, to his patience and perseverance as well as to his gracefulness and dexterity of movement—the latter extending to fingers and toes to an extent which makes even skilled Europeans awkward and clumsy. The usual denial of power of continued hard work, of patience and of endurance to the savage is based once more upon trying him by a foreign standard—interest in ends which involve a long series of means detached from all problems of purely personal adjustment. Patience and persistence and long-maintained effort the savage does show when they come within the scope of that immediate contest situation with reference to which his mental pattern is formed.

I hardly need say, I suppose, that in saying these things I have no desire to idealize savage intelligence and volition. The savage paid for highly specialized skill in all matters of personal adjustment, by incapacity in all that is impersonal, that is to say, remote, generalized, objectified, abstracted. But my point is that we understand their incapacities only by seeing them as the obverse side of positively organized developments; and, still more, that it is only by viewing them primarily in their positive aspect that we grasp the genetic significance of savage mind for the long and tortuous process of mental development, and secure from its consideration assistance in comprehending the structure of present mind.

I come now to a brief consideration of the second main point—the extent to which this psychic pattern is carried over into all the relations of life, and becomes emotionally an assimilating medium. First, take art. The art of the Australian is not constructive, not architectonic, not graphic, but dramatic and mimetic.[8] Every writer who has direct knowledge of the Australian corroborees, whether occasional and secular, or state and ceremonial, testifies to the remarkable interest shown in dramatic representation. The reproduction by dances, of the movements and behavior of the animals of the chase is startling. Great humor is also shown in adapting and reproducing recent events and personal traits. These per-

[8] There are of course pictures, but comparatively speaking, few and crude. Even the carvings, if originally pictorial, have mostly lost that quality, and become conventional.

formances are attended with high emotional attacks; and all the accompaniments of decoration, song, music, spectators' shouts, etc., are designed to revive the feelings appropriate to the immediate conflict-situations which mean so much to the savage. Novelty is at a distinct premium; old songs are discarded; one of the chief interests at an intertribal friendly meeting is learning new dance songs; and acquisition of a new one is often sufficient motive for invitation to a general meeting.

The ceremonial corroborees are of course more than forms of art.[9] We have in them the sole exception to the principle that the activities of the hunter are immediate. Here they are weighted with a highly complicated structure of elaborated traditional rites—elaborated and complicated almost beyond belief.[10] But it is an exception which proves the rule. This apparatus of traditionary agencies has no reference to either practical or intellectual control, it gets nowhere objectively. Its effect is just to reinstate the emotional excitations of the food conflict-situations; and particularly to frame in the young the psychic disposition which will make them thoroughly interested in the necessary performances.[11]

It is a natural transition to religion. Totemism and the abundance of plant and animal myths (especially the latter) and the paucity of cosmic and cosmogonic myth testify to the centering of attention upon the content of the combat, or hunting situation. It would be absurd to attempt in a parenthesis an explanation of totemism, but certainly any explanation is radically defective which does not make much of the implication of tribe and animal in the same emotional situation. Hunter and hunted are the factors of a single tension; the mental situation cannot be defined except in terms of

[9] It is, of course, a historic fact that the actual origin of dramatic art (through the Greeks) is in mimetic dances of a festival and ceremonial sort.

[10] The best account is of course Spencer and Gillen. Certain ceremonies take weeks.

[11] Not, of course, that all these ceremonies are initiatory in character; on the contrary, many are "magical," intended to promote the productivity of their chief food supplies. But even these were conducted in dramatic fashion, and in such way as to reproduce the emotional disposition involved in the actual occupational life.

both. If animals get away, it is surely because they try; and if they are caught it is surely because after all they are not totally averse—they are friendly. And they seal their friendliness by sharing in one of the most intense satisfactions of life —savory food to the hungry. They are, as a matter of fact, co-partners in the life of the group. Why then should they not be represented as of close kin? In any case, attention and interest center in animals more persistently than in anything else; and they afford the content of whatever concentrated intellectual activity goes on. The food taboos, with their supernatural sanctions, certainly create tensions or reinstate conflict-situations, in the mind; and thus serve to keep alive in consciousness values which otherwise would be more nearly relegated to the mechanically habitual, or become sensuous, not idealized or emotionalized.

I turn now to matters of death and sickness, their cause, and cure, or, if cure is hopeless, their remedy by expiation. Here the assimilation to the psychosis of the hunting activity is obvious. Sickness and death from sickness are uniformly treated as the results of attacks of other persons, who with secret and strange weapons are hunting their victim to his death. And the remedy is to hunt the hunter, to get the aid of that wonderful pursuer and tracker, the medicine man, who by superior ability runs down the guilty party, or with great skill hunts out the deadly missile or poison lodged in the frame of his victim.

If death ensues, then we have the devices for tracking and locating the guilty party. And then comes actual conflict, actual man-hunting. Death can be avenged only by the ordeal of battle—and here we have the explanation of the wars and warlike performances of which so much has been made. It is, however, now generally admitted that the chief object of these warlike meetings is to reinstate the emotion of conflict rather than to kill. They are, so to speak, psychological duels on a large scale—as one observer says, they are "fights with a maximum of noise, boast, outward show of courage and a minimum of casualties." [12] But the maneuvering, throwing

[12] Horn, *Expedition*, Vol. IV, p. 36.

and dodging that take place are a positive dramatic exercise in the utilities of their occupational pursuits.

Finally, as to marriage, and the relations between the sexes. What was said concerning the impossibility of an adequate account of totemism applies with greater force to the problem of the system of group relationships which determine marital possibilities. It is clear, however, that the system of injunctions and restrictions serves to develop a scheme of inhibitions and intensified stimuli which makes sex satisfaction a matter of pursuit, conflict, victory and trophy over again. There is neither complete absence of inhibition, which, involving little personal adjustment, does not bring the sexual sensations into the sphere of emotion as such; nor is there a system of voluntary agreement and affection, which is possible only with a highly developed method of intellectual control, and large outlooks upon a long future. There is just the ratio between freedom and restraint that develops the dramatic instinct, and gives courtship and the possession of women all the emotional joys of the hunt—personal display, rivalry, enough exercise of force to stimulate the organism; and the emotion of prowess joined to the physical sensations of indulgence. Here, as elsewhere in the hunting psychosis, novelty is at a premium, for the mind is dependent upon a present or immediate stimulus to get activity going. It requires no deep scientific analysis to inform us that sex relations are still largely in the dramatized stage; and the play of emotion which accompanies the enacting of the successive stages of the drama gives way to genuine affection and intelligent foresight only slowly through great modifications of the whole educative and economic environment. Recent writers, I think, in their interest on the institutional side of marriage (for we are going through a period of reading back Aryan legal relationships just as we formerly read back Aryan theogonies and mythologies) have overlooked the tremendous importance of the immediate play of psychic factors congruous to hunting as such.[13]

[13] For a statement doing justice to the psycho-physic factors involved, see Thomas, "Der Ursprung der Exogamie," *Zeitschrift für Socialwissenschaft,* Bd. V, 1.

In conclusion, let me point out that the adjustment of habits to ends, through the medium of a problematic, doubtful, precarious situation, is the structural form upon which present intelligence and emotion are built. It remains the ground pattern. The further problem of genetic psychology is then to show how the purely immediate personal adjustment of habit to direct satisfaction, in the savage, became transformed through the introduction of impersonal, generalized objective instrumentalities and ends; how it ceased to be immediate and became loaded and surcharged with a content which forced personal want, initiative, effort and satisfaction further and further apart, putting all kinds of social divisions of labor, intermediate agencies and objective contents between them. This is the problem of the formation of mental patterns appropriate to agricultural, military, professional and technological and trade pursuits, and the reconstruction and overlaying of the original hunting schema.

But by these various agencies we have not so much destroyed or left behind the hunting structural arrangement of mind, as we have set free its constitutive psychophysic factors so as to make them available and interesting in all kinds of objective and idealized pursuits—the hunt for truth, beauty, virtue, wealth, social well-being, and even of heaven and of God.

18

PSYCHOLOGY AND SOCIAL PRACTICE

IN coming before you I had hoped to deal with the problem of the relation of psychology to the social sciences—and through them to social practice, to life itself. Naturally, in anticipation, I had conceived a systematic exposition of fundamental principles covering the whole ground, and giving every factor its due rating and position. That discussion is not ready today. I am loath, however, completely to withdraw from the subject, especially as there happens to be a certain phase of it with which I have been more or less practically occupied within the last few years. I have in mind the relation of Psychology to Education. Since education is primarily a social affair, and since educational science is first of all a social science, we have here a section of the whole field. In some respects there may be an advantage in approaching the more comprehensive question through the medium of one of its special cases. The absence of elaborated and coherent view may be made up for by a background of experience, which shall check the projective power of reflective abstraction, and secure a translation of large words and ideas into specific images. This special territory, moreover, may be such as to afford both signposts and broad avenues to the larger sphere—the place of psychology among the social sciences. Because I anticipate such an outcome, and because I shall make a survey of the broad field from the special standpoint taken, I make no apology for presenting this discussion

Address of the President before the American Psychological Association, New Haven, 1899. From *The Psychological Review*, March, 1900; 105-124.

to an Association of Psychologists rather than to a gathering of educators.

In dealing with this particular question, it is impossible not to have in mind the brilliant and effective discourses recently published by my predecessor in this chair. I shall accordingly make free to refer to points, and at times to words, in his treatment of the matter. Yet, as perhaps I hardly need say, it is a problem of the most fundamental importance for both psychology and social theory that I wish to discuss, not any particular book or article. Indeed with much of what Dr. Münsterberg says about the uselessness and the danger for the teacher of miscellaneous scraps of child study, of unorganized information regarding the nervous system, and of crude and uninterpreted results of laboratory experiment, I am in full agreement. It is doubtless necessary to protest against a hasty and violent bolting of psychological facts and principles which, of necessity, destroys their scientific form. It is necessary to point out the need of a preliminary working over of psychological material adapting it to the needs of education. But these are minor points. The main point is whether the standpoint of psychological science, as a study of mechanism, is indifferent and opposed to the demands of education with its free interplay of personalities in their vital attitudes and aims.

I

The school practice of today has a definite psychological basis. Teachers are already possessed by specific psychological assumptions which control their theory and their practice. The greatest obstacle to the introduction of certain educational reforms is precisely the permeating persistence of the underlying psychological creed. Traced back to its psychological ultimates, there are two controlling bases of existing methods of instruction. One is the assumption of a fundamental distinction between child psychology and the adult psychology where, in reality, identity, reigns; *viz.*: in the region of the motives and conditions which make for mental power. The other is the assumption of likeness where marked difference is the feature most significant for educational purposes; I mean the specialization of aims and habits in the adult, compared with the absence of specialization in the child, and the connection of undifferentiated status with the full and free growth of the child.

The adult is primarily a person with a certain calling and position in life. These devolve upon him certain specific responsibilities which he has to meet, and call into play certain formed habits. The child is primarily one whose calling is growth. He is concerned with arriving at specific ends and purposes—instead of having a general framework already developed. He is engaged in forming habits rather than in definitely utilizing those already formed. Consequently he is absorbed in getting that all-around contact with persons and things, that range of acquaintance with the physical and ideal factors of life, which shall afford the background and material for the specialized aims and pursuits of later life. He is, or should be, busy in the formation of a flexible variety of habits whose sole immediate criterion is their relation to full growth, rather than in acquiring certain skills whose value is measured by their reference to specialized technical accomplishments. This is the radical psychological and biological distinction, I take it, between the child and the adult. It is because of this distinction that children are neither physiologically nor mentally describable as "little men and women."

The full recognition of this distinction means of course the selection and arrangement of all school materials and methods for the facilitation of full normal growth, trusting to the result in growth to provide the instrumentalities of later specialized adaptation. If education means the period of prolonged infancy, it means nothing less than this. But look at our school system and ask whether the 3 R's are taught, either as to subject matter or as to method, with reference to growth, to its present demands and opportunities; or as technical acquisitions which are to be needed in the specialized life of the adult. Ask the same questions about geography, grammar and history. The gap between psychological theory and the existing school practice becomes painfully apparent. We readily realize the extent to which the present school system is dominated by carrying over into child life a standpoint and method which are significant in the psychology of the adult.

The narrow scope of the traditional elementary curriculum, the premature and excessive use of logical analytic methods, the assumption of ready-made faculties of observation, memory, attention, etc., which can be brought into play if only the child chooses to do so, the ideal of formal discipline—all these find a large measure of their explanation in neglect of just this psychological distinction between the child and the adult. The hold of these affairs upon the school is so fixed that it is impossible to shake it in any fundamental way, excepting by a thorough appreciation of the actual psychology of the case. This appreciation cannot be confined to the educational leaders and theorists. No individual instructor can be sincere and wholehearted, to say nothing of intelligent, in carrying into effect the needed reforms, save as he genuinely understands the scientific basis and necessity of the change.

But in another direction there is the assumption of a fundamental difference: Namely, as to the conditions which secure intellectual and moral progress and power.[1] No one seriously questions that, with an adult, power and control are obtained through realization of personal ends and problems, through personal selection of means and materials which are relevant, and through personal adaptation and application of what is thus selected, together with whatever of experimentation and of testing is involved in this effort. Practically every one of these three conditions of increase in power for the adult is denied for the child. For him problems and aims are determined by another mind. For him the material that is relevant and irrelevant is selected in advance by another mind. And, upon the whole, there is such an attempt to teach him a ready-made method for applying his material to the

[1] I owe this point specifically (as well as others more generally) to my friend and colleague, Mrs. Ella Flagg Young.

solution of his problems, or the reaching of his ends, that the factor of experimentation is reduced to the minimum. With the adult we unquestioningly assume that an attitude of personal inquiry, based upon the possession of a problem which interests and absorbs, is a necessary precondition of mental growth. With the child we assume that the precondition is rather the willing disposition which makes him ready to submit to any problem and material presented from without. Alertness is our ideal in one case; docility in the other. With one, we assume that power of attention develops in dealing with problems which make a personal appeal, and through personal responsibility for determining what is relevant. With the other we provide next to no opportunities for the evolution of problems out of immediate experience, and allow next to no free mental play for selecting, assorting and adapting the experiences and ideas that make for their solution. How profound a revolution in the position and service of textbook and teacher, and in methods of instruction depending therefrom, would be effected by a sincere recognition of the psychological identity of child and adult in these respects can with difficulty be realized.

Here again it is not enough that the educational commanders should be aware of the correct educational psychology. The rank and file, just because they are persons dealing with persons, must have a sufficient grounding in the psychology of the matter to realize the necessity and the significance of what they are doing. Any reform instituted without such conviction on the part of those who have to carry it into effect, would never be undertaken in good faith, nor in the spirit which its ideal inevitably demands; consequently it could lead only to disaster.

At this point, however, the issue defines itself somewhat more narrowly. It may be true, it is true, we are told, that some should take hold of psychological methods and conclusions, and organize them with reference to the assistance which they may give to the cause of education. But this is not the work of the teacher. It belongs to the general educational theorist: the middleman between the psychologist and the educational practitioner. He should put the matter into such shape that the teacher may take the net results in the form of advice and rules for action; but the teacher who comes in contact with the living personalities must not assume the psychological attitude. If he does he reduces persons to objects, and thereby distorts, or rather destroys, the ethical relationship which is the vital nerve of instruction.

That there is some legitimate division of labor between the general educational theorist and the actual instructor, there is of course no doubt. As a rule, it will not be the one actively employed in instruction who will be most conscious of the psychological basis and equivalents of the educational work, nor most occupied in finding the pedagogical rendering of psychological facts and principles. Of necessity, the stress of interest will be elsewhere. But we have already found reason for questioning the possibility of making the somewhat different direction of interest into a rigid dualism of a legislative class on one side and an obedient subject class on the other. Can the teacher ever receive "obligatory prescriptions"? Can he receive from another a statement of the means by which he is to reach his ends, and not become hopelessly servile in his attitude? Would not such a result be even worse than the existing mixture of empiricism and inspiration?— just because it would forever fossilize the empirical element and dispel the inspiration which now quickens routine. Can a passive, receptive attitude on the part of the instructor (suggesting the soldier awaiting orders from a commanding general) be avoided, unless the teacher, as a student of psychology, himself sees the reasons and import of the suggestions and rules that are proffered him?

I quote a passage that seems of significance: "Do we not lay a special linking science everywhere else between the theory and practical work? We have engineering between physics and the practical workingmen in the mills; we have a scientific medicine between the natural science and the physician." The sentences suggest, in an almost startling way, that the real essence of the problem is found in an *organic* connection between the two extreme terms—between the theorist and the practical worker—through the medium of the linking science. The decisive matter is the extent to which the ideas of the theorist actually project themselves, through the kind offices of the middleman, into the consciousness of the practitioner. It is the participation by the practical man in the theory, through the agency of the linking science, that determines at once the effectiveness of the work done, and the moral freedom and personal development of the one engaged in it. It is because the physician no longer follows rules which, however rational in themselves, are yet arbitrary to him (because grounded in principles that he does not understand), that his work is becoming liberal, attaining the dignity of a profession, instead of remaining a mixture of empiricism and quackery. It is because, alas, engineering makes only a formal and not a real connection between physics and the practical workingmen in the mills that our industrial problem is an ethical problem of the most serious kind. The question of the amount of wages the laborer receives, of the purchasing value of this wage, of the hours and conditions of labor, are, after all, secondary. The problem primarily roots in the fact that the mediating science does not connect with his consciousness, but merely with his outward actions. He does not appreciate the significance and bearing of what he does; and he does not perform his work because of sharing in a larger scientific and social consciousness. If he did, he would be free. All other proper accompaniments of wage, and hours, healthful and inspiring conditions would be added unto him, because he would have entered into the ethical kingdom. Shall we seek analogy with the teacher's calling in the workingmen in the mill, or in the scientific physician?

It is quite likely that I shall be reminded that I am overlooking an essential difference. The physician, it will be said, is dealing with a body which either is in itself a pure object, a causal interplay of anatomical elements, or is something which lends itself naturally and without essential loss to treatment from this point of view; while the case is quite different in the material with which the teacher deals. Here is personality, which is destroyed when regarded as an object. But the gap is not so pronounced nor so serious as this objection implies. The physician after all is not dealing with a lifeless body; with a simple anatomical structure, or interplay of mechanical elements. Life functions, active operations, are the reality which confronts him. We do not have to go back many centuries in the history of medicine to find a time when the physician attempted to deal with these functions directly and immediately. They were so overpoweringly present, they forced themselves upon him so obviously and so constantly, that he had no resource save a mixture of magic and empiricism: magic so far as he followed methods derived from uncritical analogy, or from purely general speculation on the universe and life; empiricism so long as he just followed procedures which had been found helpful before in cases which somewhat resembled the present. We have only to trace the intervening history of medicine to appreciate that it is precisely the ability to state function in terms of structure, to reduce life in its active operations to terms of a causal mechanism, which has taken the medical calling out of this dependence upon a vibration between superstition and routine. Progress has come by taking what is really an activity as if it were only an object. It is the capacity to effect this transformation of life activity which measures both the scientific character of the physician's procedure and his practical control, the certainty and efficacy of what he, as a living man, does in relation to some other living man.

It is an old story, however, that we must not content ourselves with analogies. We must find some specific reason in the principles of the teacher's own activities for believing that psychology—the ability to transform a living personality into an objective mechanism for the time being—is not merely an incidental help, but an organic necessity. Upon the whole, the best efforts of teachers at present are partly paralyzed, partly distorted, and partly rendered futile precisely from the fact that they are in such immediate contact with sheer, unanalyzed personality. The relation is such a purely ethical and personal one that the teacher cannot get enough outside the situation to handle it intelligently and effectively. He is in precisely the condition in which the physician was when he had no recourse save to deal with health as entity or force on one side, and disease as opposing agency or invading influence upon the other. The teacher reacts *en bloc*, in a gross wholesale way, to something which he takes in an equally undefined and total way in the child. It is the inability to regard, upon occasion, both himself and the child as just objects working upon each other in specific ways that compels him to resort to purely arbitrary measures, to fall back upon mere routine traditions of school teaching, or to fly to the latest fad of pedagogical theorists—the latest panacea peddled out in school journals or teachers' institutes—just as the old physician relied upon his magic formula.

I repeat, it is the fundamental weakness of our teaching force today (putting aside teachers who are actually incompetent by reason either of wrong motives or inadequate preparation), that they react in gross to the child's exhibitions in gross without analyzing them into their detailed and constituent elements. If the child is angry, he is dealt with simply as an angry being; anger is an entity, a force, not a symptom. If a child is inattentive, this again is treated as a mere case of refusal to use the faculty or function of attention, of sheer unwillingness to act. Teachers tell you that a child is careless or inattentive in the same final way in which they would tell you that a piece of paper is white. It is just a fact, and that is all there is of it. Now it is only through some recognition of attention as a mechanism, some awareness of the interplay of sensations, images and motor impulses which constitute it as an objective fact, that the teacher can deal effectively with attention as a function. And, of course, the same is true of memory, quick and useful observation, good judgment and all the other practical powers the teacher is attempting to cultivate.

Consideration of the abstract concepts of mechanism and personality is important. Too much preoccupation with them in a general fashion, however, without translation into relevant imagery of actual conditions is likely to give rise to unreal difficulties. The ethical personality does not go to school naked; it takes with it the body as the instrument through which all influences reach it, and through control of which its ideas are both elaborated and expressed. The teacher does not deal with personality at large, but as expressed in intellectual and practical impulses and habits. The ethical personality is not formed—it is forming. The teacher must provide stimuli leading to the equipment of personality with active habits and interests. When we consider the problem of forming habits and interests we find ourselves at once confronted with matters of this sort: What stimuli shall be presented to the sense organs and how? What stable complexes of associations shall be organized? What motor impulses shall be evoked, and to what extent? How shall they be induced in such a way as to bring favorable stimuli under greater control, and to lessen the danger of excitation from undesirable stimuli? In a word, the teacher is dealing with the psychical factors that are concerned with furtherance of certain habits, and the inhibition of others—habits intellectual, habits emotional, habits in overt action.

Moreover, all the instruments and materials with which the teacher deals must be considered as psychical stimuli. Such consideration involves of necessity a knowledge of their reciprocal reactions—of what goes by the name of causal mechanism. The introduction of certain changes into a network of associations, the reinforcement of certain sensorimotor connections, the weakening or displacing of others— this is the psychological rendering of the greater part of the teacher's actual business. It is not that one teacher employs mechanical considerations, and that the other does not, appealing to higher ends; it is that one does not know his mechanism, and consequently acts servilely, superstitiously and blindly, while the other, knowing what he is about, acts freely, clearly and effectively.[2]

---

[2] That some teachers get their psychology by instinct more effectively than others by any amount of reflective study may be unreservedly stated. It is not a question of manufacturing teachers, but of reinforcing and enlightening those who have a right to teach.

The same thing is true on the side of materials of instruction—the school studies. No amount of exaltation of teleological personality (however true, and however necessary the emphasis) can disguise from us the fact that instruction is an affair of bringing a child into intimate relations with concrete objects, positive facts, definite ideas and specific symbols. The symbols are objective things in arithmetic, reading and writing. The ideas are truths of history and of science. The facts are derived from such specific disciplines as geography and language, botany and astronomy. To suppose that by some influence of pure personality upon pure personality, conjoined with a knowledge of rules formulated by an educational theorist, an effective interplay of this body of physical and ideal objects with the life of the child can be effective, is, I submit, nothing but an appeal to magic, plus dependence upon servile routine. Symbols in reading and writing and number are, both in themselves, and in the way in which they stand for ideas, elements in a mechanism which has to be rendered operative within the child. To bring about this influence in the most helpful and economical way, in the most fruitful and liberating way, is absolutely impossible save as the teacher has some power to transmute symbols and contents into their working psychical equivalents: and save as he also has the power to see what it is in the child, as a psychical mechanism, that affords maximum leverage.

Probably I shall now hear that at present the danger is not of dealing with acts and persons in a gross, arbitrary way, but (so far as what is called new education is concerned) in treating the children too much as mechanism, and consequently seeking for all kinds of stimuli to stir and attract—that, in a word, the tendency to reduce instruction to a merely agreeable thing, weakening the child's personality and indulging his mere love of excitement and pleasure, is precisely the result of taking the psycho-mechanical point of view. I welcome the objection for it serves to clear up the precise point. It is through a partial and defective psychology that the teacher, in his reaction from dead routine and arbitrary moral and intellectual discipline, has substituted an appeal to the satisfaction of momentary impulse. It is not because the teacher has a knowledge of the psychophysical mechanism, but because he has a partial knowledge of it. He has come to consciousness of certain sensations, and certain impulses, and of the ways in which these may be stimulated and directed, but he is in ignorance of the larger mechanism (just as a mechanism), and of the causal relations which subsist between the unknown part and the elements upon which he is playing. What is needed to correct his errors is not to inform him that he gets only misleading from taking the psychical point of view; but to reveal to him the scope and intricate interactions of the mechanism as a whole. Then he will realize that while he is gaining apparent efficacy in some superficial part of the mechanism, he is disarranging, dislocating and disintegrating much more fundamental factors in it. In a word he is operating not as a psychologist, but as a poor psychologist, and the only cure for a partial psychology is a fuller one. He is gaining the momentary attention of the child through an appeal to pleasant color, or exciting tone, or agreeable association, but at the expense of isolating one cog and ratchet in the machinery, and making it operate independently of the rest. In theory, it is as possible to demonstrate this to a teacher, showing how the faulty method reacts unhappily into the personality, as it is to locate the points of wrong construction, and of ineffective transfer of energy in a physical apparatus.

This suggests the admission made by writers in many respects as far apart as Dr. Harris and Dr. Münsterberg—that scientific psychology is of use on the pathological side—where questions of "physical and mental health" are concerned. But is there anything with which the teacher has concern that is not included in the ideal of physical and mental health? Does health define to us anything less than the teacher's whole end and aim? Where does pathology leave off in the scale and series of vicious aims and defective means? I see no line between the more obvious methods and materials which result in nervous irritation and fatigue; in weakening the power of vision, in establishing spinal curvatures; and others which, in more remote and subtle, but equally real ways, leave the child with, say, a muscular system which is only partially at the service of his ideas, with blocked and inert brain paths between eye and ear, and with a partial and disconnected development of the cerebral paths of visual imagery. What error in instruction is there which could not, with proper psychological theory, be stated in just such terms as these? A wrong method of teaching reading, wrong I mean in the full educational and ethical sense, is also a case of pathological use of the psychophysical mechanism. A method is ethically defective that, while giving the child a glibness in the mechanical facility of reading, leaves him at the mercy of suggestion and chance environment to decide whether he reads the "yellow journal," the trashy novel, or the literature which inspires and makes more valid his whole life. Is it any less certain that this failure on the ethical side is repeated in some lack of adequate growth and connection in the psychical and physiological factors involved? If a knowledge of psychology is important to the teacher in the grosser and more overt cases of mental pathology, is it not even more important in these hidden and indirect matters—just because they are less evident and more circuitous in their operation and manifestation?

The argument may be summarized by saying that there is controversy neither as to the ethical character of education, nor as to the abstraction which psychology performs in reducing personality to an object. The teacher is, indeed, a person occupied with other persons. He lives in a social sphere—he is a member and an organ of a social life. His aims are social aims; the development of individuals taking ever more responsible positions in a circle of social activities continually increasing in radius and in complexity. Whatever he as a teacher effectively does, he does as a person; and he does with and toward persons. His methods, like his aims, when actively in operation, are practical, are social, are ethical, are anything you please—save merely psychical. In comparison with this, the material and the data, the standpoint and the methods of psychology, are abstract. They transform specific acts and relations of individuals into a flow of processes in consciousness; and these processes can be adequately identified and related only through reference to a biological organism. I do not think there is danger of going too far in asserting the social and teleological nature of the work of the teacher; or in asserting the abstract and partial character of the mechanism into which the psychologist, as a psychologist, transmutes the play of vital values.

Does it follow from this that any attempt on the part of the teacher to perform this abstraction, to see the pupil as a mechanism, to define his own relations and that of the study taught in terms of causal influences acting upon this mechanism, are useless and harmful? On the face of it, I cannot understand the logic which says that because mechanism is mechanism, and because acts, aims, values, are vital, therefore a statement in terms of one is alien to the comprehension and proper management of the other. Ends are not compromised when referred to the means necessary to realize them. Values do not cease to be values when they are minutely and accurately measured. Acts are not destroyed when their operative machinery is made manifest. The statement of the disparity of mechanism and actual life, be it never so true, solves no problem. It is no distinction that may be used offhand to decide the question of the relation of psychology to any form of practice. It is a valuable and necessary distinction; but it is only preliminary. The purport of our discussion has, indeed, led us strongly to suspect any ideal which exists purely at large, out of relation to machinery of execution, and equally a machinery that operates in no particular direction.

The proposition that a description and explanation of stones, iron and mortar, as an absolutely necessary causal nexus of mechanical conditions, makes the results of physical science unavailable for purposes of practical life, would hardly receive attention today. Every skyscraper, every railway bridge, is a refutation, compared with which oceans of talk are futile. One would not find it easy to stir up a problem even if he went on to include, in this same mechanical system, the steam derricks that hoist the stones and iron, and the muscles and nerves of architect, mason and steelworker. The simple fact is still too obvious: the more thoroughgoing and complete the mechanical and causal statement, the more controlled, the more economical are the discovery and realization of human aims. It is not in spite of, nor in neglect of, but because of the mechanical statement that human activity has been freed, and made effective in thousands of new practical directions, upon a scale and with a certainty hitherto undreamed of. Our discussion tends to suggest that we entertain a similar question regarding psychology only because we have as yet made so little headway—just because there is so little scientific control of our practice in these directions; that at bottom our difficulty is local and circumstantial, not intrinsic and doctrinal. If our teachers were trained as architects are trained, if our schools were actually managed on a psychological basis as great factories are run on the basis of chemical and physical science; if our psychology were sufficiently organized and coherent to give as adequate a mechanical statement of human nature as physics does of its material, we should never dream of discussing this question.

I cannot pass on from this phase of the discussion without at least incidental remark of the obverse side of the situation. The difficulties of psychological observation and interpretation are great enough in any case. We cannot afford to neglect any possible auxiliary. The great advantage of the psychophysical laboratory is paid for by certain obvious defects. The completer control of conditions, with resulting greater accuracy of determination, demands an isolation, a ruling out of the usual media of thought and action, which leads to a certain remoteness, and easily to a certain artificiality. When the result of laboratory experiment informs us, for example, that repetition is the chief factor influencing recall, we must bear in mind that the result is obtained with nonsense material—*i.e.*, by excluding the conditions of ordinary memory. The result is pertinent if we state it thus: The more we exclude the usual environmental adaptations of memory the

[309]

greater importance attaches to sheer repetition. It is dubious (and probably perverse) if we say: Repetition is the prime influence in memory.

Now this illustrates a general principle. Unless our laboratory results are to give us artificialities, mere scientific curiosities, they must be subjected to interpretation by gradual reapproximation to conditions of life. The results may be very accurate, very definitive in form; but the task of reviewing them so as to see their actual import is clearly one of great delicacy and liability to error. The laboratory, in a word, affords no final refuge that enables us to avoid the ordinary scientific difficulties of forming hypotheses, interpreting results, etc. In some sense (from the very accuracy and limitations of its results) it adds to our responsibilities in this direction. Now the school, for psychological purposes, stands in many respects midway between the extreme simplifications of the laboratory and the confused complexities of ordinary life. Its conditions are those of life at large; they are social and practical. But it approaches the laboratory in so far as the ends aimed at are reduced in number, are definite, and thus simplify the conditions; and their psychological phase is uppermost—the formation of habits of attention, observation, memory, etc.—while in ordinary life these are secondary and swallowed up.

If the biological and evolutionary attitude is right in looking at mind as fundamentally an instrument of adaptation, there are certainly advantages in any mode of approach which brings us near to its various adaptations while they are still forming, and under conditions selected with special reference to promoting these adaptations (or faculties). And this is precisely the situation we should have in a properly organized system of education. While the psychological theory would guide and illuminate the practice, acting upon the theory would immediately test it, and thus criticize it, bringing about its revision and growth. In the large and open sense of the words, psychology becomes a working hypothesis, instruction is the experimental test and demonstration of the hypothesis;

the result is both greater practical control and continued growth in theory.

II

I must remind myself that my purpose does not conclude with a statement of the auxiliary relation of psychology to education; but that we are concerned with this as a type case of a wider problem—the relation of psychology to social practice in general. So far I have tried to show that it is not in spite of its statement of personal aims and social relations in terms of mechanism that psychology is useful, but because of this transformation and abstraction. Through reduction of ethical relations to presented objects we are enabled to get outside of the existing situation; to see it objectively, not merely in relation to our traditional habits, vague aspirations and capricious desires. We are able to see clearly the factors which shape it, and therefore to get an idea of how it may be' modified. The assumption of an identical relationship of physics and psychology to practical life is justified. Our freedom of action comes through its statement in terms of necessity. By this translation our control is enlarged, our powers are directed, our energy conserved, our aims illuminated.

The school is an especially favorable place in which to study the availability of psychology for social practice; because in the school the formation of a certain type of social personality, with a certain attitude and equipment of working powers, is the express aim. In idea at least no other purpose restricts or compromises the dominance of the single purpose. Such is not the case in business, politics, and the professions. All these have upon their surface, taken directly, other ends to serve. In many instances these other aims are of far greater immediate importance; the ethical result is subordinate or even incidental. Yet as it profiteth a man nothing to gain the whole world and lose his own self, so indirectly and ultimately all these other social institutions must be judged by the contribution which they make to the value of human life. Other ends may be immediately uppermost, but these ends must in turn be means; they must subserve the interests of conscious life or else stand condemned.

In other words, the moment we apply an ethical standard to the consideration of social institutions, that moment they stand on exactly the same level as does the school, *viz.*: as organs for the increase in depth and area of the realized values of life. In both cases the statement of the mechanism, through which the ethical ends are realized, is not only permissible, but absolutely required. It is not merely incidentally, as a grateful addition to its normal task, that psychology serves us. The essential nature of the standpoint which calls it into existence, and of the abstraction which it performs, is to put in our possession the method by which values are introduced and effected in life. The statement of personality as an object, of social relations as a mechanism of stimuli and inhibitions, is precisely the statement of ends in terms of the method of their realization.

It is remarkable that men are so blind to the futility of a morality which merely blazons ideals, erects standards, asserts laws without finding in them any organic provision for their own realization. For ideals are held up to follow; standards are given to work by; laws are provided to guide action. The sole and only reason for their conscious moral statement is, in a word, that they may influence and direct conduct. If they cannot do this, not merely by accident, but of their own intrinsic nature, they are worse than inert. They are impudent impostors and logical self-contradictions.

When men derive their moral ideals and laws from custom, they also realize them through custom; but when they are in any way divorced from habit and tradition, when they are consciously proclaimed, there must be some substitute for custom as an organ of execution. We must know the method of their operation and know it in detail. Otherwise the more earnestly we insist upon our categorical imperatives, and upon their supreme right of control, the more flagrantly helpless we are as to their actual domination. The fact that conscious, as distinct from customary, morality and psychology

have had a historic parallel march, is just the concrete recognition of the necessary equivalence between ends consciously
conceived, and interest in the means upon which the ends
depend. We have the same reality stated twice over: once as
value to be realized, and once as mechanism of realization.
So long as custom reigns, as tradition prevails, so long as
social values are determined by instinct and habit, there is no
conscious question as to the method of their achievement, and
hence no need of psychology. Social institutions work of their
own inertia, they take the individual up into themselves and
carry him along in their own sweep. The individual is dominated by the mass life of his group. Institutions and the
customs attaching to them take care of society both as to its
ideals and its methods. But when once the values come to
consciousness, when once a Socrates insists upon the organic
relation of a reflective life and morality, then the means, the
machinery by which ethical ideals are projected and manifested, comes to consciousness also. Psychology must needs be
born as soon as morality becomes reflective.

Moreover, psychology, as an account of the mechanism of
workings of personality, is the only alternative to an arbitrary
and class view of society, to an aristocratic view in the sense of
restricting the realization of the full worth of life to a section
of society. The growth of a psychology that, as applied to
history and sociology, tries to state the interactions of groups
of men in familiar psychical categories of stimulus and inhibition, is evidence that we are ceasing to take existing social
forms as final and unquestioned. The application of psychology to social institutions is the only scientific way of
dealing with their ethical values in their present unequal distribution, their haphazard execution and their thwarted development. It marks just the recognition of the principle of
sufficient reason in the large matters of social life. It is the
recognition that the existing order is determined neither by
fate nor by chance, but is based on law and order, on a system of existing stimuli and modes of reaction, through
knowledge of which we can modify the practical outcome.
There is no logical alternative save either to recognize and

search for the mechanism of the interplay of personalities that controls the existing distributions of values, or to accept as final a fixed hierarchy of persons in which the leaders assert, on no basis save their own supposed superior personality, certain ends and laws which the mass of men passively receive and imitate. The effort to apply psychology to social affairs means that the determination of ethical values lies not in any set or class, however superior, but in the workings of the social whole; that the explanation is found in the complex interactions and interrelations which constitute this whole. To save personality in all, we must serve all alike—state the achievements of all in terms of mechanism, that is, of the exercise of reciprocal influence. To affirm personality independent of mechanism is to restrict its full meaning to a few, and to make its expression in the few irregular and arbitrary.

The anomaly in our present social life is obvious enough. With tremendous increase in control of nature, in ability to utilize nature for the indefinite extension and multiplication of commodities for human use and satisfaction, we find the actual realization of ends, the enjoyment of values, growing unassured and precarious. At times it seems as if we were caught in a contradiction; the more we multiply means, the less certain and general is the use we are able to make of them. No wonder a Carlyle or a Ruskin puts our whole industrial civilization under a ban, while a Tolstoi proclaims a return to the desert. But the only way to see the situation steadily, and to see it as a whole, is to keep in mind that the entire problem is one of the development of science, and of its application to life. Our control of nature with the accompanying output of material commodities is the necessary result of the growth of physical science—of our ability to state things as interconnected parts of a mechanism. Physical science has for the time being far outrun psychical. We have mastered the physical mechanism sufficiently to turn out possible goods; we have not gained a knowledge of the conditions through which possible values become actual in life, and so are still at the mercy of habit, of haphazard, and hence of force.

Psychology, after all, simply states the mechanism through which conscious value and meaning are introduced into human experience. As it makes its way, and is progressively applied to history and all the social sciences, we can anticipate no other outcome than increasing control in the ethical sphere—the nature and extent of which can be best judged by considering the revolution that has taken place in the control of physical nature through a knowledge of her order. Psychology will never provide ready-made materials and prescriptions for the ethical life, any more than physics dictates offhand the steam engine and the dynamo. But science, both physical and psychological, makes known the conditions upon which certain results depend, and therefore puts at the disposal of life a method for controlling them. Psychology will never tell us just what to do ethically, nor just how to do it. But it will afford us insight into the conditions which control the formation and execution of aims, and thus enable human effort to expend itself sanely, rationally and with assurance. We are not called upon to be either boasters or sentimentalists regarding the possibilities of our science. It is best, for the most part, that we should stick to our particular jobs of investigation and reflection as they come to us. But we certainly are entitled in this daily work to be sustained by the conviction that we are not working in indifference to or at cross-purposes with the practical strivings of our common humanity. The psychologist, in his most remote and technical occupation with mechanism, is contributing his bit to that ordered knowledge which alone enables mankind to secure a larger and to direct a more equal flow of values in life.